C000165112

African Arguments

Written by experts with an unrivalled ._____

African Arguments is a series of concise, engaging books that address the key issues currently facing Africa. Topical and thought-provoking, accessible but in-depth, they provide essential reading for anyone interested in getting to the heart of both why contemporary Africa is the way it is and how it is changing.

African Arguments Online

African Arguments Online is a website managed by the Royal African Society, which hosts debates on the African Arguments series and other topical issues that affect Africa: http://africanarguments.org

Titles already published

Alex de Waal, *AIDS and Power*

Tim Allen, *Trial Justice*

Raymond W. Copson, *The United States in Africa*

Chris Alden, *China in Africa*

Tom Porteous, *Britain in Africa*

Julie Flint and Alex de Waal, *Darfur: A New History of a Long War*

Jonathan Glennie, *The Trouble with Aid*

Peter Uvin, *Life after Violence: A People's Story of Burundi*

Bronwen Manby, *Struggles for Citizenship in Africa*

Camilla Toulmin, *Climate Change in Africa*

Orla Ryan, *Chocolate Nations: Living and Dying for Cocoa in West Africa*

Theodore Trefon, *Congo Masquerade*

Léonce Ndikumana and James Boyce, *Africa's Odious Debts*

Mary Harper, *Getting Somalia Wrong?*

Neil Carrier and Gernot Klantschnig, *Africa and the War on Drugs*

Alcinda Honwana, *Youth and Revolution in Tunisia*

Marc Epprecht, *Sexuality and Social Justice in Africa*

Lorenzo Cotula, *The Great African Land Grab?*

Michael Deibert, *The Democratic Republic of Congo*

Adam Branch and Zachariah Mampilly, *Africa Uprising*

Celeste Hicks, *Africa's New Oil*

Morten Jerven, *Africa: Why Economists Get it Wrong*

Theodore Trefon, *Congo's Environmental Paradox*

Paul Richards, *Ebola: How a People's Science Helped End an Epidemic*

Forthcoming titles

Odd-Helge Fjelstad, Wilson Prichard, Mick Moore, *Taxing Africa*

Kris Berwouts, *War and Failed Peace in Eastern Congo*

Published by Zed Books and the IAI with the support of the following organizations:

The principal aim of the **International African Institute** is to promote scholarly understanding of Africa, notably its changing societies, cultures and languages. Founded in 1926 and based in London, it supports a range of seminars and publications including the journal *Africa*.
www.internationalafricaninstitute.org

Now more than a hundred years old, the **Royal African Society** today is Britain's leading organization promoting Africa's cause. Through its journal, *African Affairs*, and by organizing meetings, discussions and other activities, the society strengthens links between Africa and Britain and encourages understanding of Africa and its relations with the rest of the world.
www.royalafricansociety.org

The **World Peace Foundation**, founded in 1910, is located at the Fletcher School, Tufts University. The Foundation's mission is to promote innovative research and teaching, believing that these are critical to the challenges of making peace around the world, and should go hand in hand with advocacy and practical engagement with the toughest issues. Its central theme is 'reinventing peace' for the twenty-first century.
www.worldpeacefoundation.org

About the author

Louisa Lombard is an assistant professor of anthropology at Yale University. Previously she held a Ciriacy-Wantrup postdoctoral fellowship in natural resource economics at the University of California at Berkeley. She has published widely on politics and conflict in Central Africa. In addition to her academic research, she has worked in the Central African Republic as a field consultant to several international organizations, including Human Rights Watch, Small Arms Survey, Refugees International, and the World Bank. Her previous books include *Making Sense of the Central African Republic*, co-edited with Tatiana Carayannis (Zed Books, 2015).

STATE OF REBELLION

VIOLENCE AND INTERVENTION IN THE CENTRAL AFRICAN REPUBLIC

LOUISA LOMBARD

ZED

Zed Books

LONDON

In association with
International African Institute
Royal African Society
World Peace Foundation

State of Rebellion: Violence and Intervention in the Central African Republic was first published in 2016 by Zed Books Ltd, The Foundry, 17 Oval Way, London SE11 5RR, UK.

www.zedbooks.net

Copyright © Louisa Lombard 2016.

The right of Louisa Lombard to be identified as the author of this work has been asserted by her in accordance with the Copyright, Designs and Patents Act, 1988.

Typeset in Haarlemmer by seagulls.net
Index by John Barker
Cover design by Jonathan Pelham
Cover photograph © William Daniels/Panos

A catalogue record for this book is available from the British Library.

ISBN 978-1-78360-885-0 hb
ISBN 978-1-78360-884-3 pb
ISBN 978-1-78360-886-7 pdf
ISBN 978-1-78360-887-4 epub
ISBN 978-1-78360-888-1 mobi

Printed and bound by CPI Group (UK) Ltd, Croydon, CR0 4YY

CONTENTS

Acknowledgements .... *ix*

Abbreviations and acronyms .... *xiii*

Map of the Central African Republic .... *xvi*

Introduction 1

1.   Conflict and the state in the peace-kept world 27

2.   The nativeness of 'foreign' violence 59

3.   Mobility as power 85

4.   Long and short histories of rebellion 113

5.   DDR and the frustration of desires for entitlement 141

6.   War as the violence of the pack 177

7.   World champion of peacekeeping 213

Conclusion 243

Notes 255

References 265

Index 277

ACKNOWLEDGEMENTS

On a recent visit to CAR I drank a grapefruit soda with my Central African sister, Aminata. After spending her childhood in Bangui, Aminata left, settling first in Ontario and then in the Philadelphia area. She saw her two children into their teenage years and then returned to Africa to help with her family's businesses and other enterprises. Aminata told me of the excellent education she had received as a child in Bangui a few decades earlier. Entry to the best schools depended on the moral reputation of the family, not just on one's wealth. No one had ever heard of electricity cuts – one could have the lights on even during the bright sunshine of midday if one so desired. Aminata sighed at how far the country had fallen since those days. Young people graduate with their baccalaureate yet often cannot write or calculate basic sums; electricity is far more off than on for the few who have it in their homes. And yet, she said, 'I keep coming back. Because I know that somehow, this country made me who I am.'

With those words, Aminata had described my connection to CAR better than I had yet been able to. I lament the difficulties my Central African friends and colleagues face in furthering their lives. I complain about the challenges of getting anything done in the country. (Budget at least four hours for a simple bank transaction, and ideally have a friend on call who can bring water in the event of an extended wait.) But I keep coming back, because in so many ways, the country has made me who I am. It has shaped my career and my thinking as a scholar. More broadly, it has shaped my understanding of justice and the problems facing the world. And personally, it has expanded my sense both of generosity and stinginess, of ways of including and excluding.

An entire book-worth of people have spoken with me, fed me, sheltered me, transported me, corrected me, challenged me, or otherwise helped me find my way. In all of these ways and more, I know that I have gotten more from this benighted place than I have given. The analysis I offer here is, in the peculiar way of the academic, a paean to the various people concerned with Central Africa, both CAR nationals and others. Perhaps, amid the tragic dynamics described, it will help us recognize strengths and create more opportunities for people from this part of the world.

To the Central Africans (by nationality and by spirit) who welcomed me into your offices, homes, and lives despite my endless queries, I owe an enormous debt of gratitude. Here is the first instalment, due to: Faouzi Kilembe, Sylvain Batianga-Kinzi, Charlotte Mararv, Aminata Gaye, Pichou Stone, Patrick Bonazoui, Louis Bainilago, Arsène Sende, Hippolyte Donossio, Marcel Dimanche, Fortune Kinguelewa, Sylvain Yakara, Gisèle Willybiro-Maidou, Stanislas Mbangot, Guy-Florent Ankogui-Mpoko, John Hanson, Wendy Rice, Meike van Ginneken, David Tchouinou, Magloire Kolisso, Erick Kpakpo, Soumaine Ndodeba, Marcel Sendema, Eric Massi, Joseph Benamse, Henri Zana, Jean-Jacques Demafouth, Mireille Vonguiabode, Robert Goffet, Aziza Kassara, Habiba Mohammed, and Didier Kassai.

Institutionally and financially, research for this book has been supported by the Social Science Research Council, both the International Dissertation Research Fellowship and the Conflict Prevention and Peace Forum; the National Science Foundation (Cultural Anthropology and Law and Society divisions); the Wenner-Gren Foundation; the United States Institute of Peace Jennings-Randolph Fellowship; the Ciriacy-Wantrup Postdoctoral Fellowship in Natural Resource Economics at the University of California at Berkeley; Yale University, both the Department of Anthropology and the MacMillan Center for International and Area Studies; the Aegis Trust; and Duke University.

At Duke, Charles Piot's guidance achieved the feat of letting me retain my distinctive features while being reshaped as a scholar along disciplinary lines. Along the way, with astute mentoring from Charlie as well as from Orin Starn, Peter Redfield, Mack O'Barr, Stephen W. Smith, Anne Allison, Ian Baucom, and Janet Roitman, anthropology became my vocation, one for which I am deeply grateful. Colleagues at the University of California at Berkeley, especially Michael Watts, Mariane C. Ferme, Nancy Peluso, Nathan Sayre, Joshua Craze, Alice Kelly, and Hannah Appel, were models of generosity and stimulated and broadened my thinking. Now at Yale, my good fortune has continued. Colleagues in Anthropology, the Council on African Studies, the MacMillan Center, and the Agrarian Studies Program have helped both deepen and broaden my analysis, and also helped me find my place here. Particular thanks in this regard to Anne Underhill, Kalyanakrishnan Sivaram-akrishnan, David Watts, Marcia Inhorn, Catherine Panter-Brick, Helen Siu, Douglas Rogers, Erik Harms, William Honeychurch, Karen Nakamura, Paul Kockelman, Claudia Valeggia, Eduardo Fernandez-Duque, Ian Shapiro, Dan Magaziner, Stephanie Newell, Inderpal Grewal, Chris Udry, Michael Cappello, Kate Baldwin, and Unni Karunakara. Graduate students Aalyia Sadruddin, Adrienne Cohen, and Miríam Juan-Torres Gonzalez have been a source of energy and inspiration.

Fellow-travellers in research on conflict and intervention, espe-cially in Africa, have inspired and asked hard questions throughout: Morten Bøås, Tatiana Carayannis, Alex de Waal, Marielle Debos, Donald L. Donham, Kevin C. Dunn, Pierre Englebert, Rebecca Hardin, Danny Hoffman, René Lemarchand, Roland Marchal, Mike McGovern, Mary Moran, William Reno, Mats Utas, Henrik Vigh, and Luise White. For fellowship as well as for critical and wide-ranging discussions, I thank Adam Baczko, Andrea Behrends, Eric G. Berman, Ledio Cakaj, Andrea Ceriana Mayneri, Phil Clark, Mirjam de Bruijn, Lotje de Vries, Pierre-Marie David, Jatin Dua, Matthew Ellis, Tamara Giles-Vernick, Brian Goldstone, Robert J.

Gordon, Julie Kleinman, Benoît Lallau, Andreas Mehler, Madeleine Reeves, Nicholas R. Smith, Kevin Sobel-Read, Claudio Sopranzetti, Eddie Thomas, Simon Narcisse Tomety, Jérôme Tubiana, Denis M. Tull, and Henri-Michel Yéré. The late Dennis D. Cordell was a paragon of generous scholarship, as was Bruno Martinelli.

Ken Barlow at Zed Books, Stephanie Kitchen at the International African Institute and the editorial board of the African Arguments series fostered this project, including as it grew into something different (and bigger) than initially envisioned. Philip Burnham, Paul Richards, and Stephen W. Smith's careful and generous readings of the manuscript helped sharpen and nuance the arguments in important ways. Ben Healy's precise and smart editing brought me as close to my goal of a semi colon-free book as an academic type like me can manage.

A value my parents instilled in me from a young age was to seek always to understand where other people were coming from first and judge only later, if at all. That spirit gave me the courage to wander afar, toward Central Africa and anthropology, while knowing I remained always securely connected to home. In nearly every way, Graeme Wood has pushed me to learn more, and to do more, and this book is evidence of that support. To Zuleika: this is what Mamma does at work. Strange, perhaps. But it is one way I endeavour to make myself of use in the world.

ABBREVIATIONS AND ACRONYMS

APRD   Popular Army for the Restoration of Democracy (*Armée populaire pour la restauration de la démocratie*)

AU   African Union

BBC   British Broadcasting Corporation

BINUCA   United Nations Integrated Peacebuilding Support Office in the Central African Republic (*Bureau intégré de l'Organisation des Nations Unies en Centrafrique*)

BONUCA   United Nations Peacebuilding Support Office in the Central African Republic (*Bureau des Nations Unies pour la Consolidation de la Paix en République Centrafricaine*)

CAR   Central African Republic

CEEAC   Economic Community of Central African States (*Communauté économique des états de l'Afrique centrale*)

CEMAC   Central African Economic and Monetary Community (*Communauté économique et monétaire de l'Afrique centrale*)

CFA   Central African franc (*Coopération financière en Afrique centrale*)

CNDDR   National Commission for Disarmament, Demobilization, and Reinsertion (*Commission nationale de désarmement, démobilisation et réinsertion*)

CPJP   Convention of Patriots for Justice and Peace (*Convention des patriotes pour la justice et la paix*)

DDR	disarmament, demobilization, and reintegration
DRC	Democratic Republic of the Congo
ECHO	European Commission Humanitarian Office
EU	European Union
EUFOR-RCA	European Union Force in Central African Republic
EUMAM	EU Military Advisory Mission in the Central African Republic (*Mission militaire européenne de conseil en République centrafricaine*)
FACA	Central African Armed Forces (*Forces armées Centrafricaines*)
FDPC	Democratic Front of the Central African People (*Front démocratique du peuple centrafricain*)
ICC	International Criminal Court
IDP	internally displaced person
INGO	international non-governmental organization
LRA	Lord's Resistance Army
MDRP	Multi-Country Demobilization and Reintegration Program
MICOPAX	Mission for the Consolidation of Peace in Central African Republic (*Mission de consolidation de la paix en Centrafrique*)
MINUSCA	United Nations Multidimensional Integrated Stabilization Mission in the Central African Republic (*Mission multidimensionnelle intégrée des Nations Unies pour la stablisation en République centrafricaine*)
MISCA	African-led International Support Mission to the Central African Republic (*Mission internationale de soutien à la Centrafrique sous conduite africaine*)
MLCJ	Movement of Central African Liberators for Justice (*Mouvement des libérateurs centrafricains pour la justice*)
NGO	non-governmental organization
PCS	practice of charlatanism and sorcery (*Pratique du charlatanisme et sorcellerie*)

PJA	daily food allowance *(Prime journalière d'alimentation)*
PRAC	Programme for Reintegration and Support to Communities *(Programme de réinsertion et appui aux coummunautés)*
SSR	security sector reform
UFDR	Union of Democratic Forces for Unity *(Union de forces démocratiques pour le rassemblement)*
UFR	Union of Republican Forces *(Union des forces républicaines)*
UN	United Nations
UNDP	United Nations Development Programme
UNICEF	United Nations Children's Fund
UPC	Union for Peace in Central African Republic *(Unité pour la paix en Centrafrique)*
USD	US dollar

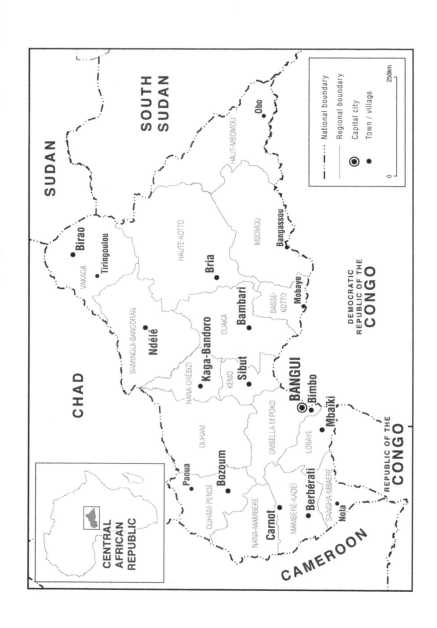

SUDAN

SOUTH SUDAN

CHAD

CAMEROON

DEMOCRATIC REPUBLIC OF THE CONGO

REPUBLIC OF THE CONGO

National boundary
Regional boundary
Capital city
Town / village

250km

0

Obo

HAUT-MBOMOU

MBOMOU

Bangassou

Birao

VAKAGA

Tiringoulou

HAUTE-KOTTO

Bria

Bambari

Mobaye

BASSE-KOTTO

BAMINGUI-BANGORAN

Ndélé

OUAKA

Kaga-Bandoro

NANA-GRÉBIZI

KEMO

Sibut

BANGUI

Bimbo

OMBELLA M'POKO

LOBAYE

Mbaïki

OUHAM

DUHAM

Paoua

Bozoum

OUHAM-PENDE

NANA-MAMBÉRÉ

Carnot

MAMBÉRÉ-KADÉI

Berbérati

SANGHA-MBAÉRÉ

Nola

CENTRAL AFRICAN REPUBLIC

INTRODUCTION

Where is the Central African Republic?

If you asked that question in picking up this book, you are not alone: it is one of the questions I am most frequently asked. (Hint: the country's name includes a clue.)

That location is among the first things a person might wonder about regarding the Central African Republic (CAR) is understandable. Though it lies at the geographical centre of the African continent, it often escapes notice. Map readers' eyes are drawn to coasts and cities, and CAR has none of the former and only one place with a claim to the latter, namely its capital, Bangui. During the colonial period, CAR was known as the Cinderella of the French empire (big game hunters loved its vast spaces home to few people, but lots of other animals), or, less charitably, as the 'trash can' (of little strategic or economic importance, it was the dumping ground for colonial training school graduates with the lowest grades). Either way, it was a backwater. The decades of relative calm that followed independence in 1960 have been overtaken by twenty years of militarized politics – armed groups, coups, international intervention – as leading an armed group has become a surer way to power than standing in elections. CAR never 'failed' in spectacular fashion, like Somalia. Instead, it became durably 'fragile', to borrow the current organization-speak descriptor.

While overlooking CAR is from a certain perspective understandable, doing so has impoverished our understanding not just of Equatorial Africa, but of states and conflict in Africa and the world

more broadly. Rather than an anomaly, CAR is better thought of
as a limiting case – 'an instance marking one end of a continuum
of different configurations that can be taken by a particular set of
dynamics' (Rutherford 2003: 229) – of the state. An extreme case, in
other words, and one that draws out elements that might be harder
to spot, but still present, in less pronounced cases.

For the problems Central Africans currently confront are not
at all unique to the country. In particular, CAR highlights the interplay between a few key elements. The first concerns the current
rigidity of our idea of 'the state'. The Weberian ideal type (claim to
a monopoly on legitimate violence, controlling borders, providing
some security and welfare for a population of citizens through
rational-bureaucratic means) has been drained of his important
insight that modes of political organization are always hybrid and
combine multiple forms of authority, and instead become the only
legitimate architecture for political organization. Anything else is
aberrant, illegitimate, a piece that doesn't fit. Everyone – Central
Africans and international actors intervening in CAR in whatever
capacity – hold tightly to that state ideal, like an element of religious
dogma. It remains the vision par excellence of how the world *should*
be. However, though CAR has been given considerable resources of
the type required to impose/create any such state – its ministries have
for instance received French aid continuously since independence,
and it was a pilot case for the United Nations Peacebuilding Fund
– it has never come close to achieving that goal. This problem could
alternately be phrased as the gap between the realities of the context
(which include a history of a state that has shown little interest in
public welfare, as well as Central Africans' ambivalence about state
control of their lives) and the tools international state-builders have
in their kit. This problem is frequently lamented, but never causes
people to re-draw the state blueprints in any considerable way.

None of these elements are CAR's lot alone. The strong desire
Central Africans feel for a certain ideal of the state form (one
founded on security and provision of salaries as welfare) is wide-

spread. It can for instance be seen in the fact that the collapse of the Siad Barre regime in Somalia in 1991 resulted not in the end of the state but rather a proliferation of them – notably Somaliland and Puntland – as well as decades of intervener focus on creating and supporting a Somali government, for a long time in exile.

That people desire a state is not a bad thing. It evidences a wish for collective action, social support, and other services that will allow people more opportunities and security. The problem is that the factors outlined above combine to smother any organic state-making initiatives, such as people who take it upon themselves to provide security or taxation and services, which diplomat-donors providing life support to the polity label illegitimate. Perhaps this helps explain why those countries that have had greatest success in rebuilding after armed conflict are those that have eschewed the dictates of international aid and charted their own course (Englebert 2015). Of course, international interventions are marshalled only where domestic leadership has failed, so one should not necessarily blame the interventions themselves – they are embedded in larger systems of failure. However, there is an important conclusion to draw here: that the usual tendency to divide politics into 'internal' state spheres and 'external' intervener spheres is an analytical fiction, and an unhelpful one at that. They exist only through their relationships with each other; they create each other.

The CAR case also reveals the traditional distinction between 'the economy' and 'the state' to be an unhelpful fiction. The usual post-conflict prescription is to 'rebuild the state and restart the economy'. In terms of the former project, the emphasis is always on supporting ministries. In terms of the latter, natural resources – in CAR's case, diamonds, oil, gold, uranium, timber – are often named as a source of hope, and a future source of jobs.[1] 'This is a rich country', I have heard again and again – from French officers, from Central Africans in the neighbourhoods, from international journalists, from government officials, from NGO employees. This line of thought argues that CAR simply hasn't taken advantage of its potential, and the resources are currently being exploited in an informal way and to the benefit of the wrong people (e.g. armed group leaders). To which I respond: perhaps. But if the solution is a government that provides services and a private sector that provides jobs, we must at the very least recognize that CAR's every historical tendency has worked against these ideals. Moreover, that they were not achieved in the past was not for lack of agreement about their importance. Indeed, these tenets have long been a 'gospel truth' for everyone involved in CAR and similar places, and yet they have only slipped further away. The time has therefore come to recognize that holding on to these ideals may well be an example of 'millenarian thinking, as if Jesus will come and remake the world, as if there is a thing called magic' (Steinberg in Ferguson 2015: 19).

So another lesson of CAR is that rather than distinguish between the economy as a source of production and incomes, and the public sector as a source of (however limited) services, we should address these concerns through a unified political economy of distribution, particularly distribution of money. This should not be a stop-gap (a short-term labour-intensive project, for instance, or an occasional 'cash transfer') but a long-term commitment in a place like CAR that will likely never see much in the way of industrialization or even wage labour, and where a state salary has historically been a source of entitlement – that is, of the Central African version of accountability and meaningful citizenship (dignity and legitimacy) (Lombard 2016b).

In short, taking CAR seriously requires turning many dogmatic assumptions about states – and especially the solutions for 'fragile' states – sideways or upside down, to reveal connections and disconnections that the usual frameworks and assumptions hide. Doing so shows why and how the predominant modes of thinking about the state and intervening to support it have not worked and suggests ways this dire situation might be improved.

CAR: *Setting the scene*

But I am getting ahead of myself. When you asked where CAR is, you had something else in mind. As its name suggests, it does indeed contain the geographic centre of the African continent. Today, the UN has told us, we should replace the term 'landlocked' with 'land-linked', which is a nice positive spin but inappropriate here, in this Texas-sized place that is at the centre of the continent but not really on the road to anywhere. Among its neighbours are four countries that have seen chronic violent conflict: Chad to the north; Sudan and South Sudan to the east; and the Democratic Republic of the Congo to the south. Even the one neighbour that had long avoided armed conflict, Cameroon to the west, has recently been pulled in. Cameroon moreover profits from its position by squeezing imports into CAR with heavy official and unofficial duties.

CAR is a country with a lot of land, few people, and little physical infrastructure. There is wide ecological diversity. In the south-west, one finds swathes of towering rain forest, interspersed with villages, manioc fields, and banana and mango trees. It is humid all year, and could rain on nearly any day. In the opposite corner of the country, in the northeast, one finds semi-forested savannah, which is alternately scorched and swampy, in the dry and rainy seasons, respectively. Here, you are more likely to find groundnut and millet fields. Climatically, the rest of the country is somewhere between these two extremes – frequent downpours during about half the year and mostly dry for the rest.

Most Central Africans farm, or have people who farm for them. Hunting and gathering are also important sources of both nourishment and income. Only about four million people call CAR home. Most live in the western (near Cameroon) and central regions; the east is home to very few people. The capital, Bangui, is the only place that can call itself a city, with a population of nearly 800,000, and everything official is centralized there.

People having been living in the lands now known as CAR for

centuries, if not longer. People moved around a lot within the region, but less between the region and further afield. Already by the 1700s, the area's residents were farming the New World crops of manioc, maize, and tobacco, evidence that they were in contact with traders and processes reaching across the Atlantic. But until the nineteenth century, almost all lived in dispersed villages without institutionalized, centralized leadership that could coerce or control (Cordell 1983).

Around that time, Muslim traders and raiders were making incursions into the area. They set up trading posts as part of networks leading north into present-day Cameroon, Nigeria, Chad, and Sudan. They brought new ways of life, new goods, and new modes of seizure (e.g. raiding of people and goods), production (e.g. slave plantations), and exchange (e.g. there were hundreds of currencies in use in the area in the 1800s [Cordell 1985; Guyer 1993]). With time their presence was institutionalized in sultanates that were themselves vassals of the more-powerful northern polities like Wadai and Sokoto. The last decades of the 1800s were a period of massive upheaval and change, on a scale arguably not seen since, as European (chiefly French) and Muslim trading and raiding operations intensified in the area (Cordell 2003). Though these two sets of imperialists initially found each other useful, the French eventually decided the Muslim leaders were not sufficiently tractable, and so executed or otherwise sidelined them.

French attention was dilettantish, however. As one colonial official wrote in 1903, five years after the French developed a plan for administering their colony of Oubangui-Chari, this was a country that 'earlier reports, too pompous, described as rich, which is far from the case' (Colonie du Congo 1903: 32). In 1915, the government tried to trade Oubangui-Chari to Britain for a speck of land on the Gulf of Guinea, but the British declined (Brégeon 1998: 272). The French had neither money nor much domestic political will supporting colonization. Seeing the riches King Leopold was reaping just to the south, in his private colony, the Congo Free State, French officials wondered if privatization might offer a solution. By carving nearly the entire French Equatorial Africa territory into private concessions and leasing them to profit-seeking companies, the theory went, they could outsource the costs of economic development, and later recuperate them for the benefit of imperial France. The first leases, granted in 1899, were for thirty years. In 1910, seeking to wrest back some control, colonial officials reduced them to ten. (To get this through they had to grant the companies additional privileges, though.) The cost (material and human) of building roads and other infrastructure in this isolated region was (as it remains) immense. Therefore, the concessionary companies did the only economically rational thing: they enlisted local chiefs to brutally compel people to exploit rubber, ivory, and other natural resources. They earned as much as they could as quickly as they could, and then left. Despite these draconian measures, many companies did not even turn a profit.[2]

Throughout the thirty years of the concessionary experiment (1899–1930), the French colonial government and the French public were repeatedly made aware of the companies' brutality and abuses. André Gide's *Voyage au Congo* (1927) is the most famous example, but also one of the last. Before his reporting on executions and overwork, a number of official and unofficial missions to the colony described widespread murders and torture. Each time, these abuses were described as a scandal (that is, as aberrant) and protective legislation was enacted. There was never enough funding to actually enforce the new laws, however, and the abuses continued (Coquéry-Vidrovitch 1972) to such an extent that one could argue they were more structural/systemic than scandalous (Lombard in preparation). Technology proved more helpful than legislation. For instance, motorized vehicles meant less reliance on human porters, which had been a brutal toil (Mollion 1992).

Central Africans were not passive during the concessionary period. Some appreciated the new ways of life and goods brought by the increased European presence, but many resisted fiercely. Oubangui-Chari became known for a number of rebellions. The most famous of these was the Kongo-Wara rebellion (1928–1931), in what is today western CAR, but there were many others as well, primarily carried out by individuals and small groups.

After the concessionary period, the colonial government tried a new tactic: cotton cultivation, particularly in the northern and western regions, where this crop did well. However, Central Africans naturally did not want to cultivate it, as they were paid very little for very difficult work. They had to be compelled, by various means (Brégeon 1998). Thus one of the foremost historians of CAR, Pierre Kalck, described French colonization as 'thirty years of concessions followed by thirty years of forced cotton' (1959: 151).

After the Second World War (during which French Equatorial Africa was an outpost of Free France) there was a brief effort to build schools and other public infrastructure. Barthélemy Boganda, a Catholic priest defrocked for being too blatantly married, became a champion for independence and Central African rights, but died in a plane accident in 1958. Independence came for most of the French African colonies in 1960. Of all of these, Oubangui-Chari, which at independence became the Central African Republic, was the least prepared to stand on its own. And it did not. French advisers remained in all the ministries, and security agreements and other treaties assured that France would remain actively involved in politics and production. For most Central Africans, independence brought few changes. From their perspective, the 'munju' (white/foreigners) who ruled them had been replaced by 'munju voko' (black-skinned white/foreigners; this term was coined by Boganda) (Kalck 1971; Zoctizoum 1983).

Nevertheless, the first decades of independence were filled with optimism. Jean-Bédel Bokassa, who claimed power from the ineffective David Dacko in a bloodless coup on 1 January 1966, is best known today for his megalomaniacal tendencies, but he also had a vision for the country, and he built things – a university, futuristic ministry buildings – and started projects. Economic decline began in the 1970s, however, due to the departure of foreign businesspeople, the drop in global commodity prices, and mismanagement of the country's money, and has never really recovered. Structural adjustment, the slimming of civil service rolls in the 1980s, and presidents who ruled in increasingly clientelistic ways, combined with a donor-led push for multi-party democracy in the early 1990s, made for an unstable mix. Army mutinies broke out in the mid-1990s. Coup attempts and rebellion followed. Two rebellion-coups were successful. François Bozizé, the former head of the army, claimed power in March 2003. He was himself ousted by Michel Djotodia, a former civil servant, and his alliance of armed men, the Seleka, in March 2013. Since the mid-1990s, then, the country has been under the tutelage of regional heads of state, France, the United Nations, and various regional organizations. Over the same period, CAR's neighbours have become sites of militarized politics, with long-running wars in Chad and in Sudan, and by the late 1990s unrest in the Democratic Republic of the Congo (DRC) as well.

Amid this upheaval, schooling has frequently been interrupted by violence, or else by teacher and student strikes, such that even graduates lack many basic academic skills. The main employer is the civil service, and salaries have often gone unpaid, with dramatic ripple effects throughout the informal economy. CAR has always depended on aid and concession kickbacks, but the decline of the minimal private sector that existed until the 1980s has made this dependence nearly total. Though the concessionary system ended long ago, concessionary politics have only expanded in practice. Previously, concessions were primarily granted for resource extraction, but now, through foreign aid, all government prerogatives have been turned into concessions as well, amounting to the wholesale outsourcing of the country's sovereignty (Smith 2015b).

This is important because it runs counter to the assumptions that underlie all international development aid. Development aid assumes that the will to govern is latent, just not actualized for lack of human or material resources. That assumption, however, is contrary to the dominant historical tendencies in CAR's governance. Concessionary politics, while not a particularly exalted mode of operating, has the advantage of short-term monetization of incompetence and penury for government officials (Smith 2015b). Given the combination of political instability and short funding cycles, neither Central African politicians nor international aid officials are able to make effective long-term plans. More specifically, while the goals are always far-off and long-term ('build the state'), only short-term work is possible. A better recipe for shortcomings in accountability – and frustration for everyone involved – could not be found.

That long-term vision of a functioning state holds regular Central Africans in thrall too. For Central Africans, this vision of an ideal state, the state they would like to have, is focused on provision of entitlements, such as salaries. In contrast, the state they do have is focused on extraction from regular people, such as in the form of crippling informal taxation that goes directly into government employees' pockets (Marchal 2015a; Lombard 2013a). People see those working for the government as wholly corrupt. As a Central African expression puts it, if the head of a fish is rotting, the rest of the fish is spoiled too.

But while the country is in most senses poor and dysfunctional, it is rich in two things: land and water. It is huge (the size of France and Benelux combined), home to very few people, and much of its land is suitable for agriculture and/or grazing. While the north is rapidly drying out and the once-massive Lake Chad is today less than one-twentieth of its 1963 size (UNEP 2008), CAR's plentiful rivers and streams are attracting cattle herders in far larger numbers than before.

And while most outside the region view CAR as at best a backwater and more properly a basket case, since the 1970s, businesspeople, mostly Muslim, from throughout the region have seen CAR as a place where one could get rich (Kilembe 2015). For a variety of reasons, non-Muslim Central Africans are not particularly active in running businesses (Marchal 2015a). This leaves many business opportunities for Muslims and for people from elsewhere. Nearly all the permanent market shops (car parts, clothes, imported soda, household goods, stationery) are owned and run by Muslims.[3] The country has thus seen high rates of Muslim migration from both neighbouring countries (Cameroon, Chad, Nigeria) and further afield (e.g. West Africa) (Filakota 2009). Non-Muslim Central Africans invite these foreigners in, but remain anxious about getting ripped off. They worry these foreigners are making off with the country's 'riches'.

Concern about dispossession (material and existential) by more-powerful foreigners has become the main source of nationalist mobilization in CAR. Who counts as Central African is partly determined by language. Almost all Central Africans speak Sango. Prior to colonization, this language was spoken only by a few people near Bangui, but its use spread as a result of colonization, missionaries, and music (Diki-Kidiri 1979). Formerly seen as a colonial import, Sango has become one of the few markers of Central African nationalism, and an exclusionary one at that – that is, if you don't speak it, you can't truly be a Central African. (At home, however, particularly outside of the capital region, people are likely to speak their 'dialect', as they term their ethnic group's language.)

Religion is also a marker of nationality. Thanks to colonial history, everything to do with the official state codes as southern/Bangui and Christian, whereas Islam codes as foreign, dangerous, and imperialist. This leaves Muslim Central Africans in a bind, because while not legally stateless, in effective terms they are frequently denied citizenship and/or otherwise made the object of suspicion.

There is a distinction, however, between Muslims with family networks reaching toward West Africa, and Muslims with family networks or ancestral roots in Chad and Sudan. Non-Muslim Central Africans see people in this latter category as especially dangerous, for both long-term and short-term historical reasons. When François Bozizé took power in Bangui in March 2003, and when Michel Djotodia did the same in March 2013, a majority of their armed supporters were Muslims from Chad or Darfur, and they were rapacious in achieving their goal and paying themselves for the work afterwards (violence, looting, etc. – activities in which, admittedly, many Central Africans took advantage of the mayhem to participate in as well). People living in CAR but with family and ancestral connections to the north were thus viewed with suspicion by extension. Non-Muslim Central Africans thus sometimes say of their country's northeastern residents, 'They are Central Africans, but they act like Chadians', which is almost as bad as really being Chadian.

Moreover, regional heads of state both actively and passively supported the violent changes in power in 2003 and 2013, further augmenting Central Africans' sense of powerlessness and anxiety over the erosion of their sovereignty.

These concerns are felt on multiple levels. There is the visible level of blatant political manoeuvring, armed conflict, and looting. At the same time, this is joined by an invisible level, the realm of spirits and other forces that act in the world but cannot be seen. These forces can be summed up, to use a very problematic word, as sorcery.[4] A widespread understanding in Equatorial Africa holds that every person contains the capacity for witchcraft in his or her body. This force is localized in the abdomen. Some people do not develop it, and it remains latent. Others strengthen it such that it augments their capacity for action in the visible world. While the extent to which individual Central Africans think about these occult forces varies, few would repudiate their existence outright.

Today, one major focus of Central Africans' uncertainty has to do with the fact that danger and dispossession are not confined to the visible world but also manifest in ways that use special, occult knowledge and which require a response in kind. The majority of Central Africans are part of the ethno-linguistic cluster known as 'Ubanguian' peoples; these include the Azande and Nzakara in the east, the Banda and Manja in the centre, and the Gbaya in the west. For all of these people, witchcraft is a substance housed in the human body. This substance is like a small animal. That is, it is alive and its will and power are not wholly under the control of the human body in which it is located. The substance can grow large in the case of people who very successfully manipulate the occult, or it can stay small in others, but it is present in everyone and represents a *potential* for occult power. (In her research in CAR, Aleksandra Cimpric witnessed surgeries to remove this witchcraft substance. The entity removed was the appendix [Cimpric 2010].) Great rulers are understood to have cultivated and expanded their witchcraft substance. In pre-colonial times, in those Central African societies with stratification and centralized authority structures (e.g. the Azande), rulers and their oracles possessed special tools that helped them effectively control witchcraft and sorcery, preventing them from becoming socially destructive. Commoners in those societies cited control of witchcraft as the main benefit of living in a state. In those Central African societies without much centralization of authority, instability due to witchcraft was a constant element of village life.

These visible/invisible world dynamics make many Central Africans feel dispossessed and invaded by a disorder that they cannot strike back against (Ceriana Mayneri 2014a, 2014c; Marchal 2015a). There are both short-term and long-term reasons for this, aptly summed up by the historian Florence Bernault as the 'destructive understandings' between Equatorial Africans and colonial officials of all kinds (2006: 239). By this she means that Africans and colonizers did not necessarily have diametrically opposed views of the sources of occult power (as many have argued), but rather that African and European views resonated with each other in ways that ultimately destabilized Equatorial Africans' confidence in their own abilities to counter nefarious occult forces.

In that spirit, the belief that surface-level appearances might not be what they seem does not solely affect people for whom the occult plays a large role in life. More broadly, it presents itself as a general concern about what could lie beneath: Is a person who he or she seems to be? What motives or profits might she or he be hiding? And if one is inclined to ask those questions, suspicion and vigilance become part of one's behavioural and interpretive repertoire. This curiosity about what might be beneath/behind the surface is moreover not at all unique to Central Africans – it is widespread among international interveners as well. Thus this book argues, as Bernault did for the colonial period, that the present, too, is marked by destructive understandings among Central Africans and international actors.

Even so, there is a major difference between most Central Africans and interveners, namely material status. To attract people to work in CAR, international organizations attempt to reproduce rich-country luxuries in the midst of Central African poverty – spacious houses, air-conditioning, Land Cruisers to drive, fast internet. Poor Central Africans approach interveners for handouts, and higher-status Central Africans seem, in their conversations with interveners, to be not just dependent on donor aid but to see it as a birthright. These tendencies make it easier for interveners to overlook just how humiliating many Central Africans find their position in the world. A shoeless village chief cannot visit a minister. In the aftermath of a coup, a family cannot protect itself from violation – of their material goods, of their bodies. And overall, 'The rest of the world is moving forward. But we just keep going backward,' Central Africans will frequently say. Or, 'Of all the countries in the world, we're the last.'

But despite these formulations, it is striking that Central Africans do not accept them as the way things have to be. 'How and why are we the last?' they ask. They do not take for granted their ranking – as one looking at the bare economic statistics about the country might do – but actively look for answers as to why and how this came about. In doing so, Central Africans often blame others rather than looking at their own potential responsibility, which may be immense. Still, this inquisitive tendency, this refusal to accept that the status quo is 'simply the way things must be', is not just solely a process of buck-passing but also a means of cultivating hope amid despair.

Rebellion becomes war

Of despair, there has been far too much recently. In the years after Bozizé took power in 2003, a number of rebellions broke out in rural areas. But, at least on the surface, life in the capital remained relatively calm. The prospects for most Central Africans remained dismal, however. With time, the network of people benefiting from the Bozizé government became smaller and more concentrated around the leader's family and evangelical church. Throughout the decade of *la Bozizie*, as Bozizé's clientelistic mode of operating became known, CAR went through internationally-led peace-building and state-building initiatives meant to address the ongoing rural rebellions by fostering inclusiveness. Inclusiveness existed in name only, however, a fact Central Africans and international interveners alike knew but felt they had few means of addressing. From the perspective of diplomats and donors, Bozizé seemed like the least bad option. Without him there, chaos seemed likely.

However, Central Africans, interveners, diplomats, and side-lined politicians and politico-military entrepreneurs became increasingly frustrated with Bozizé. In mid-March 2012, a few of these sidelined politicians and entrepreneurs of rebellion met in Niamey, Niger to begin planning a takeover. By the end of 2012, they formed a heterogeneous coalition of rebels from Chad, Sudan, Central African Republic, and a few other countries called Seleka ('alliance' in Sango) that soon took the northeastern town of Ndele and began marching toward Bangui. Regional heads of state didn't yet intervene, thinking perhaps that Seleka would scare Bozizé into being more cooperative.

But when Seleka's seriousness about taking Bangui became clear, regional heads of state took notice. Chadian President Idriss Déby Itno dispatched extra soldiers for MICOPAX, the sub-regional peacekeeping mission in CAR, who prevented Seleka from breaching the Damara line, about 70 km from the capital. In early January 2013, President Bozizé and Seleka leaders, along with a few civil society representatives thrown in mostly for appearances, were brought to Libreville, Gabon, to negotiate. These were peace talks without much talking, in that regional leaders largely determined both the agenda and favoured solutions ahead of time (Tumutegyereize and Tillon 2013). The non-Central African participants leading the process had their own issues, and the plight of CAR was secondary. They were interested in CAR to the extent that its troubles could provide leverage in regard to their own concerns. They moreover wished to avoid potentially de-stabilizing spillover. But, for the most part, no one wanted to get stuck with the mess of CAR. A quick fix was proposed and everyone signed. It quickly became clear that neither Bozizé nor Seleka leaders would show each other much good faith in implementing its terms, an outcome no one could reasonably find surprising (Tumutegyereize and Tillon 2013).

Seleka started a new advance in March 2013. The Chadian soldiers at Damara and along the route to Bangui did not stop them. The Central African army, not a particularly fearsome force at the best of times, effectively dissolved. South African troops (in the country for reasons everyone found a bit unclear, not to say suspicious – were they after the diamonds or other natural resources?) were the only forces to try to stop Seleka's advance. The South Africans seemed to be taken by surprise by the rebels' military sophistication. Thirteen South Africans were killed, in the largest loss of South African soldiers abroad since the end of apartheid, and Michel Djotodia claimed the capital on behalf of Seleka. International organizations and diplomatic actors from the region and beyond condemned the violent change of power, but no one stepped forward to claim leadership over resolving the situation. Bozizé had disrespected the terms of the peace agreement and there was little support for the return of such an intransigent big man (in a region of bigger men). Seleka's Michel Djotodia was not a legitimate leader because he took power violently and not in elections, but perhaps a democratic transition could be brought about.

In the meantime, insecurity reigned. Since its emergence in late 2012, Seleka had been ruling CAR towns and villages as fiefdoms, but without the long-term interest a fiefdom usually entails. Killings, dispossession, and other violence occurred on a massive scale. With Bozizé gone, Seleka fighters moved into most of the country's west and north (they largely ignored the southeast, in part because residents pulled ferries to the far eastern side of their crossings, making it difficult to bring vehicles across the Ubangui River and toward the capital). But even as their presence grew, very little united the various armed groups that called themselves Seleka. Without a unified command-control hierarchy, *ad hoc* pillaging and violence were among their primary tactics of profit and rule.

Central African armed group members from the northeast, whom I first met in 2009 and who went on to join Seleka, blamed opportunistic, late-arriving foreign Seleka recruits for the destruction of their country. In saying this, however, they conveniently skirt the fact that only the military bulk provided by the foreigners allowed them to steamroll into the capital so successfully. Moreover, by many accounts these Central African rebels were themselves the latecomers to Seleka, whose earliest recruits were from Chad and Sudan. But one can nevertheless extend a little sympathy to the Central African members of Seleka, who felt rebellion was their only effective means of expressing their grievances over being ignored and treated as foreign. Djotodia and his associates created a monster, and though everyone involved should have foreseen dire consequences from the alliance's course of action, once its strength became apparent it was difficult for people from the region to decline to join.

Between late 2012 and early 2013, embassies in Bangui pulled out their expatriate staff, as did the UN Integrated Peacebuilding Support Office in CAR (BINUCA). Humanitarian organizations were thoroughly looted and most pulled out their staff as well. A few diplomats and Central African politicians argued that a sustained and geographically dispersed peacekeeping presence would be needed to restore even the rather dire status quo, but the international and regional response was fairly inert overall. Donors and diplomats expressed dismay from afar, but were all reluctant to claim leadership over resolving problems in what they had come to consider a perennially hopeless mess.

In September 2013, Djotodia, unable to control the men who helped him take power, officially disbanded Seleka. This left him with even less leverage. Meanwhile, Central Africans had begun mobilizing militarily against Seleka, and against Chadian/Sudanese/Muslim profiteering more broadly. These mobilizations were consistent with a long tradition of self-defence groups throughout most of CAR. These groups are less standing forces than networks that can be activated when the need arises. The new groups drew on existing networks and traditions but also transformed in new ways.

The actors that mobilized in the wake of Seleka abuses called themselves the Anti-Balaka. Anti-Balaka has two commonly-cited etymologies. First, it references its initiation ceremonies, which members saw as making them impervious (a countering force, or anti-) to Kalashnikov bullets (*balles-AK*, or *balaka*). And second, *balaka* is the term for machete in the Gbaya language, which is spoken in the area around Bozizé's home region of Bossangoa, and hence the Anti-Balaka are those who counter the use of violence (machetes, etc.) against them and their kin. Some of the Anti-Balaka drew support from the Bozizé political networks. Others had more localized protection objectives, while others were more flatly criminal. As with Seleka, the Anti-Balaka name described a number of different segments whose members did not share the same interests or objectives and certainly had no unified system of organization.

As the Anti-Balaka introduced a sectarian dimension to CAR's upheaval around September 2013, bilateral and international diplomatic rabble-rousers began to advocate and mobilize for a response, in the form of peacekeepers and humanitarian aid. The 'genocide card' (or, more precisely 'verge of genocide' card) was played to describe the Anti-Balaka's targeting of Muslims. For better and worse, the 'genocide card' continues to be the main source of leverage in mobilizing interventions for ongoing conflicts (de Waal 2013; Lombard 2013b). CAR was in 'crisis' as a popular advocacy hashtag (#CARcrisis) put it. France and the African Union both authorized and deployed peacekeepers in December 2013 and January 2014. The French called their mission Sangaris, after one of CAR's many butterfly species; the AU mission was MISCA, the African-led International Support Mission to CAR. These authorizations coincided with one of the periods of most intense violence in Bangui, directed primarily against Muslims, such as the 5 December rampage in which Muslim neighbourhoods were looted and destroyed and many people were killed. Throughout the west and centre of the country, thousands were killed (Human Rights Watch 2013). At the height of the fighting, in 2014, a quarter of the population (more than one million people) was displaced, most moving within CAR but still hundreds of thousands settling in Cameroon, Chad, and the DRC.

Even with peacekeepers arriving, violence remained widespread. In early January, President Déby decided to intervene, calling CAR's entire transitional government to Ndjamena. He convinced Djotodia to step down, and organized the process whereby the government selected Catherine Samba-Panza, a businesswoman, lawyer, and former mayor of Bangui, as the new transitional president. In Bangui, Central Africans were disappointed by the peacekeepers' mode of operating, which as far as they could tell focused on protecting government installations rather than preventing violence against people in the neighbourhoods (Cinq-Mars 2015). French and AU peacekeepers became a visible presence in the capital, but for the most part they stuck to the main roads even though much of the violence happened on side streets and alleys.

Even more damaging to perceptions of the intervention's neutrality and effectiveness, many of the AU peacekeepers came from the neighbouring countries (Cameroon, Chad, and the two Congos) that were among the first to step forward for the mission.

These troops were deployed along their respective borders, which, though understandable from an operational perspective, encouraged the soldiers to put their own countries' needs first and gave them more opportunities for commerce and other cross-border activities. This only strengthened Central Africans' suspicions that these troops were in the country not to help its people but for their own personal gain.

Violence remained intense in the early months of 2014. In one notorious incident, peacekeepers perpetrated the carnage. Although accounts of what exactly happened vary, at the end of March nearly thirty people were killed in a market in central Bangui during a patrol by Chadian MISCA troops. President Samba-Panza criticized the killings and, in a move interpreted as anger at her demand for accountability, President Déby immediately called the peacekeepers home. This probably should have happened far earlier given that Chadian soldiers – whether wearing an AU beret or not – were seen not as neutral but as parties to the conflict (a number of the Seleka were ex-Chadian military).

Throughout this period, diplomatic actors – the French chief among them – advocated replacing MISCA with a UN military-civilian mission. The reasons for this were several. For one, Central African officials preferred a UN mission, the luxury model of peacekeeping operations. In part, this preference stemmed from mistrust of the AU, which Central Africans saw as beholden to South Africa – and what had those South African soldiers been doing in CAR, anyway? Undoubtedly something collusive and profiteering, and perhaps reflective of an ongoing relationship with Bozizé, the Central African politicians worried. From the French perspective, a UN peacekeeping presence would make it easier to draw down their own involvement in CAR, which had lasted longer than expected and was costing 800,000 Euros a day.

A UN mission, MINUSCA (the UN Mission in the CAR), was indeed authorized in April 2014, with resolution 2149. The transition from MISCA to MINUSCA occurred in September 2014.

MINUSCA was given a Chapter 7 mandate, meaning it would engage in 'peace enforcement' rather than 'peacekeeping' (with greater force authorized in the former than in the latter). The transition took several months. Initially, it was a re-hatting, with MISCA troops operating under UN rather than AU procedures. But over the course of a year these soldiers were replaced by people who at least theoretically met the more stringent UN requirements. In addition to the peacekeepers, civilian staffers began to fill the MINUSCA compound as well. While talking about the need to do things differently compared to previous peacebuilders, the proposals they developed with the government looked much like those of their predecessors: political dialogue; disarmament, demobilization, and reintegration (DDR); presidential elections.

There was also a massive expansion in the number of humanitarian organizations in the country. From about twenty-five international non-governmental organizations (INGOs) pre-Seleka, by March 2016 they totalled well over a hundred. This is impressive enough, and the INGOs already present dramatically expanded as well. For instance, before Seleka the Danish Refugee Council had a small office with a handful of expatriate staffers. Today, there are around thirty-five expatriates on staff and five hundred Central Africans on the payroll as well. And while regional organizations, sub-regional organizations, France, and the UN have marshalled dozens of peacekeeping missions over the past two decades, those forces were smaller and had limited mandates in comparison to MINUSCA, which combines military and civilian elements.[5] Nevertheless, the peacekeepers have struggled to respond effectively when violence has flared, such as in Bangui in late September and early October 2015.

As of September 2016, MINUSCA comprises about twelve thousand peacekeepers and civilian staff. A European Union force, EUFOR-RCA/EUMAM, has been present in a couple of neighbourhoods of Bangui since April 2014, first in support of MISCA and now MINUSCA. The French Sangaris troops (leaving at the end of 2016) also support MINUSCA. A political dialogue, the Bangui Forum, brought together armed groups, the government, and civil society to talk about the sources of the country's troubles and how to secure a more peaceful future in May 2015. The electorate selected Faustin Archange Touadéra, a former prime minister and university administrator, as president in February 2016. Conditions for the elections were procedurally defensible if not wholly optimal, and there were even some campaign innovations such as a televised debate during which each candidate had to respond to the same questions. (Few people in CAR have access to a TV, but the debate was still a useful nod in the direction of making candidates explain themselves to voters.)

Despite public will for it, disarmament has largely not happened, and armed groups continue to be present, either as standing forces or as networks that could easily be re-mobilized. In Bangui it is not difficult to find people who describe themselves as Anti-Balaka, though most do not declare it publicly. Ex-Seleka members are also encamped at three sites in the city. Outside the capital, the number of armed groups may even be growing, spreading across much of the country's territory. Alliance and factionalization are both common, and often temporary. What form the DDR (disarmament, demobilization, and reintegration) will eventually take remains contested; armed group members expect integration into the army, while international DDR planners envision only a short-term assistance, given more to communities than armed group members themselves.

That will serve as an overview. Policy and advocacy researchers who have inundated CAR since 2013 have thoroughly documented both violence and peacekeeping activities, and their reports offer a trove of additional detail about those matters. MINUSCA's reports to the UN Security Council are also full of such data, as are the reports of the UN Panel of Experts on CAR. Having sketched this background, my focus in what follows will be on the nature of relationships among people involved in these processes of intervention and violence in CAR. How do people understand each other, and how do those perceptions shape their collaborations and conflicts?

Methods

People often ask me how I came to study CAR. As is perhaps common with short-term projects that end up becoming vocations, the answer owes something to hubris. About to graduate from college with a degree that included an area focus on Africa, I figured I knew basically everything I needed to about the continent. Then I happened to attend a talk about a country I had hardly heard of before – CAR. Deciding my ignorance needed to be rectified, I proposed myself to Eric G. Berman as a research assistant. That job evolved into a research consultancy on armed groups in Central Africa and lasted several years. Without fully realizing what was going on, I developed a range of both personal and intellectual commitments to Central Africa. This book grows out of thirteen years of engagement with and attempts to respond to the seemingly simple question, posed to me by one of my PhD advisers, the anthropologist Peter Redfield, 'What is "the state" in CAR?'

Even readers who might not share my investment in Central Africa can be enriched by taking the country seriously. As an anthropologist, I am committed to understanding politics in all its diversity. And as I have suggested, CAR is particularly compelling in that respect as a limiting case of the concept of the state. In order to understand CAR for *what it is*, rather than *what it is not* or what we think it *should someday be*, one must flip the major tenets of the Weberian state ideal type. For instance, one of the most fundamental characteristics of such states is that they are territorial entities. Even those literatures that are devoted to understanding the diversity of the state form (e.g. Young 1994) consider territorialization a defining criterion. But the CAR state is not primarily a geographically delimited territory. The most important meetings about the government and the country's future are taken in Ndjamena,

Paris, Nairobi, or New York. For instance, when, at the end of 2013, Michel Djotodia had still not managed to assure any security in the country and opposition was growing by the day, Chadian President Idriss Déby Itno flew the entire government to Ndjamena, forced Djotodia to step down, and demanded that the government select a new leader. CAR simply would not exist without these far-flung connections. Moreover, CAR's history of concessionary politics means that the ideal-type distinction between the public sphere (the state) and the private sphere (everything else) does not work. The state has always been privatized, to such an extent that the distinction loses any purchase. Given a non-territorialized, privatized state, power becomes very strongly linked with mobility – who can move, and who cannot – rather with being fixed in place and fixing others in place, as in classic state systems and ideas.

To the extent that one could speak of the collapse of the state in CAR, as many policy reports do, it is related to the ways that these different aspects of Central African stateness have intensified, and the backlash against that. That is, the insecurity and dispossession caused by the extreme porousness and non-territorial nature of the CAR state have fed a desire for a more stable and closed system. However, a less porous state would require something entirely new, something nearly impossible to imagine given the history of violent extraversion (that is, of Central African participation in creating their dependent relations with the rest of the world). By definition, such a bounded state could not be achieved by 'external' actors – the UN, INGOs, etc.

Where does that leave us? While CAR's peculiar history might make it seem marginal or an otherwise odd place to look to for broadly applicable lessons, it nevertheless has a great deal to show us, perhaps especially in understanding what is misleadingly referred to as neocolonialism and/or the problems of 'fragile' (World Bank 2011) states. Specifically, while much of the literature sees places like CAR as falling victim to 'state collapse' – a frame that suggests, wrongly, that colonial states worked well, and the chaos of recent years is a result of African stupidity/venality – CAR shows instead that violence has always had a role in shaping the state.

I have conducted ethnographic field research in CAR every year since 2003 except for 2005 and 2013. When not in the country, I am in email and phone/Skype contact (as well as, increasingly, Facebook and WhatsApp contact) with other CAR-interested friends and colleagues both in the country and outside of it, and I closely follow news reports and other developments. I have also done archival research both in Bangui (for instance at the offices of the EU) and in Paris (at the Historical Service of the Ministry of Defence) and in Aix-en-Provence (at the National Archives for France Overseas).

Since 2007, I have provided expert analysis on CAR to high-level UN officials through the Conflict Prevention and Peace Forum, which has in turn helped me understand many of the modes of thinking and operating in these realms. I have co-edited a book, and written a number of peer-reviewed articles, reports, briefings, and op-eds on CAR and related dynamics.

Ethnography does not have a clear start and end; there is no 'on' and 'off' switch that makes certain things relevant for analysis and others off-limits. Rather, it is a long-term process, one that necessitates constant circling back, re-evaluation, and adjustment of one's views. And though others may now label me an 'expert' on CAR, I feel less that I have definitively understood the place and its dynamics than that my ethnographic research has cultivated 'new habits of mind'.

What are these habits? The primary one is willed suspension of interpretive judgment, a radical form of self-distancing. You are obliged to abandon prior understandings of how the world works and, to steal a phrase from Gregory Bateson, recalibrate your understanding of the differences that make a difference. Another is humility. Much of what you already know will be of little value. You have no choice but to start over: with language, rules of deportment, expectations as to how bodies are held, used, adorned, fed. Allied with that painful self-reinvention is the obligation to listen, a challenge for scholars, whose vocation celebrates speaking with authority. The ethnographer's hosts also experience 'new habits of mind'. The very awkwardness of the encounter may change their understanding of what they do and why. It may nudge the more analytically inclined to seek a rationale for practices that normally require no explanation. (Brown 2014: 276–277)

With ethnographic research, it is not simply that everything is game for inclusion in the analytical mix at a point in time, but that the composition of the mix and one's take on it are always up for revision. The required long-term commitment and necessary openness to new habits of mind do much to separate anthropology from its non-academic cousins, like journalism or travel writing. Thus, while this book contains many stories, its analysis is far from anecdotal. For every story I tell, I could have shared many more that would have evinced similar dynamics. For those who find these methods vague, I challenge you to read and see what you learn from them, and I look forward to your counter-arguments.

Chapter 1

CONFLICT AND THE STATE IN THE PEACE-KEPT WORLD

Welcome to CAR

In June 2003 I arrived in Bangui for the first time, on a Cameroon Airlines flight from Douala. The aircraft was dilapidated and my seat was broken, creating a perma-recline that perfectly assuaged the fever I'd gotten by eating bad watermelon while waiting an entire day for the flight to leave. This was three months after François Bozizé's successful takeover of the presidency. In the centre of Bangui, locked, heavy metal doors and shuttered windows made many buildings unusually faceless. Others had been ransacked, leaving their entrails exposed. Waves of paperwork flowed across the floors of the looted offices of civil servants. A statue of the ousted president, Ange-Félix Patassé, was dressed daily in colourful drag, one of the few signs of playfulness in an otherwise tense and heavy climate. It seemed like everyone was waiting. Would people be able to go about their lives without fear of violence? Responses to this question were hopeful, but decidedly uncertain. Even in the centre of town, traffic was sparse enough for me to cross the street without looking both ways.

My task on that trip was to document the socio-economic toll of small arms and light weapons in CAR. Canvassing the humanitarian organizations for statistics and stories was quick work. There were only four: *Cooperazione internazionale*, Handicap International,

Oxfam-Quebec, Doctors Without Borders-Spain. The then-current UN peacebuilding mission, BONUCA,[1] occupied a compound on the Avenue Barthélemy Boganda that seemed fairly empty and deserted, as if several sizes too large. Once or twice, I was able to check my email at the BONUCA office. I arranged meetings from the landline at my hotel. (My recollection is that the only mobile service available had to be cadged from across the river in DRC. As much as Central Africans and others lament the slow pace of 'progress' in CAR, some things have changed!)

Early one morning, a police officer arrested me for taking a photograph. From my perspective, I was attempting to get a shot of an impossibly decrepit multi-story building (a former ministry) that nevertheless contained many camped-out residents. From his, I had captured an image of the monument to the founder of the nation, a site of prime national security interest. It was only after he pointed it out that I even noticed the pile of rubble and concrete that had been a memorial to Barthélemy Boganda. The ironies of the incident – the officiousness with which a once-proud, now-crushed legacy was treated – seemed telling.

Just over a decade later, in December 2014, I returned to Bangui for the first time since mid-2012. What had begun as a rebellion and an attempt to claim the presidency by Michel Djotodia and the Seleka in late 2012 had become a war with sectarian dimensions, with Christian nationals fighting those they perceived as Muslim foreigners. By the time I arrived, armed violence was minimal, but just two months before it had been commonplace in the capital (and it would return). Before arrival, my plane did a fly-over to assure that none of the tens of thousands of internally displaced persons (IDPs) who had made the airport their temporary home were loitering in our landing path.

I expected to find a climate like the one I had experienced more than a decade earlier: a state of suspended animation, a partially inhabited ghost town. Instead, I found traffic jams – the first I had ever experienced in Bangui, thanks to a greater number of cars and of the daily proliferation of potholes caused by heavy, armoured peacekeeping vehicles and a general lack of maintenance. Vendors with gaudy Christmas gifts (half-deflated beach balls, neon-coloured tinsel) crowded the sidewalks and streets, along with the usual boys balancing pyramids of boiled eggs and women expertly carving green oranges to reveal fragrant, glowing orbs beneath. The four INGOs of 2003 had become about fifty, accompanied by a massive UN peacekeeping mission, MINUSCA, which had outgrown the old BONUCA compound. Even with unofficial curfews in place, European-standard restaurants did brisk business. A new Lebanese-owned fast-ish food place was packed every day for lunch, both because it served decent burgers and falafel and suited the frantic pace of humanitarian work: always in a rush, if only to write the next report. Offices and expat-standard housing (a perimeter wall, good running water, on a favoured part of the electricity grid and ideally with a generator) were in short supply, with rents higher than ever. But not everything had changed: civil servants were waiting for their salaries, and every Central African I met seemed to have a story of trauma and dispossession.

Why did I find a bustling, almost overflowing metropolis in 2014, rather than the not-yet-post-conflict purgatory I had expected? Why had peacebuilding not made itself redundant, but become more prominent, in concert with escalating conflict? And how could a situation of such immiseration and violence be accompanied by such apparently robust economic activity?

These are, of course, somewhat naive questions. That war can offer opportunities for enrichment has long been noted and lamented. Carolyn Nordstrom (2004) argues simply: war is always profitable. And yet, what is striking about CAR in 2014 and today is that while a few intrepid (or foolish, or corrupt) people overtly take advantage of the war to make money, the vast majority of the people working in and on the country claim other motivations.

This is certainly the case for the various players usually referred to as the 'international community'. Rather than a community, though, these actors are more properly a crowd – an assortment of people all present at the same place, but who have diverging interests and backgrounds and might not even get along. What they share is their location – their position as part of the crowd – and their sense of self as motivated primarily by good intentions (which implicitly if not explicitly means they are less concerned with accountability for outcomes). Hence my preferred term: the good intentions crowd.[2]

They can make a lot of money doing this work, but for most money is not the draw. Members of rebel groups find ways to make money, too, but their interest in it is also inseparable from what it does for them in terms of dignity and social status. And then there's me. I make money studying these issues, and I would not do it if I didn't (one must feed one's family). But I place the money factor far down on a list of motivations topped by deciphering the puzzle of CAR: why has this persisted in being such a tough place – and even become tougher – for so many of its inhabitants?

So while I came to this project with a sense of the changes I had seen over thirteen years of studying the country foremost in my mind, finding answers to my questions required going further back in time to understand which dynamics are new and which are not. What I have found is that the ever present but always changing role of violence in Central African politics has had a lot to do with the state form itself. As I've alluded to, building a state in the classic, Weberian mould has been very difficult in CAR. For much of its history, its 'statelessness' – or in contemporary parlance, its 'fragility' (World Bank 2011) – has been ignored or considered part of its charm. (For instance, CAR's erstwhile safari/game hunting industry depended on this being the 'real' or 'wild' Africa.) At the same time, there are specific forms of violence and other problems that arise in CAR given that a state form ideal that is in this context difficult to flesh out and fulfil nevertheless monopolizes the box accorded legitimate political organization.

As the region has militarized over the past few decades, inter-national organizations and other diplomatic actors have come to see 'weak' states as a problem with only one solution: the creation of the ideal-type state that has already proved elusive. This concern has drawn a range of actors, new and old, to the table in CAR. But though united by the primacy they assign the state as a form, that same nation-state form – in particular, its status as the unit of identification and analysis in a ranked international order – divides them, allowing some at the table to see themselves as 'internal' or 'national', and others to see themselves as 'external' or 'expatriate'. In different ways, then, the idea of the state becomes a 'bond' – both a point of connection and a chain that structures those relationships in ways that the individuals involved cannot transcend.

Therefore, understanding the entrenchment of armed conflict in CAR today requires shifting the analytical frame. Rather than acting as if the people interested in conflict and politics in CAR – in whatever capacity – constitute separate, bounded cultures unto themselves (e.g. 'venal' Central African politico-military entrepreneurs, 'well-intentioned' UN and humanitarian employees, 'meddling' regional actors, 'occasionally insightful but mostly irrelevant' researchers), we must look at the nature and structure of their relationships.

Although anthropologists have long critiqued the bubble model of culture (i.e. that each culture is a self-contained bubble unto itself), it remains current in popular understandings, and it is also perpetuated by the nationalist international order. It's much easier and more comfortable to focus on 'their' culture or 'our' culture than it is to look at how these categories are given meaning through their relationships with each other. And perhaps more to the point, working to create a sense of who 'we' are as opposed to who 'they' are can be socially useful for the sake of mobilization and action, and loyalty and belonging. With analysis, however, our goal is not simply to reproduce 'native' categories but to understand and explain them – to see what they do. We want to understand the hows and the whys, and doing so shows that the differences people see as socially salient are in fact produced by their relationships with those they see as other.

Thus this book has a very simple argument, with more detailed corollaries and implications: understanding conflict in Africa today requires looking at the relationships among all of the people present and how those relationships structure what people do. I come to this argument from an interest in the good intentions crowd's newfound and growing institutionalization over the past two decades and its effects. But, given the always-outsourced nature of CAR's politics and economy (Smith 2015b), or put otherwise, given its longstanding extraversion, the country's tricky when not tragic politics have *always* been produced by the interplay among a number of actors who see themselves as different from each other – who claim different entitlements and different timeframes for involvement with this place. So in this book I navigate that longer history of unequally structured relationships and its contemporary manifestations, in part to reflect on both what really is different and what has persisted. It is always easier to see injustice in the past than in the present, but perhaps the recognition of significant similarities will spur critical reflection on the current moment as well.

Still fighting for the rainforest?

Twenty years ago, Paul Richards published what has become a manifesto for the anthropology of war, *Fighting for the Rainforest: War, Youth, and Resources in Sierra Leone*. The Cold War had recently ended, and in its aftermath violent conflict had broken out in various places around the world, with a notable concentration in West and Central Africa. At the time, the reigning explanation came from the journalist Robert D. Kaplan, who explained these conflicts as but the beginning of 'The Coming Anarchy' in a 1994 article in *The Atlantic*. He argued that in an age of environmental destruction and scarcity, senseless conflict would become increasingly prevalent. Kaplan's article was infamously faxed (those were the days) by the United States State Department to every US embassy. In a similar vein, Samuel Huntington argued in *The Clash of Civilizations*

(1996) that coming wars would be fundamentally about identity and incompatible worldviews. The dominant thrust of these journalistic and political science accounts was that whatever these post-Cold War wars were about, it would not be politics. Enter Richards, an anthropologist with a decades-long engagement with Sierra Leone. Richards showed that in Sierra Leone – one of Kaplan's main cases of coming-anarchy-in-the-present – fighting that appeared senseless or at best tied to scarce resources was in fact born of long-festering political grievances about how society should be structured. He further demonstrated that even the brutal techniques used in the war, such as amputations, had a logic in the minds of people committing them. In doing so, he showed that rather than a 'new barbarism' (Richards' term for Kaplan-style analysis), post-Cold War wars grew from political struggles over distribution, status, and belonging.

In this way, Richards charted a course for a new genre of anthropological accounts of contemporary wars. My work has consistently seconded Richards' contention that it is analytically vacuous to describe wars in terms of degrees of 'barbarism', that is, to describe the West's interest in long-distance killing (Lindqvist 1993) as more evolved than those who continue to fight face to face. I have also striven to understand why people engage in violence – what violence communicates and why. This approach has limits, but it has nevertheless been a useful corrective to the journalistic accounts that focus on barbarism and 'blood-letting', which tend to tell us more about the prejudices of the people writing than they do about the fighting taking place.

Alongside the possible resurgence of barbarism, observers also wondered whether post-Cold War wars reflected a fundamental alteration of the classic Clausewitzian model of battles between state armies. Was this a 'new' mode of warfare? Military historian Martin van Creveld (1991) and political scientist Mary Kaldor argued yes. Kaldor coined the term 'new wars' to serve as an ideal type, a guide for policy and research. (She did not mean to imply that such wars never occurred in the past; rather, she wanted to make the limitations of the usual war model – 'old war' – explicit.) What set 'new wars' apart, she argued, was that 'whereas old wars tended to extremes as each side tried to win, new wars tend to spread and to persist or recur as each side gains in political or economic ways from violence itself rather than "winning"' (Kaldor 1999; 2013). Other terms used to describe 'new wars' include non-conventional wars, small wars, asymmetrical wars, or insurgency. The key throughout is that these other varieties of war involve non-state actors, and are in large part about the economic benefits that accrue to certain people during wartime.

So while the extent to which post-Cold War conflicts reflect new trends is debatable, they have undoubtedly prompted a new emphasis on the social context and study of war. In this book, I pause to ask where we are today. I contend that since the early 2000s there have been major shifts in the prosecution and management of violent conflict, and we cannot understand conflict without including these shifts – that is, without making all the people present the objects of the analysis. When Kaplan, Richards, and Kaldor were writing, international intervention in conflict zones was moving from its Cold War logics into UN-led, humanitarian modes. Some of the older players (e.g. France in its former colonies, African regional heads of state and their soldiers) continued to exert important influences, but various international conflict-response agencies also swelled and came to take on an increasingly wide range of functions. While there were only eighteen UN peacekeeping missions between 1948 and 1990, since 1990 there have been more than fifty.

These new interventions and modes of helping are shaped and constrained by the nation-state form, and the fictive conception that the world is composed of equal nation-states.[3] The term 'fictive' (as opposed to 'fictional') highlights that people treat it as socially real, even though aware of the flimsiness of its empirical basis. Anthropologist-turned-novelist Amitav Ghosh presciently pinpointed the problem of the rigid state form in his notes on an early UN mission, in Cambodia:

> there is an unspoken and unwritten agreement that underlies the UN's actions, not merely in Cambodia, but wherever it goes: an agreement that derives ultimately from what might be called the primal mandate of the UN itself. The UN represents the totality of the world's recognized nation-states, and the fundamental logic of its functioning is to recreate the image of its membership wherever it goes. Elections are, thus, only a step in restoring or conjuring up a nation-state, and wherever the demands of democracy or humanitarianism run contrary to the exigencies of the nation-state, it is the latter that will always win out. (1994: 421)

The problem is that while in theory these nation-states are equal, in practice they are anything but. The international system is constructed to insist upon perpetuating a single political form (i.e. the state as holder of an *a priori* monopoly on legitimacy it has done little to earn). This can make it impossible to focus on organic processes of accountability and democratic participation while staying agnostic on the ultimate administrative shape of things. The insistence on the state form also determines a great deal about the kinds of relationships that the various people involved in Central African political economies are able to have. That is to say, despite the apparent institutional frailty of the state, the state form nevertheless organizes the possible relationships and ideas about what can be done, and introduces hierarchies, power dynamics, and incentives that to a large extent structure relationships and privileges. Curiously, these hierarchies, dynamics, and incentives are perhaps most constraining for the people who are most privileged.

Consider, for instance, the chain of events that led to the nomination of a new Central African prime minister in August 2014. It was widely known that French diplomats preferred Karim

Meckassoua, a long-time minister and a Muslim. When President Catherine Samba-Panza met with French officials to discuss who to choose, she expressed interest in Meckassoua. The French officials were pleased she had on her own arrived at the person whom they saw as the right choice. A few days later, however, Samba-Panza gave a speech in which she criticized the French for imposing Meckassoua on her. We are a sovereign nation, she said, and we must make our own choices. She appealed to popular sentiment that the country has been dispossessed and otherwise buffeted by more powerful foreigners – and by France in particular. In Meckassoua's place, she chose Mahamat Kamoun, a long-time civil servant with a reputation as a technocrat who would have little chance of effectively countering the president's excesses or other bad choices. She claimed the choice had been made based on an internal review of the possible candidates following 33 criteria, and that Kamoun had received the highest score. (Unstated was whether friendship with the president was one of the factors; Kamoun's wife, the head of customs and notoriously corrupt, is a close friend of Samba-Panza's [Africa Confidential 2014].)

In the end, Kamoun proved a competent prime minister, to the extent that the prime minister can exercise a role in the pros-ecution of politics. International donors and organization staffers in particular were thankful for his attention to policy and help in moving the transition process forward. So in this case, things worked out more or less. But what does the story tell us about the nature of power and sovereign authority in CAR? Had Samba-Panza not taken her own course, it was entirely plausible that French diplomats would play a decisive role in determining the Central African prime minister. Of CAR's eight presidents, French actors had important (if not entirely decisive) roles in the rise to and main-tenance of power for five or six. And yet that tendency also gives Central African politicians a framework in which to make their own choices, in part by playing with the vagaries of sovereignty and the state form. In places like CAR, the question of who is in charge is not just obscured by the fiction of the sovereign nation-state, but becomes genuinely impossible to determine. Central Africans often describe themselves as victims of foreign string-pullers, but that analysis ignores their active participation in these matters and the ways they, too, wield power.

The selection of the prime minister further demonstrates that though French and Central African politicians might try to describe themselves as fundamentally different kinds of actors (as having different cultures, or as being 'internal' and 'external') *who* they are is far less useful analytically than understanding *what* shapes their relationships and *what* they are able to do. In fact, the very process of defining themselves as 'segregated' from each other thoroughly links them together in ways that do little to resolve the major problems of the day. What gets lost is any kind of substantive democratic process — as opposed to a simply instrumentalized (i.e. a leader who appeals to popular anti-French sentiment while still remaining thoroughly beholden to French and other forms of international aid) or procedural (i.e. elections that provide no accountability) one.

The anthropologist Max Gluckman offers a powerful model for analysing relationships among all actors present in a political situation. A Jewish South African working during the entrenchment of the apartheid system (1930s–1970s) and critical of it, Gluckman recognized that segregation was an important social value for the government and many whites. However, this did not square with his experience of life there. Rather, he noticed that people of different races had all sorts of relationships with one other. In a now-famous article (published in 1940), he illustrated this point by describing a ceremony in Zululand to inaugurate a new bridge. Ditching the previously commonplace anthropological tendency to focus on one social group at a time – for instance, to look at Zulus unto themselves, or (less often) to look at white government officials unto themselves – he mentioned everyone present, including himself (where he was, to whom he spoke and in which languages, etc.). He described and diagrammed the protocols for interaction, and how he was treated when he breached them. He found that 'segregation' was in fact produced out of pomp and practice – such as these ceremonies – in which all participated. Thus, 'segregation' was fictive. Or as he put it, it lacked any 'real content' (1940: 14). There was an *appearance* of cultural separation: blacks and whites 'were sharply separated by custom and language, standards of living, types of work, marriage barriers, and social exclusiveness' (1955: 151). However,

> they were held together largely in the cohesion of a common social system – by money and cultural ties, as much as by the Maxim gun. ... I want to emphasize that the system worked because from the beginning divisions of interest in the Zulu group led certain of its sections and individuals to seek alliances with certain White groups or individuals. Zulu kings sought the aid of White muskets against their Black enemies. Later, desires for peace, for White technical assistance, and for White money and goods, introduced conflicts in Zulu allegiances, and thus led some Zulu – eventually almost all Zulu – into co-operation with Whites. The whole process of establishing cross-linkages across the main Black-White division was quickly at work. (ibid.: 151)

Gluckman's close attention to micro-level processes – the protocols at bridge openings, the position of a Zulu 'agricultural demonstrator' among his people – led him to conclude that all people in South Africa had created new 'equivocalities' in their positions by entering into relationships with one another. That is, they had relationships with conflicting obligations and loyalties. The result was entanglement and difficulty acting on the basis of principle.

Gluckman explains equivocality through reference to the tricky position of the Zulu native chief. His position was 'equivocal' because the popular legitimacy he gained from fellow Zulu was based on the degree to which he opposed the government, but his 'effective authority' (that is, his powers of taxation and use of force) came from the white government. Chiefs thus had to balance these allegiances, which they did, for example, by going along with government directives and then neglecting to implement them. Moreover, even among Zulu there were many important divisions – such as between Christians and non-Christians – and they would switch allegiance flexibly in pursuit of their interests. Yet they did so in the context of the colour-bar, which created hierarchies and inequalities while nevertheless fastening a range of people into cross-cutting relationships. The colour-bar linked people, yet without providing a shared moral order or sense of purpose for everyone involved. As a result,

> The ability of the Zulu to play off Commissioner against chief in different situations did not enable the Zulu to solve the problems of poverty, deteriorating land, inadequate wages, cultural strain, restrictive controls, and so forth, which they considered oppressed them. ... Changes of the incumbents of offices, alterations of jobs, movements to new areas – no shifting of allegiances – could redress the fundamental cleavage of the colour-bar. (Gluckman 1955: 163)

Today, there is no official colour-bar in Africa. There is even a Central African maxim that *zo kwe zo* – every person is a person, which implies that equality should be the basis for the social order. And yet when people invoke that aphorism today it carries at best an aspirational connotation, and more often an ironic or even cruel one, given how limited people's life chances are in this part of the world, both compared to their country's elites and compared to people in most other places.

A quantitative political scientist might devote herself to determining the causal reasons for CAR's unenviable human development statistics. I could certainly contribute a litany of historical and ongoing injustice and exploitation to consider. But as an anthropologist, I am particularly interested in what *gives form to* the relationships among people involved in this place called CAR. Why is it that an international employee of the UN has a set of entitlements and a salary scale that is so different from that of a national staff member? Perhaps in part it has to do with skills – that is, with which skills and what kind of knowledge are valued (e.g. thematic knowledge is seen as more valuable than 'local' or 'contextual' knowledge [Autesserre 2014]). But a local with impeccable thematic knowledge does not suddenly become an international employee, with an international salary. And that offers a hint that the differences people take for granted as natural are in fact socially produced (and therefore changeable).

The system of independent nation-states (a characterization that is more ideological-aspirational than analytical given the hierarchies, power dynamics, and relationships that are its foundation) is crucial here. Its philosophy is quite different from that of the colour-bar, but it has a similar ability to structure relationships. It moreover shapes how we talk about what the problems are and what solutions are possible. When Ghosh happened upon the UN mission in Cambodia in the early 1990s, he was surprised the UN staffers had made it their business to determine people's proper nationality and citizenship and escort them to the appropriate side of the Cambodia/Vietnam border. Why was that the priority? He concluded,

It is my belief that we are currently witnessing a fundamental change in the political institutions of this century, one that will probably result in a two-tier system of nation-states. In the first of those tiers, the boundaries of the nation-state, as traditionally understood, will become increasingly blurred; in the other, conversely, those boundaries will become increasingly rigid and will serve as a mechanism for the maintenance of a pattern of global order. Thus, the very institution that was (and is) so eagerly embraced by the peoples of the colonized world, as the embodiment of their liberty, will become, effectively, the instrument of their containment. This two-tier system will probably reflect global realties more accurately than did the international order of the Cold War era. But fundamentally the principles of that order will not be new. Throughout the period of Western expansion over the last two centuries, the nation-state has repeatedly supplied models of containment: we have only to think of the reservations of America or the Bantustans of South Africa. The transformation we are witnessing today may well be another step in the ascendancy of that pattern. What is novel in it perhaps is that now the peoples of the regions in which it is becoming ascendant are fully complicit in the taking of that step. (1994: 421–422)

Ghosh's claim that the world is becoming a global reservation will no doubt strike many as polemical. It does, however, seem pertinent to note that when the UN was dealing primarily with a European refugee crisis after the Second World War, its fundamental mission was to protect the 'right to leave' (that is, the right for persecuted peoples to flee their countries of origin); once the refugee problem became a matter of Asians and Africans in flight the principle of the 'right to return' (that is, to go home as soon as a peace agreement had been struck) took precedence (Hyndman 2000).

In any event, the reservation claim is most useful for the kinds of questions it spurs us to ask and respond to. In the poorer states of the world we often find anaemic governments supported by high levels of development aid and peacebuilding initiatives of a wide variety and scope. (More-powerful neighbouring heads of state and their militaries frequently become players in these unlucky places as well.) And all of these people are adapting to each other, drawing in new and old players in new and old ways, in the process shifting relationships and creating new entanglements. Yet rather than re-centring the analysis away from the ideal-type state model to better align with the empirical context, people often end up sticking with the old state-based labels and categories. This ideal-type state form is a kind of phantom limb, albeit one the patient never had in the first place.

And yet as much of an eidolon as it is, it places parameters on the imaginations of doctors and patients alike as to what can be done to improve the situation. It is the limb that is needed, nothing else. The patient's body – the state as it actually exists – occupies an extremely dependent and debased position in comparison.

To the extent that debased position is made the starting point for analysis, it is usually for polemical purposes, such as the cunning victimhood that is the foundation of Central African foreign policy: posing as a victim (I am but the poor, weak cousin in a dangerous neighbourhood) in order to make an implicit threat (if you don't support me, all hell will break loose). (In the words of an Anti-Balaka leader I interviewed, 'The origin of the crisis in CAR is the international community!' What international community, I asked? 'France!' he replied.) More often, people focus on diagnosing particular categories of actor, while taking the structure of their interactions for granted. So we find reports on the venality of Central African politicians, and endless evaluations of UN peacebuilding blunders, and efforts to track every dollar accumulated by an armed group leader.

This 'bounded cultures' approach can nonetheless yield some useful data and observations. For instance, peacebuilders have recently turned to analysis of their own 'nation', 'Peaceland' (Autesserre 2014), and describe the transplantation of projects and ways of working from one place to another (for a similar analysis of 'Aidland' see Mosse 2011). Though the citizens of these 'lands' describe their work as a kind of solidarity, their daily practices distance them from the people on whose behalf they see themselves as working. Describing the culture of Aidland or Peaceland can thus help us see the contradictions between rhetoric and practice among the diverse people and institutions involved in these efforts. It can also suggest everyday ways of changing those dynamics.

However, framing the issue as one of separate cultures (aid givers unto themselves, and aid recipients unto themselves) is not a simple description of facts. It is itself the reproduction of the separations people want (to varying degrees) to maintain, but which are belied by the relationships that link them. An expatriate international organization staffer might be segregated in a white Land Cruiser with tinted windows, but that vehicle will be driven by a Central African. In this sense the effort to describe a Peaceland has resonances with the efforts of oil executives in Equatorial Guinea to describe themselves as 'offshore' and hence not embedded in any particular place, despite the vast local resources (human and otherwise) required to perpetuate their offshore vision (Appel 2012).

Perhaps more to the point, the recommendation that Peacelanders should use local context as the starting point for programme design and daily practice is limited in terms of its possible effects. I may understand the Central African context brilliantly; I might be in solidarity with Central Africans and them with me. But I have not just one but two passports (US and Norwegian) that permit me to travel anywhere I wish, while even the rarefied few Central Africans who obtain a passport find it but the first of many difficult steps toward travelling abroad. And no project, no matter how contextually aware, can change that.

Comparison may clarify: a few years ago, another international intervener called for 'local context' in order to improve its operations. In that case, it was the US military, and the initiative was the Human Terrain System, which would incorporate anthropologists and historians into operations, with the aim of promoting cross-cultural understanding and reducing recourse to violence. But, whether equipped with context or not, the US military is still the US military, and it occupies a hegemonic position in the world, with a tendency toward adventurism guided by American assessments of geosecurity. Peacelanders are not the equivalent of the US military, but they do benefit from certain structural immunities and privileges in relation to the people they work among. Ten thousand Haitians died of cholera when Nepali peacekeepers in the UN Stabilization Mission in Haiti were not properly screened and inadvertently introduced the disease to the country after an earthquake in 2010. The screening failure could be ascribed to a technical slip-up. The fact that UN officials have prevented attempts to seek redress cannot. It is, rather, rooted in relationships made unequal by structural considerations, not just by the choices of the individuals within them.

But this book is not a diatribe against international interveners or any other category of actor. In fact, that is my point: no matter how smart or dedicated the individual – whether a Central African politician, someone in the good intentions crowd, or a peasant – she is constrained by her relationships with other people and the underlying principles shaping those relationships. Nor do I argue that international intervention and peacebuilding cause or exacerbate violent conflict, causal findings that my research was not designed to test. Nor is the state my target, except insofar as the state ideal/ system places counter-productive limits on the imagination. Rather, to do justice to everyone we must consider all of the actors involved and the nature of their relationships with each other – the interplay of personal and structural factors that shape what people do and why. And that requires treating 'native categories' such as the construction of 'us' and 'them' as themselves *projects* rather than given facts of the world.

Classically, anthropologists have sought to show the insights that come from making the taken-for-granted features of our world – that which strikes us as 'familiar' – strange, to draw attention to the social construction of the everyday. This can occur through juxtaposing the present with perhaps surprising similarities in the past, as in Ghosh's comparison of contemporary peacekeeping to the Bantustans of yore. And it can be achieved by vigilant curiosity around why things are the way they are, and never accepting what you find as *necessary*. I draw on both techniques in this book. As a result, my focus is not on sterile questions of 'effectiveness', such as whether peacebuilding interventions are good or bad, but on the range of effects they have, and especially the kinds of relationships they involve. As Soumaine Ndodeba, a rebel leader and children's rights advocate who became one of my most important armed group interlocutors, reflected one day, 'Sometimes I ask myself why I was born here. This sure is a bizarre country.' Probing every aspect of that bizarreness requires awareness of what is new and different about the newly-institutionalized modes of intervention in the post-Cold War as well as how they resonate with long-standing trends.

The early critics of international conflict management and humanitarianism, such as Ghosh and Alex de Waal (1997), were far more trenchant in their critiques of these modes of intervention than many contemporary accounts aimed at reforming such institutions. De Waal, for instance, wondered whether the humanitarian mode of power had the ability to impose a changed political order, one based in a real way on a contract between rulers and ruled. In the nearly two decades since he wrote, many advocates and academics seemed to take for granted that the US military was unable to do anything similar (in Iraq and Afghanistan in particular) but were far less sceptical of international agencies' ability to do the same. And it is indeed possible that humanitarian aid and international interveners have been learning from past mistakes and are doing things more effectively than they once were. However, it is equally possible that many of us have simply gotten used to the current modes of managing and responding to violent conflict and forgotten that they, too, are bizarre.

However 'new' war and rebellion in CAR may be in the Kaldorian sense, their protagonists have also developed techniques of conventionalization that help them better collaborate with the bureaucratic organs and prerogatives of international organizations. To be clear, this is a project undertaken both by members of rebel groups and by the international diplomats and bureaucrats called on to help resolve these conflicts. In the middle stands the sovereign nation-state form, in nothing more than an aspirational sense. This form is sacrosanct and privileged, such that while all the people involved in 'building' it develop cross-cutting ties, they are never able to broach the fundamental issues of distribution that most trouble CAR today. Why, for instance, does it seem natural to describe a person who falsifies personal data in order to benefit from

DDR – a benefit of maybe a thousand dollars at most – as corrupt, or a profiteer, or his superior's dupe, while it would seem odd to describe the UN staffer running the project – who is likely banking USD100,000–200,000 a year tax-free – in any of the same ways? Perhaps there are good reasons. But the main reason these kinds of questions are impossible to raise is the nation-state logic that fixes some people as 'nationals' and others as 'expatriates'. That is simply the way of the world today. But it is important not to forget that it has important political and economic effects, such as in terms of who gets what, and who can move where, and the solutions that can be tried. Thus I focus on connections, and the nature and dynamics of connections and the equivocalities that fester when people who are divided (and who divide themselves) in various ways nevertheless become part of the same system.

The book focuses on the past decade of conflict in CAR. I draw on a longer-term history in order to show how relationships and ideas operating today have developed through the highly unequal and often violent manner in which Central Africa has been integrated into long-distance trades and processes. The crisis, as many refer to the period from 2013–2014 (and beyond), drew much international attention to CAR. While 'crisis' might be a useful galvanizer for hashtag advocacy, it is not particularly useful analytically, because it implies a departure from a prior state of normalcy. In CAR, the disruption of normalcy *is* the new normal (Carayannis and Lombard 2015). Conflict and international intervention have adapted to each other, drawn in new and old players, and in the process created new relationships and entanglements. These processes of adaptation involve figuring out how to communicate with (and influence) each other, as well as how to collaborate. These processes trend toward conventionalization, by which I mean the development of shared languages, forms, and tools that create a platform for working together while leaving all the countervailing elements in the shadows.

For instance, where rebellion in CAR used to be fairly *ad hoc* and unorganized, in the 2000s rebel groups began to develop patriotic names and their associated acronyms, the better to communicate to the government and international organization/diplomatic players the threat they represent (Lombard 2016b). A new name and an officer rank did not erase a person's history of road banditry or otherwise problematic status, but it made it easier for those international actors that take an intermittent interest in responding to conflict in CAR to understand the particular kind of threat such a person and the men behind him represented, and to identify a particular tool (e.g. peace processes) to put forward as a solution. One could say that as irregular war has been regularized in Central Africa over the past two decades, so have the improvised yet bureaucratic conflict management apparatuses offered in response.

Conventional rebellion in CAR lasted about a decade, from the emergence of the *Armée populaire pour la restauration de la démocratie* (Popular Army for the Restoration of Democracy, APRD) in 2005 to 2012. Seleka's emergence in late 2012 marked a shift. The greater proportion of men-in-arms from the Chad/Darfur borderlands in the group contributed to a more rapacious governing style as rebels took on governing functions in areas far from their homes. During conventional rebellion, members of rebel groups had primarily operated in their home regions, and while their mode of rule could be brutal, they considered these areas their past, present, and future homes and so had incentives not to go too far. But things changed once Seleka arrived on the scene, composed not just of once-conventional rebels but also people with shallower roots in CAR and histories of region-spanning politico-military entrepreneurship. (Changes in the forms and organization of violence will be the focus of Chapter 6.) From their initial assaults to the aftermath of their taking the presidency (December 2012 – September 2013), members of Seleka ruled the towns they occupied as fiefdoms. As has been shown elsewhere (Ferme and Hoffman 2004), operating far from home is associated with extra brutality. People in occupied towns, as well as Bangui, began to rise up in anger. Some were supported by the ousted president, François Bozizé, or his associates; many drew on longstanding, intermittently-organized self-defence initiatives. Together, they began to call themselves the Anti-Balaka.

Neither Seleka nor the Anti-Balaka were ever unified groups, or even alliances of groups. They had certain features in common, but they did not have a unified identity. Just as anthropologists have struggled in the past to describe 'stateless' societies, it is difficult to refer precisely to these kinds of entities. Smith (1974) coined the term 'corporate category' to describe people who share certain cultural features like language or descent rules but do not have unified institutions or a sense of themselves as a group. This is also something of what Deleuze and Guattari meant to convey with their idea of the 'war machine', but that term carries misleading associations in that the mode of power/organizing they are describing neither concerns war nor is a machine.

The violence that flared between Seleka and the Anti-Balaka looked less like conventional rebellion and more like the anger and necessity-driven processes of popular punishment (Lombard and Batianga-Kinzi 2015) and what political scientists refer to as 'inter-communal violence'. Certain self-styled leaders worked to conventionalize their forces, with greater success among the former Seleka than among the Anti-Balaka. But the anger and opportunistic violence are not gone, and have spiked at particularly fraught political moments such as presidential elections that had been scheduled for October 2015. (The presidential election's first round was eventually held on 30 December 2015, and the run-off on 14 February 2016, events that were thankfully marked by little violence.)

While the process of conventionalization and the political marketplace it requires (de Waal 2015) evolved into something new and much more violent, the ways these various armed actors, Central African politicians, aid donors, and diplomats collaborate have certain constant features. And all of those relationships are mediated by the form of the state and the constraints it imposes, even despite the chasm between the actual practices and capacities of the Central African government and ideal-type tenets. That state form remains rigid, just as Ghosh pointed out, and people adapt in relation to it, developing cross-cutting ties that further entangle them. That is to say, everyone has relationships with a range of people, and conflict in one kind of relationship (e.g. between a rebel leader and a diplomat) can create solidarity in another set of relationships (e.g. between that rebel leader and the people fighting under him). When multiplied over and over, you see why allegiances that are multiple, overlapping, and even sometimes at cross purposes (such as the obligation not to engage in corruption and the obligation to provide for one's family), can make it so difficult to achieve the kind of collective action that could transform the mode of politics once and for all.

Gluckman described these processes in relation to the entrenchment of apartheid rule in South Africa. In that system, whites imposed segregation in order to cement their position at the top of a hierarchy. Gluckman pointed out that this left them with far less leverage to work with people of other races and hence quite hemmed in by comparison. (In titling his talk 'The Bonds in the Colour-Bar' he referred to the chains whites had unwittingly imposed on themselves.) Today, the de-politicizing force of the colour-bar has been replaced by the de-politicizing force of the state form, and the ideal type of the sovereign nation-state. This fiction of a sovereign nation-state continually obscures and displaces the question of who is in charge, while nevertheless reserving particular privileges for high-level government officials and diplomats that are difficult for any individual to refuse (even if he wanted to). When a president or minister enters a room, all assembled – diplomats and Central Africans alike – rise silently and respectfully. That minister or president is hugely dependent on donor aid, and in theory donors could turn off the spigot (and therefore his authority) if they saw a need to. More often, though, they privately lament or scoff at the government's ineptitude while publicly participating in the ceremonies.

One problem with this system is that while a range of people have arrogated authorities and privileges for themselves, the question of who should be held to account if things sour is far less clear. Responsibility is divided, and hierarchies are both obscured and changeable from one interaction to another. The effects of this accountability gap are not equally felt. Diplomats and others receive salaries either way; the 'beneficiaries' of any eventual project might not. Disarmament programmes are a particularly dramatic, or tragic, case of how the centrality of the fictive sovereign nation-state form leads not just to policies that are maladapted to the Central African context, but which also seem always to prevent popular grievances – popular visions of political change – from being taken seriously.

Rituals, social emotion, and anomie

A central concern of this book is to recognize how difficult it is for people to just act as they wish, or as they see best, in any given situation. There are *structures* that shape how people interact with one another. 'Structure' is a somewhat misleading term, however, because it conjures an image of an edifice in which people move around, through fixed passages and doors. This is inaccurate. People, through the rules and rituals of day-to-day interactions, are themselves the creators and supporters of social structure. Recognizing that social structure is not a free-standing entity but is continuously re-created through social life itself does not make social structure any weaker – quite the opposite.

In fact, daily life consists of little besides these kinds of micro-supports that bolster broader social and cultural norms and tendencies. The way one says hello, the way one eats (and what one eats), taking turns speaking at a meeting: all of these activities follow rules that might be nowhere written or enforced, and yet which we all tend to obey simply because not doing so risks making us into outcasts – perhaps shunned, or maybe just avoided, but either way denied the human connections and validation that are so central to our lived experience. As Erving Goffman pointed out in his study of asylums, those diagnosed as mentally ill are not separated from the rest of us by some grand difference like an extra appendage, but by the fact that they repeatedly fail to correctly participate in minor daily rituals like those mentioned above – eating with the hands when cutlery is expected, failing to return a 'Hello, how are you?' with something from the spectrum of expected responses, etc. (Goffman 1961; Collins 2004: 20).

However, though conformity to 'ritual propriety' (Collins 2004: 20) is central to the micro-ritual creation of social life, that conformity is not limited to groups that see themselves as culturally homogeneous. In fact, the pressures might be even stronger between people who see themselves as different from each other, both because they want to mark their difference in ritual and material ways, and because their uncertainty about the other means that they work harder to make sure their interactions follow safe channels. This point is at least as old as Emile Durkheim's coining of the term 'organic solidarity' to refer to the fabric of social life in diverse places like cities, but it is often neglected in favour of studies of how a particular group sees itself, as if that group were a bounded entity unto itself and not, as is in fact the case, formed out of its relations with those it sees as both similar and different.

Consider a meeting I attended in late September 2015. Diplomats (bilateral and international), representatives of INGOs and advocacy organizations, and a few academic types like me assembled for lunch at a hotel in New York City. We were to receive the transitional president of CAR, Catherine Samba-Panza, who was in town for the UN General Assembly meetings. Central Africans and others concerned with the fate of the country were frustrated with her tenure, which seemed to prioritize pomp over substantive measures to help Central Africans. When I polled my friends and colleagues for questions I should ask her, one suggested 'How many houses have you purchased while in office?' Others wondered why there had been no progress on disarmament or said she should step down since she clearly was not pulling the country out of its crisis. One suggested she was in fact a sorcerer – prolonging the crisis so that she could enrich herself. I was primed and eager to ask a difficult question.

When the president walked into the room, however, we all stood respectfully. We listened to a speech she gave about her accomplishments. The first questioner made a statement of support for her and her government, then asked something entirely anodyne. A diplomat seconded and broadened the statement of support. Just two days before, new violence had broken out in Bangui. People were being killed, and INGOs in the centre of town (where no one expected violence) were being looted. The peacekeepers in the country seemed ill-prepared to deal with it. Central Africans and diplomats alike wondered if this was a coup attempt; not just the president but other senior government and UN officials were all out of the country. So for most of the people in the room, their statements of solidarity were a way of signalling they would support the president as she rushed home early from her trip abroad.

My concerns and interests were different, however. I, like my Central African colleagues, wanted to push back against diplomatic public relations/marketing speak. But I hesitated. The question period ended before I had a chance to craft a query that would allow me to stay true to my goal without feeling I was being mean. Going against the tide of all that ritual and formality among those otherwise diverse people in the room would have required a massive, heaving effort. (Christopher Hitchens used to do it all the time at Washington, DC think tank events, but there are few like him.) Afterwards, I tried to explain my inaction to myself. It hadn't been the right moment for a zinger. But that was not it, at least not entirely. Rather, it was the whole context for the interaction that demanded particular modes of comportment among everyone assembled to participate. Breaching those made-in-the-situation norms and modes would be akin to stepping into a cathedral and belting out a show tune – that is, immensely difficult, whether or not one is Catholic.

And this brings up a further crucial point: the usual term for referring to daily micro-rituals is the 'everyday', or everyday practice. But that term has a secular connotation – it suggests daily life, the mundane – when in fact such things can be imbued with a kind of sacred reverence and power. There is not a sharp line between the sacred and the profane; they are instead the two ends of a spectrum. Part of that sacredness has to do with the way that when people come together, we become more than a collection of individuals. We do things we might not otherwise do. Micro-rituals and the situational exigencies of daily life are emotionally entraining (Collins 2004) – they draw us into social complicity not just on a logical/rational basis but on an emotional one as well. On occasion, we incite each other, 'amplify' each other, and emotional entrainment becomes a collective effervescence, as Durkheim wrote of Australian aboriginal religious ceremonies:

> The initial impulse is thereby amplified each time it is echoed, like an avalanche that grows as it goes along. … Probably because a collective emotion cannot be expressed collectively without some order that permits harmony and unison of movement, these gestures and cries tend to fall into rhythm and regularity, and from there into songs and dances. But in taking on a more regular form, they lose none of their natural fury. (Durkheim 1995 [1912]: 2018)

People are caught up, complicit, in the energies of the moment. Effervescence is in a sense the stark and unruly version of emotional entrainment. But both a riled-up crowd and a meeting with a president are marked by these processes, albeit in different ways. Because of this, asking people why they do what they do in collective, ritual situations will always bump into the difficulty of (re-)capturing the spirit in which the act was committed, which was conditioned by the effervescent tendencies of the moment.

This is particularly the case when it comes to violence. As a concept, violence contains reprobation – the term itself designates something bad, unlike many of the other things about social life one might seek to understand, like kinship or exchange. Moreover, violence is inherently emotional. Reasons for violence will explain certain aspects of violence, but they will generally be offered after the fact, and thus risk missing the emotional, effervescent aspects of why and how it came to pass. As anthropologist Don Donham explains, violence presents particular challenges as an object of study:

> Violence is red. It overtakes and overwhelms. It disorients and disrupts. Under threat, with palm sweating, mouth dry, the throat so tight it cannot scream, the body no longer calmly observes. 'Being there' no longer provides the usual guarantees of narrative reliability. What happened? Is this the man who raped you? We know that victims can be both absolutely certain in their identifications of attackers and wrong. In the end, we must accept this as one of the crucial properties of violence: it has the inherent potential to 'unmake' the social world, to create murk and uncertainty. ... The point is this: violence, because it creates uncertainty, also establishes the seedbed in which people can change their attitudes, commitments, and identities. In this sense, it can 'speed up' history. This means that narratives created after violence, particularly by victims, can unconsciously project back upon the past attitudes and identities in fact created by the experience of violence. ... This tendency to read the present (after violence) into the past necessarily overemphasizes and overplays the role of hatred of the other as an explanation for violence. ... The analysis of violence, consciously or not, moves into [a] fast-moving stream, with all of its undertows and cross-currents. ... Analysts distinguish themselves from participants to the degree that they deal critically and self-consciously

with the demands posed by the epistemology of extraordinary situations. That means retrieving the complexities of a situation that the experience of violence nearly always simplifies. (2006: 28–29)

In Africa today, it is not just violence that creates uncertainty. In CAR, funerals occur far more frequently than weddings. Mysterious illnesses (and/or nearly-non-existent medical facilities) claim many lives. Many people experience life as a precipice: a stronger-than-usual breeze, and they risk falling. People are resilient, of course – impressively so. They move when a home, for whatever reason, becomes unsafe, and build another, sometimes a temporary one next to their fields, other times a longer-term one in another town. But the uncertainty, and the distance between the ideals and aspirations people hold and the confusion or futility that attach to how they might be achieved remain determining aspects of life.

Durkheim is helpful here too: he describes such situations as marked by anomie, which he defined as the kind of limitless desire that emerges at times when change (whether for the better or the worse) is rapid enough to create a gap between values/norms (which are themselves in flux) and what people are able to achieve in their lives.

Irrespective of any external regulatory force, our capacity for feeling is in itself an insatiable and bottomless abyss. But if nothing external can restrain this capacity, it can only be a source of torment to itself. Unlimited desires are insatiable by definition and insatiability is rightly considered a sign of morbidity. Being unlimited, they constantly and infinitely surpass the means at their command; they cannot be quenched. Inextinguishable thirst is constantly renewed torture. It has been claimed, indeed, that human activity naturally aspires beyond assignable limits and sets itself unattainable goals. (Durkheim 1951 [1897]: 248)

Durkheim is thus diagnosing a specific social problem. When desire is limitless, it is impossible to feel like one is making any progress towards one's goals. No matter what movement one engages in, the horizon is never any closer – it is always further away than anything one can see or imagine. Thus the world comes to seem like an infinity, and not in a wondrous sense, but in the sense of one being lost, submerged.

Anomie suffuses most Central Africans' lives today. They are acutely aware of their last-place position in the world. The distant top is that impossible-to-reach horizon. But rather than making people give up, this causes instead a proliferation of limitless desires. At the same time, many Central Africans are immensely suspicious of capitalist modes of accumulation and hoarding. Doing well in business is less likely to be ascribed to a work ethic, and more likely to be ascribed to nefarious doings, possibly of an occult nature, and otherwise anti-social behaviour. Thus the feeling of drowning in one's own insatiable, unquenchable desires, and seeing no way out.

Conclusion

Studying violence in Africa and elsewhere in the peace-kept world (Ghosh 1994) demands a few starting orientations. First, it requires rejecting the bounded cultures model for understanding the different people present in conflict zones. It is in the relations between these different actors, the factors that constrain and entangle them, such as micro-rituals, that we will begin to understand why people act as they do, and the effects of their actions, just as Gluckman did with his bridge-opening ceremony. Segregation might be an important social value for certain people, but it can be produced only through social contact and the marking of difference. Moreover, the various people involved in these processes are constantly adapting to each other in ways both tiny and large, to the extent that it makes no sense to speak of, say, an armed group's culture as if it were an impervious entity and not, as it is, shaped by the incentives and relationships made possible through international intervention. Working this way also draws out the material inequalities and social hierarchies that are so central to the experience of life in conflict-affected places in the era of the good intentions crowd.

Looking at interactions and micro-rituals also reveals the sacrality of daily practices and how they entrain people, both practically and emotionally. Sometimes, the interactions and entrainment reach the point of effervescence, such that unbridled outcomes and practices can ensue. This collective creativity and the uncertainty it entails must be a central element of attempts to understand violence; it is one aspect of Donham's call for self-awareness when it comes to the 'demands posed by the epistemology of extraordinary situations' (2006: 29).

And finally, analysis of violence and intervention must incorporate history as a central element. African states did not 'fail' in the post-Cold War period – as if they were well-oiled machines before. The present reflects longstanding trajectories linked with the political usefulness of violence and the displacement of ultimate authority outside of the terrains where the violence occurs. The present reflects, too, a long slide into all-encompassing anomie. Durkheim described anomie as part of a project of understanding how and why people commit suicide. The violence in CAR since 2013, for all its political and economic rationales, also reflects the humiliating, drowning atmosphere anomie carries with it.

Chapter 2

THE NATIVENESS OF 'FOREIGN' VIOLENCE

Introduction

> The state is often not only inept but violent and repressive. Yet
> for all its hollowness and brutal authority, its emptiness should
> not be considered a sign of uselessness. State rituals become
> a 'form' that people participate in in order to avoid 'content'.
> (Hecht and Simone 1994: 21)

Many reports about CAR include a few lines about how it is a (potentially) rich country.[1] Oil, diamonds, gold, timber, uranium, verdant
land and water: all can be found in the country. People in CAR – both
expatriates and Central Africans – often make this point too. I heard
it from French officers at community and security planning meetings
(the gist being: you could be rich; stop with this fighting and get to
work). I heard it from (ex-)rebels ('We could be ten times richer than
France with all the resources we've got if they were exploited! And
yet we are so poor.') I heard it from aid workers and journalists ('This
country has so much going for it! How could it be so poor?') I heard
it from Central Africans in the *quartier* (popular neighbourhood),
who often completed the analysis by saying that France wanted the
country's resources for itself and to keep CAR poor. To cite just one
example: in Bangui in June 2015, people were talking about a Protes-
tant church in Sibut – the town where the pavement ends, about 200
km from the capital – that was allegedly built atop reserves of oil and

diamonds. (Sibut has no known diamonds or oil.) French Sangaris troops came and demanded that the church be moved so that they could exploit these riches, but the pastor stood firm and refused to budge. This story would be met with nods of approval.

These 'potentially rich' stories are misleading, if not dangerous, for several reasons. For one, CAR's resources are all quite difficult to exploit. The gold and diamonds are widely dispersed and most profitably mined artisanally. The oil is in a part of the country that becomes a marsh for half the year. The uranium also requires treatment and is in a remote part of the country, and the cost of doing business in CAR is so high that it can only be profitably exploited when global uranium prices are high (which they have not been since the Fukushima nuclear disaster). For another, regardless of how easily they could be exploited, resources do not magically make a place rich – labour, discipline, capital, and (re-)distribution are all required. The 'rich country' idea perpetuates the myth that making money is like winning the lottery, rather than a process of producing something. Later in this chapter I will delve further into Central African conceptions of work as a matter of earning a salary more than of producing something or labouring.

This story of the 'potentially rich' CAR is the inverse to the Sentinel Project/Enough Project argument that resources perpetuate if not cause violence and rebellion in the country. Central African journalist Johnny Vianney Bissakonou, in his recent book (2015), also argues that resource exploitation-greed is a driver of violence. As Enough Project founder John Prendergast (2015) put it, 'Today's deadliest conflicts in Africa – such as those in Sudan, South Sudan, Somalia, northern Nigeria, and the Democratic Republic of Congo – are sustained by extraordinary opportunities for illicit self-enrichment that emerge in war economics, where there is a visible nexus between grand corruption and the instruments of mass atrocities.' A cottage industry has emerged around research on wartime natural-resource economics. In CAR, this means a focus on diamonds, timber, and ivory. Prendergast argues that whatever its political motivations, war is exacerbated by the ways people profit from it and that people fight in order to claim the most lucrative opportunities to make money. Therefore, he argues, if the opportunities to make money are removed, war will decline as well. In this model, ending armed actors' control of resource exploitation provides an opportunity for an *a priori* legitimate actor, 'the state', to regulate these industries (at least those that are legal – exploiting ivory is entirely prohibited in CAR) for the good of the people.

There are a few problems with this reasoning. First, while diamonds, ivory, and timber have indeed been exploited throughout the fighting in CAR, and while they have brought money – even large amounts of money – to people involved in organizing and perpetrating violence, most of these people see dabbling in natural resources as but a temporary activity as they try to attain their ideal of a state job. Interdicting armed group economic activities only intensifies armed actors' desire for access to the state and its positions. For it is this state – a 'phantom' state (ICG 2007) largely produced and enacted by international actors – that is the largest source of revenue and investment. The CAR state has always been privatized, and the higher one goes up the state organizational hierarchy, the greater the opportunities for personal enrichment. The teleology of improvement (the state may be bad now, but it is being 'aided' to align better with the ideal type) makes it difficult to confront that fact as directly as might be required.

The biggest problem with the focus on resources – whether one sees them as a problem or a solution – is that it has little bearing on what really brings everyone to the Central African Republic, namely the issue of 'statelessness' or 'state fragility' (World Bank 2011). A large number of diplomats and international organization staffers, a few businesspeople with interests in the country, and Central Africans themselves are all concerned with the 'weakness' of the state in CAR. For a few (like the fictional diplomat played by Mads Brügger in *The Ambassador*), it's a profitable prospect; for the majority, a project to work on. The problem of the state in CAR thus draws all of these actors together into sometimes-unlikely collaborations. However, as this issue brings people together, it also perpetuates the dividing lines between them (such as the difference between the salary of an expatriate and that of a national) in ways that go beyond what individuals can breach on their own initiative. As Gluckman observed of South Africa, the various people attracted to the problem of statelessness in CAR 'act by customs of co-operation and communication' stemming from their common interest, 'even though' the various actors and groups 'are divided according to the pattern of the social structure' (1940: 28), which in this case includes the international order of states.

Close analysis of the processes that cluster around the problem of the state/statelessness in CAR, then, shows that though money gets made, the people involved do not tend to think about what they are doing in terms of profit and production in a capitalist or even a mercantilist sense. Rather, they have moral visions of the proper ordering of the world that they see themselves as helping to enact. Therefore, many see their actions as a *critique* of the status quo, not simply as an attempt to profit from it (though some end up doing that as well). The details of people's visions vary, but for most the logics of distribution and bureaucratic entitlement are central, much more important than commodified production, exerting coercion over others, or even profit for the sake of accumulation. In many of these visions, the state is the node that should organize these processes. Though few would claim to themselves be that state (the state is always someone else), it remains a reference point. In fact, its absence becomes the source of their claim to act, because they can position themselves as but temporarily fulfilling roles the state should properly hold.

The CAR state – such as it is – is produced out of relationships between people resident in the area and from afar, who see themselves as having different 'cultural' or social affinities from one another, have different time horizons for their engagement with this place, and tend to self-segregate. Yet they end up engaged in all sorts of projects with each other. For some of these actors, the idea of the state (that is, the idea of a rational-bureaucratic, territorial entity, with a simple public/private divide) is central to their conception of self and sense of what they are doing. But the difficulties of realizing that ideal in this part of the world means they are constantly making compromises and deals with other ways of doing business and politics. Violence has too often been one corollary of this interplay, and practices for managing who finds out about it (e.g. incidents of violence whose authors seek to terrify people nearby, while hiding their actions from their faraway higher-ups) have developed alongside. The use of violence and tactics for manipulating its audiences are all the more prominent given that the people involved have equivocal authorities, and ultimate accountability mechanisms tend to be far from the places where the violence occurs.

Adventurist politics

When trying to understand CAR today, most people refer to the state's uselessness: it is fragile, it is repressive, it is a farce of ineptitude and failure. But while those answers tell us something about what seems broken in CAR, they tell us little about what it is. Only by taking the actual dynamics of governance as the starting point will we be able to begin to transform the dynamics Central Africans and other interested observers see as damaging (de Waal 2009). Doing that, one finds that far from the simple government/non-government distinction that people might make to explain the workings of politics elsewhere, in Equatorial Africa a wide range of people have long been involved in both governing and privatized extraction. Governing authority, rather than concentrated in state institutions, is plural (Bierschenk and Olivier de Sardan 1997). At the same time, many of the people who have made their way to this part of the world invoke the need for a unitary, territorial state, and even use it as a platform from which to engage in all sorts of other projects. In the event, many efforts justified as steps towards creating a unitary, territorialized state often end up creating a greater sense of disorder and pluralization instead. During the concessionary period, this was true of the relationships among company agents, colonizers, and the Africans with whom they worked, and, in different ways, it is true of the international organizations, donors, regional actors, and government officials who are at work today.

The people who end up in Central Africa bring diverse interests and stay for varying lengths of time. To certain extents, they might see themselves as different from each other, and even as having different 'cultures' from each other and varying levels of legitimacy underpinning their activities. For instance, in their free time, humanitarian aid workers tend to socialize primarily with other aid workers, and they tend to see their reasons for being in the country as only partly overlapping with those of international businesspeople managing diamond and timber concessions. Central African politicians also tend to go out with other politicians and hangers-on, and to see their roles and interests as different from those of the aid workers. And yet none of these people act in isolation from each other.

And while it might be important for these various constituencies to define themselves through reference to their own values, everyone becomes entangled with each other. This means that however firmly we hold onto our values in theory, in practice we adjust them, such as when donors feel elections fall far short of optimal but stay quiet rather than pay for another round. Therefore, the focus of this chapter is on the cross-cutting relationships, and the equivocalities they entail, among the people drawn to Central Africa, and the ways that violence and the state idea enter into their practices.

Between donors and Central African politicians, the dynamic of adjustment tends to be, as Jean-François Bayart put it, one of 'denunciation followed by compromise' (2000: 258) – and this dynamic goes both ways. What brings everyone together is the idea of the state (the ideal-type state), which organizes what people do formally, in public, and yet everyone involved knows that this is at best a stage set, which allows people to put on a performance while ducking in and out behind the scenery to conduct other business with varying degrees of openness. The state is the placeholder 'form' that all have agreed upon, and as such it dominates the space in which people might otherwise have a discussion about different (and possibly better) political 'content'. Instead, everyone's energy is directed towards putting on a play while doing all sorts of other things offstage.

Because the ideal-type state's primary function is to credibly claim a credible monopoly on violence (as opposed to necessarily enacting that monopoly), concerns over the organization of violence have long been central to all relevant relationships and the processes that create them. And because the ideal-type state is supposed to be fundamentally a territorial entity (a polity with policed borders), mobility – who can move and who cannot, and what that means they can and cannot do more broadly – is also a node of concern and collaboration. Yet in CAR the institutions of the state make no convincing claim to a monopoly on violence, nor has the central government had much interest in policing borders (wan colonial attempts to do so were not particularly successful). So in this chapter I look at relationships among the plural authorities in CAR and the problems of violence and movement in shaping both the 'form' and the 'content' of politics in CAR. In evolving ways, extraversion founded on violence and movement has been central to the constitution of politics over the past hundred-plus years. The importance of these dynamics has waxed and waned – both in terms of violence and movement and of the extent to which these seem a problem to outsiders – and new players arrive periodically to try to do something about them. The early colonial years were one peak; and we are at another somewhat different peak today with international interventions and the problem of statelessness.

Let's start with a story of two imperial-colonial adventurists, Emile Gentil and Mohammed al-Sanusi.[2] In 1897, Gentil was traveling through Equatorial Africa on behalf of the French colonial officials who were establishing an increasingly large administrative presence in the region. Since the early 1890s, Sanusi had been working to expand his raiding and trading prowess into a polity centred at Ndele, in what is today northeastern CAR. He'd had his men assassinate Gentil's predecessor, Paul Crampel, in 1891, largely to claim the vast weaponry and ammunition Crampel carried with him, which would help Sanusi claim more autonomy from his patron to the north, Rabah, the sultan of Wadai. By the time Gentil arrived on the scene, Sanusi's army of about 20,000 men was busily raiding (people, ivory, other goods) throughout the area. The two men thus met warily: they both saw each other as simultaneously useful and dangerous. They eventually agreed to treaty terms. After an inter-faith invocation to God (Sanusi was a Muslim; Gentil was a Christian), Sanusi gave the French monopoly rights over commerce in the area. In return, the French would give Sanusi 300 guns and 15,000 cartridges within the next nine months. In addition, Gentil promised that French officers would train Sanusi's army in European military tactics and strategy (Republic of France 1897). Thus began more than a century of security sector reform (SSR) in Central Africa.

In the following years, Sanusi complained that the French did not provide the quality and quantity of guns and ammunition promised, and that they always missed deadlines. For their part, the French complained that Sanusi had not stopped raiding, as they understood him to have promised to do. Quite the contrary: thanks to the infusion of guns and the French defeat of Rabah in 1899, Sanusi now had far greater scope for raiding. He captured thousands of people and indentured them on his plantations or sold them into slavery. Captives from Dar al-Kuti, Sanusi's kingdom, were sold as far away as the Libyan coast (Cordell 1985).

When the treaty was revised in 1903, the request that Sanusi's army undergo European military training had become a demand that his sons be sent to France to be acculturated in French military practice. On the French side, negotiators sought to enlist Sanusi for the purposes of indirect rule, rounding up porters, conducting a census, and collecting taxes, all of which were the focus of the third and final treaty, in 1908. The French recognized that this would have been a departure from Sanusi's mode of governing, but they assumed they could bring him around to their 'rational' practices.

Or did they? Both Sanusi and the French were continually attempting to assess and read each other as the obvious danger-friends they were. This entailed a lot of uncertainty and miscommunication, in a context of limited information. Sanusi's compound and the heart of Ndele lay on a rocky plateau; the French post was about two kilometres downhill. Sanusi could thus easily transport slaves in and out on the far side of the mountain, without the few French soldiers and regional guards who accompanied them knowing what was going on. For their part, the French wrote letters and reports endlessly discussing Sanusi's tractability (or intractability), which seemed to change from one day to the next. Neither Sanusi nor the French officers who rotated in and out were able to carry out the terms of the treaties to their letter. If Sanusi gave up raiding, his polity would lose the force that gave it meaning. As the perceptive French officer who eventually assassinated Sanusi put it: 'from Sanusi's perspective, slavery is a way of governing and razzias [slave raids] are the only commercial operations that are actually productive' (Modat 1909: 2). And if even the French had wished to live up to their promise to deliver guns and ammunition – a proposition that is itself debatable – their torturous supply chain (they relied entirely on conscripting human porters) made that impossible. So rather than taking the treaties at face value, we can see them as a 'form' (borrowing, again, Hecht and Simone's language) that permitted Sanusi and the French entry to the same stage, on which they could pursue their own, varied interests. To whatever extent it is interesting to discuss the cultural proclivities of either of these sides (and it *is* interesting, in a way), the features of their *relationship* played a major role in shaping their governing practices and capacities to profit (Lombard 2012).

A story from about a century later further illustrates the durability of 'forms'. In 2006 CAR president François Bozizé dispatched his Presidential Guard to deal with an insurgency in the northwestern part of the country. (Better funded than the regular army, the Presidential Guard also contained a number of Chadians with more training and a fiercer reputation than their Central African counterparts.) Though Bozizé was a born-again Christian from western CAR and Sanusi was a Muslim from northeastern CAR, the Presidential Guard's tactics were reminiscent of those employed by Sanusi's *bazingir* armies, especially with their focus on village-burning. (This similarity suggests that forms of violence derive not just from 'cultural' factors but from those related to geography and political structure [Roscoe 2011].) Like Sanusi's men before them, Bozizé's forces burned villages and attacked the people who did not flee. Human Rights Watch referred to it as a 'state of anarchy' (2007) and decried the indiscriminate operations, in which many civilians died and tens of thousands were displaced and dispossessed.

In 2006 as one hundred years before, newcomers to the zone – diplomats and donors this time around – saw the problem as the lack of a professional, national military that would act judiciously and provide effective security. They thus proposed SSR: the re-structuring and reform of the state security and justice sector so that competence and professionalism would rule. Bozizé and the relevant ministers agreed. A preliminary legal framework was drafted fairly quickly by a French adviser to the European Union (who was funding the project) and some of Bozizé's ministers – and then they waited.

The president and the parliament did not even acknowledge the framework. More than two years went by. Eventually it was signed. But in the interim, rebellions festered and grew in several northern regions. Rebel groups were growing, and rebels demanded the option of integration into the army. Most had little education and little military training but they demanded to be integrated at the ranks assigned them as rebels. These demands ran counter to the disarmament objectives of the SSR, as everyone knew. Yet only on the rarest of occasions were the full-on collision course between SSR and rebels' expectations discussed publicly. Instead, everyone went on *as if* the state ideal type would suddenly become far more workable than it had ever had been before. The public, official form – an idol if not a fetish – could not be budged, even though very nearly everyone recognized the vast gap between that ideal-type state and the plural nature of actual governance in CAR. By 2013, Bozizé was ejected from power, overthrown by (among others) some of the same Chadian men-in-arms who had helped him take over almost exactly a decade earlier.

These snapshots of SSR across one hundred years demonstrate the durability of certain facets in the relationships between Central African leaders and incomers assuming roles in governance. One is that although the various people involved are collaborating and carrying out joint projects, it remains important to them to see themselves as separate from each other. The mechanism providing a venue for the collaborations is a form – that of a territorialized, bureaucratic state with, crucially, a certain kind of a military – that bears little resemblance to the existing organs and agents of government and extraction. All involved explain away this disconnection between politics as they are and the ideal-type state form as a matter of time, progress, and aid. Privately, people may harbour doubts, but it is rare to find someone – whether Central African or expatriate – who does not share in the political vision placing the ideal-type state in the central role.

However, the theatre-set ideal-type state is also clearly useful for people in many ways. Everyone has a role in the play and an interest in a continuing the performance, and so poking around in the shadows (Reno 1998) and calling attention to what one finds is not necessarily useful. Again, no matter how much knowledge/ context is made the driver of policy, relationships will always be shaped by ideals and compromise set in larger collaborative structures. Despite certain power differentials, hierarchies are not stable, authority is fluid, and relationships cut across each other in ways that frustrate the creation of clear top-down structures of loyalty and consistent values.

Looking at a century of SSR also points to how concerns over the organization of violence have drawn people into governing relationships in CAR. Violence has in other words been a concern around which practices of extraversion have been prosecuted. 'Extraversion' is the term Jean-François Bayart coined to describe the nature of African agency in light of the continent's dependent position in the world. That is, he argues that the continent's politics are fundamentally composed of relationships that exceed the continent itself, and Africans have taken these 'external constraints' and made them into 'new creations' (2000: 240–1). Basically, extraversion entails managing the rents associated with dependence, and turning them to one's own ends. For instance, the post-Cold War 'discourse of democracy' has been one major recent source of extraversion. Heads of state and other elites engage in the discourse to obtain rents, but continue with non-democratic practices such as political violence. They know that, at least since independence, the mode of engagement between actors pushing the democracy project and themselves has been a 'dialectic of denunciation and compromise' (Bayart 2000: 258) over the use and organization of political violence. In part compromises are due to *realpolitik*, such as the 'better the devil you know' and 'better the devil than the security vacuum that would result from his ouster' tropes that seem to guide much diplomacy in Central Africa. And in part they stem from the web of relationships all are involved in, which are not the sole creations of the people involved but are shaped by the remoteness and sparse human population of the area.

In this respect, Bayart's analysis should go further. Extraversion is not an African practice, adapted from African historical-cultural practices such as 'trickery' or 'mimicry', as he suggests. Instead, it is a co-creation that evolves out of the web of relationships all are entangled in, and those actors Bayart describes as 'external' are as likely to engage in extraversion as Africans are. In this respect, 'internal' and 'external' usefully describe how people see themselves, but the terms can obscure the fundamental intertwining of the people who place themselves in these different categories. After all, consider that today, the most important meetings for determining the future of CAR occur not within the country's official territory but in Ndjamena (where President Samba-Panza was selected), Nairobi (where rebels and ousted politicians have met to discuss plans of action), Brussels (where EU aid is organized and disbursed), Paris (where French policy is made and where would-be presidential candidates campaign), and New York (where decisions about UN peacekeeping and missions are taken). In short, it takes a lot of work (Appel 2012) to be able to describe the people and places involved in those happenings as *external*, given that without them there would be no CAR.

In the following section, I will further explore the history of extraversion as it relates to violence – the use of violence as a political and governing tool, as well as its visibility and status as a 'problem' in the eyes of different audiences – and what these dynamics tell us about the relationships entangling everyone concerned with CAR. In all of these processes and relationships, the commitment to the ideal type form of the state – that 'primal mandate' of the UN – prevents fundamental change, as we will see. It is difficult to say whether this life-support mode is, on balance, the better of two far-from-ideal choices, but the persistent deterioration of life chances for Central Africans suggests that change is necessary, if not sufficient.

Violence and the problem of oversight

Extraversion explains something particular about the history (Bayart might prefer 'trajectory') of politics in Africa: given factionalization and the difficulty would-be state-builders faced in consolidating power over a mobile population, ambitious politicians found it useful to enter into relationships with outsiders, who could provide critical leverage and resources. Sanusi is a good example of this historical process. On his own, he would have been a powerful merchant but not a 'sultan'. The material benefits he drew from relationships with Rabah and the French allowed him to expand his political objectives. In this mode of polity-building, sovereignty is notably not founded on a compact between rulers and the people they putatively rule (Mbembe 2001). *Ad hoc* taxation at the 'street-level' (Lipsky 2010 [1980]) or other modes of popularly-derived extraction may support regular folks, but for leaders the key material rewards of power are the aid and concession payments they may receive as presidents and ministers who can authorize outsourcing. These tendencies tend to prevent reciprocal obligations between rulers and ruled (Bayart 2009; Mbembe 2000: 37; Eubank 2012).

In addition to eroding reciprocity, the ideal-type state stage has entailed at best 'state fragility' and at worst the widespread perpetration of violence as a political and economic tool. For a variety of reasons, including logistics, it is very difficult to build a state in Equatorial Africa. As a result, the distance between state-form ideals and the capacities for governing is vast. At this point, even large strides forward would leave a chasm. Under these circumstances, people can feel compelled into 'desperate times' measures, or else take advantage of the isolation to take a moral holiday (Collins 2009), which is especially tempting given that accountability/sanction structures are multiple and the levels with 'teeth' often displaced outside the territory.

None of this is to say that Central Africa would have been a haven of welfare and production without colonization/extraversion and its successor forms. If pre-colonial history is any guide, it would likely have been full of contestation, if not always conflict. But it is to say that *particular forms of violence are associated with the ideal state project* in this part of the world. Whatever future Central Africans and other concerned parties try to build, they will need to remove the state from its ideal-type pedestal and reckon with this tragic legacy.

When European – primarily but not solely French – adventurists began trekking through the lands newly christened Oubangui-Chari at the tail end of the nineteenth century, they found most people living in a fairly non-centralized manner. Trans-Saharan raiders like Sanusi had been increasing their presence, particularly in the east and northwest. This entailed massive population movements as well as access to new forms of knowledge and connection (Cordell 1985; Lombard 2015). Leaders in organizing these political-economic processes became known as 'sultans', titles that in some cases they adopted only at the urging of Europeans who wanted to solidify the locals' authority, all the better to piggy-back on it. The agreements between French officers and Sanusi are but one example of a widespread process through which Europeans and Central Africans negotiated treaties, the terms of which neither party expected to be fully compelled by. Signing a treaty while tacitly agreeing to look the other way (*'mbi bâ, mais mbi bâ pépé'* – 'I look, but I don't see', as a Sango expression has it) allowed all parties to use one another as suited their interests, which was indispensable given the often hostile social and geographic surroundings. Only when Sanusi endeavoured to extract himself from his relationship with the French by fleeing to a 'perfectly defensible' plateau to the east was the decision to assassinate him taken. Over time, colonial and concession actors sapped the sultans of their authority and became the dominant governing and extractive presence.[3]

The French saw their colonial endeavour as that of establishing a 'legitimate' political economy. 'Until the beginning of the twentieth century, Oubangui-Chari was only a reservoir of slaves and a hunting ground for the purveyors of black flesh' (Le Roux 1919: 7). But to whatever extent they wanted to create a bureaucratic state, their economic and political undertakings were plagued by several intertwined problems. Raiding and disease had drastically depleted the human population, and Africans were largely uninterested in participating in French governing projects. The benefits they would draw from doing so were opaque at best. The terrain was exceptionally difficult to traverse. As a 'top secret' French military assessment carried out in the late-1950s put it, the Oubangui-Chari bush is an 'eater of men' (Oubangui-Chari n.d.). And they were perpetually short on money and other material resources. Conventional wisdom had it that colonies should pay for themselves; as the poorest colony, Oubangui-Chari faced particular challenges. Indeed, though residents there were by far the poorest, their annual head taxes (a tax levied on every adult male, simply for the right to exist, frequently discharged in the form of labour) were several times higher than in other colonies (Kalck 1971). This was how the French avoided seeing themselves as slavers: they might have been forcing people to work, but it was for these poor souls' own good, as it would both help build the colony and build their own moral character. Still, the extent of the violence entailed in this project troubled some, both in the colony and afar.

The triple problem of low population, impenetrable terrain, and penury combined to promote manhunts and spectacular forms of punishment in Oubangui-Chari. Total destruction of populations would only exacerbate the population problem, but targeted terror tactics could be a useful way to force submission and labour out of people who, while perhaps curious about certain aspects of the French and their promise of an end to raiding, had little interest in the back-breaking (or neck-breaking – loads of up to sixty kilograms were heaved atop people's heads for transport [Mollion 1992: 58]) and effectively unremunerated projects of the colonial officials.

Between 1890 and 1920, forced labourers were absolutely crucial for porterage. This need was especially acute along the road between Bangui and Chad, especially around Fort Crampel (Kaga Bandoro today). The Mandja, the primary inhabitants of the area, were particularly uninterested in the beads and other trinkets the French offered *en guise de rémunération*. Guns were the only currency they would accept. (Gentil, en route to vanquish Rabah in 1899, was desperate enough to acquiesce to these terms. The French adventurist mission following him was greeted with gunfire.) In the absence of mutually acceptable currency, French attempts at administration-building became hunts for forced labourers.[4] Both

Jean-Bédel Bokassa and Barthélemy Boganda – the two people with a claim to being independence heroes in CAR – had fathers who were killed by colonial authorities. Bokassa's father, a *chef de village*, was expected to provide the colonial officials with forced labourers. When he refused, he was beaten to death in a public spectacle (Lombard and Batianga-Kinzi 2015).

Violence was central to the trans-Saharan adventurists' projects and it was further sedimented into administrative processes by colonial and concessionary officials. Yet the situation was not a free-for-all. Even in the early colonial era, violence was generally not something to trumpet as a virtue, even when perpetrated against Africans who Europeans imagined as at best differently human than themselves. Violence for the sake of conquest and 'pacification' was justifiable, but violence as a technique of administration had potential for scandal – not so much in the colonies as in the metropoles. And yet it was impossible to pursue extractive political and economic projects without violence. As a result, the crucial variables became the *visibility* of violence, and how to calibrate violence in order to achieve governing and extractive objectives without sending *all* the Africans into flight.

Yet however violent the reality, the ideal-type colony remained the stage on which people were acting. Colonial officials were expected to refrain from mentioning what went into creating that appearance. For instance, in 1903, fifty-eight African women and ten children were packed into a tiny house in a village in southern Oubangui-Chari with only small air slits near the roof, on the orders of the commissioner of native affairs. Forty-five of the women died, as did three of the children; the women had sacrificed themselves by holding the children up so they could breathe. A colonial doctor arrived in the aftermath and alerted his superiors to the massacre. His reward was a sanctioning for insubordination. Though it was not always as deadly as this particular incident, locking up women and children as a way of forcing men to work was a common tactic (Mollion 1992).

While this mass murder was an extreme example, it was not isolated. It was very difficult for Europeans to even move around, let alone 'administer', without using some violence to convince people to work for them. The French had urgent needs and neither the time nor money for a more humanistic approach. Yet, again, there was squeamishness about using too much force. The French public was not particularly interested in the colonial project, and if it was revealed to be primarily a violent endeavour, support would fall still further. Investigative commissions as well as journalists like André Gide exposed abuses to the French public, beginning at the very opening of the twentieth century with the Brazza mission and subsequent report in 1905.[5]

Given that violence was both officially disapproved of and difficult to avoid, certain incentives emerged. Colonial officials were expected to write reports on their undertakings. Those who detailed the ease with which they met their labour and other administrative needs were promoted and described as credits to their profession. Those who related how difficult it was to build an administration without any resources to speak of would be demoted, sent to less favourable posts, or otherwise slotted into the category of unfit for advancement (Mollion 1992).

As automobiles became more widespread and roads better trodden in the 1920s, the need for porters declined. However, between concession companies' demands for rubber and other goods, and colonial officials' cotton-growing agenda, forced labour continued until at least the 1950s in some areas. Africans were not completely unprotected from abuses in Oubangui-Chari. After the concessionary scandals, for instance, sweeping reforms were passed. But given the combination of an anaemic administration in Oubangui-Chari – perennially short on money and therefore constrained in terms of oversight – and centrally derived demands such as road construction, many colonial officials and concessionaires saw it as expedient to ignore the protective laws. They generally faced no sanction for doing so. They also kept their distance by passing the dilemma on to the West African and Gabonese regional guards, who ultimately authored the violence much of the time.

For instance, in the 1930s, the annual head tax was supposed to be fifteen days' labour. But in Oubangui-Chari there were very few people and so the required tasks would not be completed unless labourers were kept for longer. Thus they were employed until the arduous tasks were finished rather than released once they had acquitted their day count. These kinds of practices were open secrets. In 1937 Inspector Ruffel wrote a report describing the abuses of the forced labour system and arguing for its end. The Lieutenant Governor, Masson de Saint Félix, responded with colonial pragmatism: where would they find the millions of francs that would be necessary to keep the roads in drivable condition? (Brégeon 1998: 163–4). The question was rhetorical. Both knew the money was nowhere to be found. Better therefore not to draw too much attention to the violence. Occasional uncomfortable spotlights on the abusive practices focused not on the structural problems of imposing a state form in a context of penury, isolation, and low population, but on how to reform the system, usually through legal or other technical measures with limited follow-through.[6]

Scholars, pundits, and other concerned individuals from across the ideological spectrum have called attention to the violence inherent to state-building. Even the European states that tend to be described as most closely incarnating secure, welfare-providing state ideals emerged only out of a long process involving protection rackets and organized crime (Tilly 1985). Centralized modes of power have a greater capacity for destruction on a massive scale than do non-centralized modes of social organization (Clastres 1987). States' high-modern visions for transforming societies and rendering them more easily administrable on a large scale ended up causing major famines and mass death (Scott 1998). An opposite, neo-Hobbesian perspective ascribes to 'stateless' life a range of deleterious effects, such as the existence of a 'security vacuum' and 'naturally' high levels of violence.[7] Clearly, violence has been a part of social life in a range of ways and associated with a range of political projects.

My purpose here is thus not to take a stand on whether the state is the best mode of social organization, or to rank the violence of politics in Equatorial Africa compared to elsewhere. More important, it seems to me, is to notice the particular forms and modes of violence that accompany a case in which there is a vast gap between the legal architecture for political organization and the resources available to people to enact them, when there are moreover competing interests and objectives among the people involved. One consequence of this kind of a situation is a 'paradox of scarcity' (Smith 2015a) – any minister or official knows that the sums available for administration are so small that whether he uses them for their legal purpose or simply pockets them, it will make little difference. But some outcomes do get verified, and in those cases violence can be a useful tool for accomplishing them in the face of penury and popular dissent, especially since it is frequently possible to hide that violence from far-off and intermittent overseers (who are generally all too eager to look the other way). Whether you ascribe that violence to problems that get passed down the hierarchy or the character flaws of the people who demand or enact the violence, or some combination of these factors and more, it has been one of the consequences of the particular challenges of state-building in Equatorial Africa.

With independence, these dynamics shifted, but were not overturned. Now, concerns over security – that is, avoiding a security vacuum in these obviously weak states – became a major interest of non-Central Africans interested in Central Africa. Between the end of the Second World War and 1960, when France's African colonies gained independence, a variety of possible political configurations were discussed. The independent nation-states model that eventually came into existence was no one's ideal (Cooper 2014). However, it quickly became entrenched as an unchangeable norm. And yet, the 'independent sovereignty' of the new countries was dependent upon their diplomatic relationships, especially those with France.

French nationals continued to officially staff many Central African government positions for decades after independence, and unofficially for far longer. Again, this points to the fallacy of seeing such actors as 'external'. They may have varying allegiances, interests, and/or time frames for their presence in Central Africa, but they are fully woven into the tapestry of Central African politics.

CAR's early heads of state correctly gauged that the Europeans' main concern was stability. In 1960, as a select constitutional committee met to discuss criteria for choosing the country's first president, CAR's southern neighbour, the Belgian Congo, became embroiled in major upheaval as the Belgians sought to maintain power. The constitutional committee became deadlocked on a few issues, such as the minimum age to assume the presidency. Abel Goumba,[8] heir to independence hero Barthélemy Boganda's democratic project, proposed forty as the minimum, which would have removed both him and his main challenger, Provisional President David Dacko, from the running. In this impasse, Dacko sensed an opportunity to seize power. He knew that by advocating stability above all he could count on support from French circles in Bangui, whose priority was avoiding chaos similar to that in the Congo. As president, Dacko stripped away democratic protection after democratic protection, calculating – correctly – that he would not be denounced because he was the 'safe' choice, as opposed to possible agitators (read: people with democratic credibility) like Goumba.

Ultimately, sovereignty rested not with the Central African people (most of whom saw little difference between their colonial and post-independence leaders) but with the expatriates who continued to run the formal economy (Kalck 1971: 120–121). The National Assembly had little power to counter the president, and besides, it had other preoccupations, such as debating 'the sale-price of whisky, champagne, and lemonade, and why the prices were different in the cafes in town and in the bar attached to the Assembly' (Kalck 1971: 124). On New Year's Day 1966 Dacko was himself subjected to despotic tactics when ousted in a coup by Jean-Bédel Bokassa. For the variety of people who find themselves acting and improvising in the shadow of the far-off ideal-type state and its Leviathan-style security, anti-democratic tendencies can prove useful for pursuing one's interests, whatever they might be.

Beginning in the 1990s, the *françafrique* dynamics of which the above were a symptom began to change (see Smith 2015a, 2015b and ICG 2007 for more on *françafrique* in the case of CAR). France began pulling back, and a range of international actors – regional and international organizations, regional heads of state – began stepping in, sometimes reluctantly and sometimes with gusto. Today, CAR has by some counts hosted more peacekeeping missions than any other country (Olin 2015). In the last decade, humanitarian organizations have become a massive presence as well. The central node of interest among these actors remains that of violence in a state with a weak administrative capacity. But the ways these problems are conceptualized and responded to, and by whom, have changed.

To be sure, some of the old players are still around (France), but now with company (the European Union, the UN, the World Bank, etc.).[9] Welfare, and particularly suffering, have become preoccupations in ways that were more muted before. It is not so much that the old dynamics of concession and a government with limited capacity or interest in controlling territory have changed, as that the number of organizations arriving to intervene has increased. All of these organizations require CAR government approval to be present and work; since they see themselves as helping to build the legitimate authority of the state, abiding by local laws that would otherwise exist only as lines of type on state registers is very important to them. However, 'the state' never emerges to reclaim the farmed-out authority. In this way authority has become ever more pluralized, while the idea of the unitary state as the only possible solution has become all the more entrenched and immovable.

One way of understanding this shift has been to describe the state not just in terms of its official institutions but in terms that encompass all actors who carry out state-like tasks, such as NGOs

(Trouillot 2001). However, that approach elides the centrality of the state ideal to all of these actors. NGOs and others absolutely do not see themselves as the state. Moreover, they are eager to carry out certain state projects (censuses, distribution of basic household items and food, running health clinics, map-making), but generally refuse others, such as provision of justice and other means of accountability. Certain sovereign functions remain reserved, but they are reserved for someone who never comes to claim them. So much of the time accountability is fraught, and violence remains possible to cover up. When violent events come into view – for Central Africans and people elsewhere with at least occasional concern for understanding suffering at a distance (Boltanski 1999) – they appear as scandal, that is, as events out of the ordinary. However, scandal is repetitive in this part of the world, and the measures designed to respond to it often do little to change the structural factors militating for violence and against accountability, such as the encouragement people face not to report on it and adjudicatory systems that are geographically distant.

Of course, certain forms of violence are themselves the primary concern of these new international actors. Rebellion stands out in this regard, as many organizations constantly scan the horizon for it. But other forms of violence have a more ambiguous status, much as how one hundred years ago 'slave-raiding' was cause for immediate response and reprobation, while manhunts for forced labourers, though problematic, did not elicit the same demand for action unless someone forced the issue. Today sexual violence may appear as scandal, but demands for accountability are nevertheless ambiguous. (Another problem with an ambiguous status is corruption – for lack of a better term to describe the personal appropriation of resources intended for some other end.[10])

Sexual violence does not always become a scandal. Sexual encounters that fall short of international norms for consent are widespread around the world, of course. What's striking in the case of CAR is that the various people working in the country have a range of expectations as regards proper sexual conduct, and since they understand themselves to be part of different organizational hierarchies, the accountability mechanisms become fractured – even though they're all quite intertwined. VIPs like ministers are often given a young woman companion for their stays in rural towns. Their visits to these places may have been funded by an international agency or diplomat. But those funding agencies generally do not see it as their role to police what the VIPs do; they belong to separate disciplinary hierarchies and understand each other as having different cultures as regards these kinds of things. Their positions in relation to each other are equivocal.

Other times, sexual violence does become a scandal. A recent tragic case was the alleged sexual abuse of children by French peacekeepers in Bangui. The alleged abuses occurred in early 2014, but were only made public a year later. This was not because they were unknown; allegations of the abuse had reached the UN human rights office quickly. The office investigated and issued an internal report confirming the allegations. However, the findings of the report were kept strictly confidential until an employee, Anders Kompass, shared it with French authorities and the NGO AIDS Free World. Even the UN High Commissioner for Human Rights, Zeid Ra'ad Al Hussein, had known of the case, but did not take any action. Kompass was suspended and faced dismissal for having leaked the report. More than a century separated Kompass from the doctor who alerted colonial authorities to the suffocation of women and children, but their experiences bear more than a passing resemblance.

When yet another alleged sexual abuse scandal was reported in August 2015 (a twelve-year-old girl was raped, and two unarmed civilians killed by UN peacekeepers; additional allegations were made public later that month), the UN Secretary General, Ban Ki-Moon, asked the head of MINUSCA, Babacar Gaye, to resign. Gaye accepted. The Secretary General meant to communicate how seriously the UN takes allegations of sexual violence (Sengupta

2015). Yet until now, there remains no public accounting for why the High Commissioner for Human Rights stymied the accounting for the previous incident, and he has faced no public sanctioning. For those paying long-term attention, Gaye's resignation communicates a symbolic and partial commitment to accountability, not a transformation of the system that has for so long been producing these kinds of injustices.

And these are only some of the scandals that are known, let alone all those that pass without uproar. Nor are peacekeepers uniquely culpable in sexual violence. Government officials also sometimes engage in less-than-consensual sexual acts. The traveling employees of the myriad NGOs that have taken on a wide range of state-like functions in recent decades (Trouillot 2001) are sometimes culpable as well. When I arrived in one northeastern CAR town in late 2009, an expatriate employee of an INGO described how he had resigned because an expatriate doctor employed by the NGO had had sex with a fourteen-year-old girl in the town and no punitive action had been taken. The INGO headquarters abroad assured him they were treating the matter seriously and convinced him to stay. He was sceptical of their real commitment but decided to remain because he felt people were counting on him to complete certain projects. I returned to this northeastern town in 2015. This time, I met a female employee of the same INGO, the only woman working full time at the office. She had left her husband and two young children in the capital in order to take the post. Soon after arrival she received night-time visits from a male staff member who propositioned her. Though she managed to get him to desist, he began a character assassination campaign that eventually caused her to resign. Incidents like this can and do happen anywhere, of course. There is an additional, tragic irony when they occur in organizations that describe themselves as working to promote protection, including protection from sexual violence. But my purpose in recounting these incidents is not to shame humanitarians for being less exalted in their practices than their fund-raising and PR initiatives would suggest. We are all (only) human. But it is curious how these new actors who we might think of as altogether different from their predecessors end up recreating older patterns and dynamics of governance and exploitation. In this respect, the combination of pluralized authorities (lots of people with authority, little clarity about who is in charge) and displaced or limited accountability/oversight help support particular forms of violence.

When the resources for administration are far less than would be required to build an ideal-type state and the overseers are far away, there is little incentive to rock the boat, and much incentive to look the other way (Lombard 2015). This is not a problem of a lack of information and context; the relevant people often have the requisite knowledge. It is the combination of the primacy accorded the ideal-type state concept and the plural hierarchies at work (e.g. the state organization chart, the UN organization chart) that incentivize staying quiet and displacing accountability.

Chapter 3

MOBILITY AS POWER

Introduction

When one thinks of 'the state', one thinks of a territory, and people assigned to that territory. Even Crawford Young, in his project of accounting for the varied forms that states have taken through history (1994), argues that claiming and administering a territory is a primary element of what a state is. But in important ways, CAR is not a territory. That is to say, there is a geographic area that maps allocate to CAR, and it has borders. But if one's goal is to understand the country's politics, one must not assume that mastering that territory and the people in it is the primary objective of any actor, state or otherwise.

When explaining why the government does not control the borders, donors and diplomats often attribute it to a lack of resources. The 'paradox of scarcity' (Smith 2015b) helps explain why the scarce monies allocated for such purposes often are not ultimately used for their intended purposes. But controlling territory has never been a preoccupation of the Central African government. Controlling the presidency or ministerial positions and the ability thus to negotiate concessions, however, has been (Smith 2015b). And while being fixed in space, and the ability to fix others in space, might bring a person power in the classic model of state-building, being able to move is far more important in CAR. Being able to move has a geographic/spatial and everyday connotation, as well as an occult connotation (being able to travel into the world of the spirits and bring back their power). Who can move around, and who cannot? Who has the possibility to leave when things get bad, and who does not? What kinds of information (about violence, but also about other matters) and things are mobile, and what are not? These are the critical questions.

Sometimes, the ability to move even trumps the 'law of weapons distribution' (those with guns have power and those without do not) (Mbembe 2000, 2006) – that is, that being able to move can itself be a major source of power and resistance (Cordell 2003). Questions of mobility are equally important to international interveners in CAR. Who has a passport that allows him or her to leave when violence erupts? Who will be airlifted, and by whom? Who receives two weeks of R&R abroad every eight weeks? Social sifting occurs not just according to nationality or organization, but also through the rubric of who can move and how. Mobility is both a cause and a consequence of power, and though it has different connotations for different people, it is nevertheless an idiom that unites the varied people involved in CAR. There are many ways in which mobility enters into politics and power, not all of them connected but all of them contributing to widespread anxieties over movement. Movement is thus not just a prosaic thing one does in the world. It also indicates status, and in that vein, has moral connotations. In different ways, mobility (people who move who shouldn't be able to, people who want to move but aren't able to) has also been a major theme in the grievances of Central Africans who take up arms.

Many Central Africans think of history itself as a process of movement. For instance, one of the largest ethnic groups in CAR, the Banda, tend to view history as a process of moving through space, not just time, and past events are thoroughly intertwined with past ways of living in the world, particularly in terms of the spatial orders associated with them (Giles-Vernick 1996).[1] Thus Banda point not to *moments* in past time, but *places* on the road of history (*'na lege ti guiriri'* in Sango). This is not metaphor but a way of conceiving of the world spatially rather than temporally. Thus they speak of the time of the *lege ti Nzapa* – the road/way of Christian God. In looking at the past, they attach significance to the transformation of *kete lege* (small roads) into *kota lege* (big roads). 'Small roads' refers to the way of life organized around footpaths, scattered settlement, and the fear of raiding. 'Big roads' refers to the French colonial project of road-building and forced resettlement of villages along the roadways (for easier tax collection). Understanding history is itself a matter of *ingango ndo*, that is, of 'knowing one's place in the world', with place conceived not just as a geographic position but as practical knowledge about how to live, and one's status in relation to other people – including the dead, whose spirits continue to act in the world.

As a corollary, 'knowing one's place' also has to do with knowing other people's places and making sure they stay there. For this reason, Banda men deny women access to 'history/knowledge' on the grounds that women are unable to handle such dangerous materials responsibly. Older people lament that youth – transported to new places by education and changing values – no longer learn their place, which in the past had been transmitted through such means as elders' beating of the young (Giles-Vernick 1996). For young people, whatever freedom the new place-ways seem to offer quickly becomes anomie, because the promises of the new ways (e.g. a state salary) are so impossibly out of reach that the desire for them becomes unquenchable. Banda historiography thus shows how fundamental mobility and place – who can move, and the system of movement that is embedded in – are to power, given that they form the basis for history, knowledge, control of others, and ways of being in the world and their associated moral codes.

Mobility as power and cross-cutting tie

These conceptions of movement, place, and power take on additional material dimensions in the form of the bifurcation between capital-elites (whether Central African or expatriate) and the rest of the population. As described in the previous chapter, there has never been a substantive social-political contract between these elites and the population, and the divide is felt keenly in the form of who can move and who cannot, and how. Many if not most of the Central African elite[2] have two passports (usually Central African and French). When people obtain money, they are less likely to build a house in their natal village (as might happen in Cameroon or Côte d'Ivoire) than they are to buy or build a home in Cotonou, Douala, Dakar, and/or Paris. (Catherine Samba-Panza, for instance, purchased homes in Bangui, Douala, and Paris during her tenure as president.)

And when violence breaks out in CAR, elites head directly for the airport. Though the president does not have control over the territory or the population in any thorough-going way, she or he does exercise control at the airport, sometimes stepping in to prevent a particular person from boarding a flight. For instance, just after the presidential elections in 2011 Bozizé blocked former President – and Bozizé's main rival – Ange-Félix Patassé from boarding a plane that would have taken him on the first leg of a journey to Equatorial Guinea for medical care. Under pressure, Bozizé allowed Patassé to leave several weeks later, but illness claimed his life during a stopover in Cameroon. While one could describe CAR's sovereignty as 'negative' in the sense that it is derived primarily from its recognition as such by 'external' actors (Englebert 2009), airport blockages and the like are important domestic performances of sovereignty. International interveners have embassies that can organize their flights, if the need arises.

For the urban poor, range of movement is much more constrained, and this is a source of anger and resentment. This helps explain why, during the worst of the fighting in 2013, people in Bangui set up camp on the airport grounds. There were practical reasons for doing so. It was an area with open space in an increasingly crowded city. And there were also symbolic considerations. Locating themselves at the airport functioned as a protest that drew attention to the fact that they were stuck, while the rich and foreigners could leave. For rural residents, flight means moving to the bush, returning to the *kete lege*, the time/way/place of small roads. Their resilience and strength in doing so does not negate the dangers (illness, animals and bugs, or armed attacks) that accompany such a move.

Heading home from my second trip to CAR, in 2004, I almost missed the then-once-weekly flight from Bangui to Paris. I arrived at the airport several hours early, but hundreds of people – none of them with tickets for travel – had formed a scrum outside the entrance, and aside from jostling and shoving, no one was moving. Eventually, a fixer escorted me to the rear of the airport, where disembarking passengers entered. I walked through the security checkpoints in reverse until I found myself at the Air France counter. There was no line. By the time of my next visit, in 2006, police and gendarmes implemented ticket checks, and the airport scrum was gone. This indicates two things: one, that state forces have capacity to do things that have for whatever reason become a priority; and two, that 'abroad' is a major object of desire. This is true for all those Central Africans who rushed the airport, who dream of getting away or of receiving something from those who have been away. And it is also true of people like me who work and live there for shorter stints. Among expatriates, duty-free cheeses, chocolates, and alcohol are highly valued as a gift currency.

The airport is just one site for an enclave politics that is widespread in the country and that demonstrates the fundamental interconnection of mobility and exclusion. For instance, INGO offices, international organization headquarters, and many government buildings are surrounded by high walls (for the first two, these are often topped with barbed or razor wire). One or several security guards stand sentry at the gate. Would-be entrants must leave a form of ID with them. Most Central Africans do not have any such card or document. People who present themselves to the guards having arrived in a car or SUV with air-conditioning, and thus showing no dust or sweat stains on their clothes or perspiration on their brows, are admitted easily. Those who arrive on foot, their presence announced by a sweaty-pedestrian musk, handkerchief in hand to their brows, are more likely to be turned away out of hand. (One expatriate World Bank employee described how awkward she found it that her Ministry of Agriculture colleagues would never make it past the guards, because they smelled too much like farmers.) Central African friends will often ask me to bring them name-brand perfume from abroad. At first I thought it a strangely profligate taste. Now I understand how crucial such accoutrements are to social status. The people on the inside can forget that there is a wall at all, because they pass it with no problem; for others, it is an insurmountable barrier.

Over a person's lifetime, these distinctions as to who can move and enter, and who is stopped and excluded, become written on the body. For instance, do you wear sandals (or nothing) on your feet, or do you wear shoes? The feet of sandal-wearers are tough and calloused, the nails likely scrunched in protective positions. The feet of shoe folk are rarely seen, but on the rare occasions they are (say, when white foreigners indulge their taste for flip-flops) they are smooth and unblemished. Sandal feet show the evidence of miles walked and fields tilled; they mark a person as not belonging in the 'way of' offices and private cars and planes. The shoe folk show they belong in a 'way of' maids who wash one's clothes, vehicular travel, and entitlement to office entry. This kind of stratification starts out malleable but becomes fixed over time. If one walks long enough without shoes, shoes become painful, almost impossible to wear. If one walks long enough with shoes, doing without is excruciating.

These dynamics of mobility/entitlement and stoppage/exclusion create cross-cutting ties among people who otherwise might see themselves as members of different 'cultures'. For instance, expatriate international organization staffers and Central African politicians share membership among the mobile entitled. They all tend to take for granted their access to offices, to airport lounges, to vehicular travel. Solidarity (with the poor, with the suffering) might be a major motivating factor for some and less so for others, but elites create a shared culture through their ways of moving through the landscape and what they take for granted about their place in it. Similarly, though some might find these distinctions awkward or uncomfortable, they are not easy to extricate oneself from. For instance, when there aren't enough chairs to go around and an expatriate wishes to relinquish hers, she will often be refused. For the most part, I am part of these entitled few. But, without an organization to provide a 'bubble' for me (Allen 2015), I have occasionally slipped. I would generally take taxis to the airport, and sometimes police would stop them about 400m from the entrance and I would walk from there. As I walked, white international organization Land Cruisers would speed by, not even aware there were any police present. Clearly I remained among the most entitled of all in Bangui. But these kinds of incidents gave me an inkling as to the capricious ways exclusion can be exercised against those not obviously protected by the material markers of their social status, like Land Cruisers.

These kinds of processes – social sifting within matrices of mobility/entitlement and stoppage/exclusion – are not unique to the capital. Outside of the city, roadblocks have proliferated over the past several decades, and are a particularly fecund site for these interactions (Lombard 2013a). Roadblocks are erected and staffed by gendarmes, police, soldiers, rebels, Ministry of Water and Forests guards, and others. Members of the good intentions crowd generally blast through, perhaps even oblivious to the existence of the roadblock in the first place. (They do pay for official roadblocks, with 'official' defined as those who issue a receipt, so they can be reimbursed.) Even when red road dust obscures the door decals naming their organization, a jaunty flag flying from the towering radio antenna on the hood identifies them as people not to be hassled. These vehicles slow only long enough for the roadblock guard to saunter from his spot in the shade and lift the arm of the roadblock or, at more *ad hoc* barriers, to haul away the tree branch or other obstacles placed in the road. Government officials on infrequent forays to the hinterland blast through faster than anyone, arguing that their security depends on it. They often drive at night in order to avoid the roadblocks altogether.

And then there is everyone else: the Sudanese truckers whose overloaded tractor-trailers are the primary means of mass transport for rural Central Africans; bicyclists and motorcyclists; pedestrians. People in these categories are frequently stopped for hours, if not longer, while they are questioned and their belongings are searched. Some prefer to pay large sums up front so they won't get searched, because the searches are calculated to draw attention to the traveller's delicate social status, such as by roughly overturning the carefully-washed and folded undergarments and clothes in the dust, revealing the lack of protection from a more private vehicle. Roadblocks are sites for negotiation, and most people end up paying fees, fines, and/ or 'coffee money' of various degrees of official-ness (Lombard 2013a).

As sites where social distinctions are revealed through differences in the policing of mobility, roadblocks make people angry. For many armed group members in northeastern CAR, their experiences trying to traverse roadblocks contributed to their 'radicalization' (Weiss 1967). These members' regional provenance and the religion road blockers associate with it (Islam) combined to make them targets for additional hassling. As Abdulaye Ali, a photographer-turned-rebel from Vakaga prefecture, explained to me, he used to make many trips from the northeast to the capital – sometimes several in a year. But after Bozizé took power in 2003, the roadblocks multiplied and became harder to traverse.

> Once they see your ID card and it says 'Abdulaye' or 'Vakaga' they say you're not Central African and demand 5,000 CFA [about 10 USD]. If you can speak French or Sango, you can usually get it down to the normal rate of 1,500–2,000. But without those languages, you are stuck paying 5,000 because

they say you are Chadian or Sudanese. If you try to negotiate, the price just keeps going up.

Some Muslims, whether living in the northeast or elsewhere, took the precaution of officially changing their names to Christian ones to make it easier to move around. Many southerners are convinced that a person with a Muslim name can never be a real Central African; even if the person's family has been installed on Central African soil for generations, they are seen as not true natives and thus never as true citizens. As a result, they get detained and forced to pay extra fees and fines.

Non-Muslims argue that Muslims can simply pay their way through and hence escape any kind of control. They cite as evidence the widespread rumours as to Muslims' illicit trafficking (of children, organs, diamonds, etc.). In one infamous incident in Bangui in late May 2011, two young boys were found dead in the trunk of a car. The car belonged to a Muslim from either Chad or Nigeria (accounts differ), and it was quickly popularly understood that the man was taking the bodies to Nigeria so the organs could be sold for occult purposes. Rioting followed. Some schoolmasters reported being approached by crowds who wanted them to point out all the Muslim pupils so that they could do to them what had happened to the boys in the car. The violence was quelled by a Presidential Guard intervention and a curfew (Martinelli 2014). But the tension remained, as became painfully apparent in late 2013 with the outbreak of anti-Muslim/anti-Seleka violence.

These examples show in what ways religion is important to conflict in CAR. The differences are not so much related to belief/ideology (though that aspect has increased with the anti-Muslim preaching that occurs at some Pentecostal churches, as well as by the Wahhabi doctrines that filter into a few mosques) as they are related to what religion lets a person do and how it lets them move. Since Sanusi and even before him, Muslims, who have family connections that extend beyond the borders of CAR, have been able to innovate in trade and finance in ways that non-Muslims have not. For instance, in the absence of banks in most of CAR, Muslim market traders are the only people able to move money across long distances. You give money to a trader in your city; he calls his associate in the other city, who passes the money on to the intended recipient. But financial innovation, while useful for everyone, can also create jealousy and anxiety on the part of people not able or willing to author these shifts themselves. So non-Muslims feel that Muslims are able to move around completely un-policed, while Muslims feel that they are unable to move anywhere without being hassled. Either way, everyone agrees that the question of who can move and who cannot is of utmost importance to the proper prosecution of politics. But this doesn't happen at national borders. Roadblocks, offices, the airport: these are the sites where *what kind of person one is* is determined in a material and visceral way.

Being stopped and excluded has implications that go far beyond the practical difficulties they might cause. This is because in Central Africa travelling – and especially being abroad – is a source of power. While CAR elections take place primarily in that territory ascribed to the country, much of the campaigning happens abroad. For instance, in the run-up to the presidential elections that occurred on 30 December 2015 (first round) and 14 February 2016 (second round), Martin Ziguélé pursued connections in Paris, as did Sylvain Ngakoutou Patassé (son of former CAR president Ange-Félix Patassé) and Désiré Nzanga Kolingba (son of former CAR president André Kolingba).[3] Former minister Karim Meckassoua, who had had his passport confiscated in May 2015 over suspicions he was involved with militias, got it back and promptly decamped for Brazzaville, home of his mentor Denis Sassou Nguessou (*La Lettre du Continent* 2015).

There is a prosaic aspect to all of this: CAR is the weakest state in its regional neighbourhood, and thus currying favour with the big guys is straightforward *realpolitik*. But the connotations go deeper in Central Africa. Travel, and particularly travel abroad, allows a person to accrue power in visible/apparent ways (foreign goods, money, financing of projects, etc.), but it is founded not just on those manifestations of power that all can know and see but on what all know but cannot see, namely the person's actions and accretions in that other 'abroad', the 'invisible domain of the real, where the spirits live' (Bertrand 2002: 183; cited by Ceriana Mayneri 2014c: 70). In popular discourse, a person with political power is someone presumed to have strengthened himself by occult means. The domain of foreign countries and the domain of the spirits are both parts of the 'real world' that are nevertheless foreign and unknowable for most of the population. And the domain of foreign countries is seen as a particularly active place for trade in occult knowledge. This makes sense considering that the project of polit-ical domination itself came to Central Africa from points abroad, and abroad thus is not just another geographic location but the site of the mysterious origins of political domination.

Ceriana Mayneri, drawing on Bertrand's similar findings in Java, argues that an 'imaginary of peregrination' (that is, an imagi-nary of travel, especially travel abroad) that is fundamentally linked to the occult defines the ideal political community in Central Africa. Stories of the impressive mobility of the powerful frequently meld the geographic and the spiritual/occult, such that it becomes difficult to separate the two. Indeed, the Central African environment is not just the sum of the animate and inanimate entities visibly present; it also includes equally present but invisible spiritual forces and actors. Here is one such story: the imam in Tiringoulou, in northeastern CAR, explained to me that their sheikh had once been flying in an airplane when his plane crossed paths with another plane, which was carrying another sheikh. High in the sky, the two sheikhs walked out on the wings of their planes and shook hands before re-boarding and continuing on their way. Airplane travel is a fruitful area of expan-sion for witchcraft stories and fascination, as Peter Geschiere (1997) has documented in neighbouring Cameroon. The intertwining of mobility, including and perhaps especially airplane travel, and power

– which is understood to come from occult doings while travelling
– is also visible in Central African press reports on the president's
frequent travels abroad (Ceriana Mayneri 2014c); there is always
another heads of state conference to attend in Pretoria or Beijing.
In December 2009, then-president François Bozizé's helicopter
had to make an emergency landing while returning from a rare visit
to his home village near Bossangoa, in western CAR. In popular
understanding, there was a clear subtext to reports of the incident.
Especially having just visited his home area, where the potential for the expression of jealousy in occult form would have been
rampant, Bozizé's protection (read: occult protection) was manifest
in his ability to outwit even unseen attackers and escape unharmed
(Reuters 2009).

In these ways, mobility is thoroughly bound into the constitution of Central African conceptions of power. Colonialism in both
its trans-Saharan and European-led manifestations brought with it
new forms of power, and those have been thoroughly woven into
Central African political life. But the origins of power and how
one accumulates it remain markedly foreign. This is one paradox of
political life in Central Africa today. Many Central Africans, who
imagine themselves as of-the-soil natives, want to purge the polity
of its foreignness, but foreignness/going abroad is so fundamental
to its constitution it is impossible to speak of the state and power in
Central Africa in terms of a self-sufficient, stand-alone nation-state.
This is arguably true of most states, but it is especially pronounced
in this case. Purge it of foreignness, and whatever remained would
not be a nation-state.

Given that the powerful can move around easily, the travel
patterns of elite Central Africans strike rural residents and the
urban poor as a particular affront. Like the president, other elites
frequently jet from one international conference to another. Expatriate international organization employees frequently receive calls
from junior staffers in their headquarters who needed to find one
person from every country for this or that global conference. One

told me she drew the line at suggesting a Central African representative for the International Conference on the Tiger, to be held in Russia. Yet only on the rarest occasions do elites visit the rural areas of CAR. I alluded to one reason why above: people who have landed in positions of wealth and power fear the occult capabilities of their extended families in the village, who are likely jealous (Marchal 2015a).

The poor state of the roads and expense of travel also makes such visits difficult. Recognizing those infrastructural challenges if not also the occult ones, donors and the rest of the good intentions crowd seeking to make politicians more responsive to their ostensible constituents will pay for, organize, or otherwise encourage these politicians to go on a 'mission' to the hinterland. In the run-up to elections politicians often undertake their own campaigning visits as well. Yet these visits frequently reinforce rather than undermine the sense among those visited that the powerful are mobile, and they are stuck and voiceless. On these rare visits, the officials engage in promissory politics (Lombard 2015) – making promises about state-generated future welfare as a way of demonstrating authority yet without assuming direct personal responsibility for people's plights or otherwise giving them any direct means to claim entitlements. Elite visitors respond in seemingly munificent ways to rural folks' requests, but everyone knows these promises carry a weak obligation for follow-through given residents' distance from the places where budgets are disbursed and how difficult it is for the poor and remote to travel. Thus rather than making people feel their needs are better served, promissory politicking visits feed people's expectations about the entitlements they feel due while also making their exclusion all the more painfully apparent – desire becomes limitless when also impossible. As one rebel group member put it to me, 'Us, we don't have the kind of mouth that can speak to the government.'

Since rural folks couldn't speak on their own behalf, these politicians *en mission* often encouraged people to write letters, which the politician or functionary would promise to personally deliver to the president. The politician/functionary would say such things in order to indicate his closeness to the president and his power. But for older rural people it also was a bitter reminder that the days when there was a functioning postal service reaching them were ever further gone. There is a post office in Bangui, but the formerly regular mail service outside the capital (functional into the early 1980s) has completely ended. Letters and other correspondence (such as cash) now have to be transported by personal connections. On a recent visit to CAR I travelled with a Central African friend who straddles the NGO and business (primarily real estate) realms. We were on the same plane to visit outlying towns, and on the same plane to return to the capital, though we visited different places. Upon emerging from the Bangui airport, a polite yet insistent crowd surrounded her, and she began to pull envelopes – some evidently fat with cash, some slim – from her purse. Some of the recipients she knew, while others had to demonstrate their identity in other ways. This improvised mail service requires personal connections and underscores the importance of mobility as both a means to and an expression of power.

In the discussion above, I focused on Central African political elites and their practices when visiting rural areas, but people in these areas experience the visits by international organization/ humanitarian elites as fundamentally similar. Promises get made – perhaps in good faith – that are subsequently forgotten. And worse perhaps, when promises are not fulfilled (rural Central Africans understand better than anyone that 'development' is a challenging goal in their region), there is no effort to explain what happened. (I discuss examples of these communication failures at greater length in Chapter 5 on DDR.)

The hierarchically inferior position of the letter-writer as opposed to its deliverer and intended recipient is a dynamic that is not limited to the domain of Central African politicians alone. It has also marked the way many Central Africans experience their

relationship with INGO and international organization representatives. One person who schooled me in these matters was Laurent, a
Central African born and raised near Ndele. He had grown up poor
but with big ('rebellious', in his term of choice) dreams, his world
enlarged by the French crime novels he borrowed from missionaries and other expatriates in his midst. By dint of both struggle and
luck, Laurent made it all the way to France. For reasons he did not
particularly elaborate, he was now back in his home village, but he
retained an urban, and educated, demeanour.

When I first met Laurent, one of the INGOs in town was facing
eviction over having allegedly supported the rebels who lived and
worked on the road north of town. Laurent was unsurprised. He
had reached out to the INGO to warn them about the rebels, but
they had not so much as acknowledged the letters he had written
to their headquarters in Bangui and Paris. How could they be so
callous, he wondered. In Laurent's self-conception, he was one of
them: he had a Central African body, admittedly, but he had lived
abroad and shared their cosmopolitanism. Their failure to recognize his letters had more significance than simply not agreeing to
his terms. It was a failure to recognize that he was the same kind
of person as they were. However properly styled his letter, it had
not effectively communicated his education and integrity across the
physical distance. They ignored him and collaborated with others
instead. Their downfall was therefore predictable: 'This is what is
to be expected when one works with dishonest people.' And yet that
was a shallow consolation for Laurent, who felt his personhood had
been denied.

To say that mobility and dignity are aligned – that the person
who can move has dignity in a way others do not – is not quite right,
because mobility is fundamentally intertwined with the occult
and people's ambivalence about that kind of action/knowledge.
But mobility is certainly a source of power, and as such it is node
of contestation, policing, and desire. Tracking who can move and
who cannot, as well as popular debates about mobility, are fecund

domains for understanding people's grievances and dynamics of conflict, as well as their utopian visions. And, however they might understand themselves to be different from each other, everyone intervening in Central Africa becomes entangled in these processes.

Failure to acknowledge the differences in people's mobility and the power dynamics these create can mean missing opportunities to defuse conflict and grievance. For example, armed group members I interviewed and got to know in 2009–2010 often wondered aloud why their president so rarely came to talk with them and, more importantly, why on those few occasions he did visit their locations, he kept a distance. He did not talk to them like fellow men, and he did not eat with them. (In Central Africa, eating together is a means of beginning to construct kinship ties.) In public speeches, he would exhort them to mend their ways and make promises about what he would do for them, but the armed group members all noticed that he had stopped talking about the need for DDR prior to the upcoming elections and feared he had decided to jump over the DDR phase, which would have brought armed group members some of the entitlement they sought.

Realizing that elections would weaken their claim to largesse (an election would undermine the rebellion's claim to represent rural residents' frustrations), some armed groups tried to strengthen their position by making threats. Note how central mobility – the ability to move and to control movement – is to this APRD member's threat:

We have Francis's [the president's son and minister of defence] phone number. We say that those of us who take the Dekoa and Sibut roads to get to Bangui, we know the layout of the city because we have a map and we know where the ambassadors are located. As soon as we arrive in Bangui no flight will be able to leave because we will bombard any plane that dares to make the attempt. Even the ambassadors will not be able to leave. ... Among us [rebels] there are heavy weapons specialists and others who are not afraid of guns because these guns cannot harm us [a reference to occult bulletproofing practices].

This young man was trying to demonstrate his power, and his means of doing so was to invoke his ability to move and to stop other people from moving, that is, to create disorder in the standard system of mobility and its hierarchies.

However, later in our conversation, this (ex-)fighter became more circumspect. He said that if the president simply came and spoke to the armed group members man-to-man, they would set aside their differences and financial demands. The simple fact of being taken seriously – in the form of physical closeness and eating together and the respect they connote – would suffice. But he recognized that this was unlikely. Whereas the armed group members 'should have the president's ear', this president simply ignored them: 'The president is a big idiot' ('*Lo 'ke idiot mingi*'). This irreverence was itself a borderline threat, a way of claiming that whatever the president's current power, he would soon be shown up. (As indeed happened just over two years later, though these particular rebels were not the primary authors of his downfall.) But it did little to overturn the structural dynamics whereby the mobility/power and stoppage/exclusion distinctions get reproduced on a daily basis.

The strength of state desires

In beginning to answer the question 'what is "the state" in CAR?' I have argued that for CAR, certain conceptions of what states are and how they work are flipped upside down, particularly in relation to territory, mobility, and violence. Though the violence has often been understood as scandal and thus treatable, placing incidents in a longer history reveals it to be troublingly recursive and indicates systemic, structural dimensions to these problems. For Central Africans, the state is a 'painful absence and a hurtful presence' (Smith 2015a: 17; emphasis in original). And yet it retains a special allure as the potential solver of all problems, both from the perspective of Central Africans and from the perspective of others concerned (whether out of good intentions, desire for profit, or other reasons) about happenings in the area. Although on a daily basis people experience the state and centralized administration as more predatory than anything else, they nevertheless see 'the state' as the political container best suited to assuring protection and security. The nation-state form is thus both the UN's 'primal mandate' and something that places parameters on Central Africans' visions of the proper ordering of the world, particularly in terms of the nature of the relationships that ideal ordering is seen to consist of. It creates 'bonds' – connections that are also chains (Gluckman 1955).

Currently, many Central Africans experience the state as capricious when not completely unresponsive. Here is an incident from my fieldwork in Ndele in 2010. Though varying in particulars, incidents like these occurred with some regularity during my research (and were frequently reported during the eight-prefecture study on access to justice I led in 2010–2011). One morning I went to the market to find my friend Al-Habib, a young trader who frequently worked various deals there. I didn't find him, but his brother said Al-Habib was locked up at the gendarmerie. I walked to the gendarmerie to find that Al-Habib had recently been released after two days' detention, but another brother was still detained. He explained that two women in their family had been fighting, and he and Al-Habib had stepped in to try to break them up. A bystander saw them and, misunderstanding what was going on, reported them to the authorities, who promptly locked the brothers up. (They could be released on a kind of *ad hoc* bail.)

As we were talking, I spied another familiar face: Laurent the world traveller. He seemed shocked to be in custody, without proper shoes and other material markers of dignity. He said that a man who was a distant relative stood accused of stealing from a hunting safari operator. Since Laurent had spoken with the alleged thief the day before, he was being locked up under suspicion of involvement in the theft. I thought I saw tears in Laurent's eyes. Even witnesses can be detained indefinitely, and he was unsure when he would be released. He did not have money to pay his way out.

Experiences of arbitrary detention like Al-Habib's and Laurent's are not aberrant or scandalous, even though people decry them. Like roadblocks, they are emblematic of the capriciousness that ordinary Central Africans experience in relation to their interactions with representatives of centralized authority, whether employees of the government, NGOs, or international organizations. And yet: time and again, when I asked people who could solve their problems, they frequently replied that 'only the state' could do it. This was true both of Central Africans and of INGO and international organization employees. The state was a major source of insecurity, but it (or rather, a vision of what it could one day become) still occupied the privileged place in regard to legitimate authority.

This was the case both because of the history of the state in CAR and especially the position of the state as the distributor par excellence, and also because international interveners worked to inculcate this way of thinking in Central Africans. French diplomats would tell me about how they would fly government officials around in their military planes, so it would be easier for them to reach remote areas. Once there, they would encourage the officials to raise the Central African flag so that people could start thinking of themselves as Central African. The ways in which that Central Africanness was also fundamentally a French project seemed to escape the people planning these kinds of initiatives. Under the framework of 'protection' activities in Tiringoulou, UNICEF would give schoolchildren worksheets to practice applying for a passport or national identity card. The dissonance between the decidedly predatory state these children had experienced (state forces had attacked and burned a number of villages in the area a couple of years earlier) and the state-as-guarantor-of-rights promised on those worksheets created tension, but it did not make the children simply ignore the assignment. Rather, it heightened their sense that *their state* was falling short of the ideals, and in the process entrenched the primacy of the state ideals themselves.

Even members of rebel groups saw 'the state' as the ultimate, ideal authority in their areas of operation. They routinely took control of things like roadblock operation and, in mining areas, 'security' and mine-access fees (ICG 2008). But when they listed their region's problems, they returned to the state again and again as the only entity that could solve them. For instance, 'only the state' could stop the 'foreigners' in search of ivory, water, and other valuable resources from overrunning CAR's parklands. Couldn't you do those kinds of operations yourselves, I asked? You are, after all, a commanding rebel group. The answer was always no – sometimes for reasons of a lack of resources (money, materiel), but more deeply because doing so could never be anything other than improvised or provisional (i.e. improper) if not carried out with the legitimizing, if also fundamentally illegible, signature of the state (Das 2006). This meant that people spent a lot of time waiting, and much less time figuring out things they, on the local level, might be able to do on their own to improve their situation.

This is not to say that people would be better off without 'the state', whatever that might mean in CAR today. Nor does it imply that the state form is culturally inappropriate to the region or that people have a preference for some other mode of social organization – their thoughts on these matters are complicated and sometimes contradictory, as in much of the world. Rather, CAR is interesting to explore because it draws out what arises from the interplay between assigning *a priori* primacy to the state form – as a kind of utopian project – and the fact that for so many reasons it is difficult to conjure such a territorialized polity in the region. There is always a gap between how people understand their present positions and where they would like one day to be, on an individual or collective basis – diagnosis of a disjuncture of just that kind is the basis for social activism. But in

CAR the gap between the state as it is experienced and the state as people think it should be is so vast that real conundrums arise. One of these conundrums involves fears over the mobility of conflict in the region, which while not baseless can be exaggerated for the sake of advocacy, turning the state's failure to secure the borders into another concession to be outsourced, with mixed consequences. Consciously or not, many journalistic and advocacy accounts promote a contagion model of conflict, calling attention to the ways it can 'spill over' borders. For instance, in a front-page 2006 *New York Times* report about violence in northwestern CAR, the headline was meant to evoke a connection to the African crisis of the moment, Darfur, by alerting readers that Central Africans were 'on the run as war crosses another line in Africa' (Polgreen 2006). In fact, the region the author reported from (northwestern-most Ouham-Pende prefecture) was well over one thousand kilometres from Darfur and the violence had nothing to do with the struggles in Darfur and eastern Chad. Nevertheless, among international organizations and Central Africans alike, 'Darfur spill over' became a shorthand to refer to the risk CAR faced. Perhaps the war in Darfur had not yet 'spilled over' into CAR, but it could, and that concern could mobilize new funding. The presence of the Lord's Resistance Army (LRA) on Central African territory since 2008 has also fed these conceptions of violent conflict in Africa as being driven by mercenary interests and capable of spreading as surely as an oil spill at sea. While 'spill over' models usefully remind us that borders (that is, lines on a map) do not in and of themselves stop violence, violent conflict is not like an overturned cup of milk that will spread according to natural/physical laws unless it is actively contained. To spread, conflict requires people, social projects, interests, etc. (Richards 2005; Debos 2014).

Mobile conflict in a weak state, as a particular kind of threat, carries with it a few possible treatments. These centre on outsourcing the country's territory to a variety of international actors (e.g. the American military aid directed toward anti-LRA operations in CAR's far eastern reaches) who will 'temporarily' take over for the state. These temporary arrangements often persist, however, and more frequently end because the financiers are tired of paying than because 'the state' has magically emerged to step back in.

Security and the fear of a 'security vacuum' were two of the main watchwords of Bangui diplomats in the final years of the Bozizé regime. These diplomat-donors were increasingly frustrated with Bozizé's way of governing, but he appeared nevertheless to be the least bad option. Certainly, his staying in power would be less bad than his violent removal from office, which would inevitably entail a lot of looting and destruction, as well as necessitate the re-starting of donor and other projects almost from scratch as new ministers were put in place and looted offices restocked with necessary equipment and so forth. So when Bozizé blatantly rigged the electoral system in his favour and made a joke of the idea that the 'independent electoral commission' was anything other an extension of his own interests, these donors had little room to manoeuvre in encouraging him to do otherwise.

There are important similarities between the compromises entailed in supporting Bozizé and those involved with supporting David Dacko in 1960 (as described in the previous chapter). In both cases, Central African heads of state mobilized donor/ diplomatic fears of a bad neighbourhood in order to make their anti-democratic practices seem less objectionable – or at least, to make these seem preferable to the alternative – from the perspective of the external guarantors of Central African sovereignty. They are cunning victims, assuming the persona of the victim in such a way that it becomes a half-veiled threat, revealing a certain kind of strength nevertheless.

From the perspective of democratic ideals it is easy to critique supporting a self-interested and repressive president, but the big problem is that in the case of Bozizé's removal from power, the security-centred perspective was correct. That is to say, Bozizé's ouster did carry with it a lot of violence and chaos, which as of this writing have not been definitively vanquished, two transitional governments and one elected president later. And yet Bozizé's anti-democratic and anti-distributive practices (that is, the ways he increasingly personalized power and narrowed the circle of people benefiting from government largesse) fostered the discontent that eventually led to his ouster. When Bozizé blocked Patassé from departing the country – even after Patassé had been resoundingly beaten in the presidential elections, and even though he was seriously ill – it was popularly seen as cruel and mean-spirited. Many Central Africans experienced this as a shift from being anti-democratic in the service of one's own power (understandable, if not ideal) to gratuitously insulting his fellow Central Africans. At Patassé's funeral, parading women bared their breasts at Bozizé in an attempt to shame him. Frustration was clearly growing.

In the end, Bozizé could not contain the discontent. The Seleka rebellion was far from a democratic, popular uprising (it was born of surreptitious meetings between politico-military entrepreneurs abroad, then grew in membership once back on Central African territory), so it would be a mistake to describe Bozizé's removal as the result of a popular mobilization. But Seleka nevertheless mapped onto a widespread frustration with Bozizé's way of governing, and when Seleka first took power, many welcomed the change while deploring the violence and looting that accompanied it. Certainly, few today hope Bozizé will return, though his (former) associates have benefited from their association with him, and there is nostalgia for the relatively less chaos that marked his time in power.

And so this is one of the challenges Central Africans face today. Non-Central Africans with limited time horizons and patience as regards their interest in this place are the guarantors of Central African sovereignty and have generally 'viewed it through the lens of regional stability rather than standing firm for inclusiveness in CAR politics' (Lombard 2014b). (Not that it is clear that external actors can do such a thing, as de Waal [1997] draws attention to in his study of humanitarian modes of power.) And while promoting stability *seems* to afford greater short-term security, looking at CAR history in a longer duration shows that this president-centred model of security has repeatedly failed to deliver on its promise. The country has had few elections that could be termed democratic in spirit and content, rather than just in form. Violent changes in power, often supported in different ways by non-Central African actors, have been more common.

Another way of saying that the CAR state is a 'hurtful presence and a painful absence' (Smith 2015a: 17) would be to describe it as fetishized. In popular understanding, a fetish is a kind of a false idol. However, there is another way of thinking of what a fetish is and how it works. Following Rutherford (2003), Pietz (1985), Taussig (1992), and others, a fetish is simultaneously an idea and a thing arising out of the meeting of incommensurate systems of value (put otherwise: normative pluralism [Chauveau et al. 2001]). It is charged with a dynamic of desire and disavowal – people desire it, yet also disavow it. The dynamic of disavowal and desire is 'what accounts for the border-straddling character of the fetish: the utopian dreams it incessantly rekindles, the way it works all the better because it fails' (Rutherford 2003: 21). In CAR, 'the state' – as a form, as an ideal type – is the focus of people's utopian dreams, and these desires are intensified rather than undermined by its continual failure to live up to them. At the same time, people disavow the interventions of 'the state' in their lives – expatriates at the airport fume over the twelve security checks they go through to board their planes ('job creation', they/we scoff); market women lament the excessive *ad hoc* taxes they are forced to pay. And yet no one questions that it is 'the state' that should have ultimate authority over these domains and many others.

It is tempting to respond to the observation that the state form is fetishized by saying that we should simply remove 'the state' from its pedestal and look to alternative modes of political and social organization. However, dealing with the problems of state fetishization is unfortunately not that simple. When I question international interveners' emphasis on strengthening the state security sector (remember that hundred-plus-year history of failed SSR), they often ask what alternatives exist. What, should we just support militias? Under the 'primal mandate' nation-state system, doing so would be not just legally complicated but foolish to the point of ridiculousness. And their scepticism is well-founded. There are many conflicts that play out on Central African territory that have little to do with 'the state' and more to do with other animosities, jealousies, and grievances. 'The local' is not a magically accountable and righteous domain. It is riven with its own fault lines as well as competing personal and collective projects.

Moreover, though CAR is far from the Hobbesian war of all against all that some news and advocacy accounts would suggest, and though conflict does not spread with the capricious determination of an untreated cancer, people experience the country's porousness as a kind of dispossession (Ceriana Mayneri 2014a) and therefore dangerous and damaging. That concessionary politics and extraversion make Central Africans complicit in this dispossession does nothing to assuage the anger over the injustice of their place-in-the-world (Ferguson 2006). It is both understandable and not entirely fair that they would feel overrun by dangerous foreigners (Marchal 2009). The desire to be able to strike back from a position of strength is visceral and deep. For their part, international interveners and the good intentions crowd would find it difficult to definitively sideline the state since it is the foundational organizing structure underlying their existence.

And yet, when it comes to the position and nature of the state in CAR there must be a reckoning that goes beyond the platitudes expressed during national dialogues. At these dialogues, several of which have been held in CAR, the form of the state stands on its pedestal, its externally derived sovereignty and structural accountability problems addressed only superficially, and in such a way as to present Central Africans as victims. The violence of an anaemic bureaucracy must be dealt with in a more substantive way than simply calling for more donor funding, as tends to dominate in these discussions. Money can be transformative, but it cannot in and of itself wholly erase history and the dynamics that have been reinforced through the years. The trick, then, will be to make people's state-oriented aspirations a basis for policy without reifying the state form. One way of doing this would be to shift away from projects that aim to build the full range of ideal-type bureaucratic institutions (ministries, an army) and instead focus on the ways the state can support dignified social status, such as through distribution (primarily, provision of a salary or a basic income grant-type arrangement). I discuss these suggestions further in the the book's conclusion.

Conclusion

In this chapter I have discussed the modes of violence, mobility, and extraversion that have been central to processes of accumulation and the exercise of power in Central Africa over the last hundred-plus years. I included this longer historical perspective in order to show that, rather than aberrant, scandalous incidents, these processes have been the core of the CAR state through the years. Moreover, they arise out of the situation of pluralized authority and pluralized yet frequently displaced and intermittent oversight. During the colonial era, an example would be those members of the French public and the government who took Gide's *Voyage au Congo* as a call to arms; today, one could include human-rights monitors. In both cases, the concerned people involved are far from the scenes of the crimes and not ultimately in charge of doing something about them. The end result is a highly extraverted state, such that it makes no sense to speak of CAR as a state except through reference to these 'external' relationships (Marchal 2015b).

Looking at CAR for what it is, rather than what it is not, reveals a durably fragile assemblage of relationships in which mobility, and frequently violence, allow certain people to move and accrue power while leaving others all the more thwarted and excluded. Looking at these processes in detail makes it far less compelling to diagnose the failings of the different categories of actor who meet in CAR (e.g. venal Central African politicians, out-of-touch aid workers, mostly irrelevant but occasionally interesting researchers, profiteering businesspeople) and more useful to understand how they become bound to each other, entangled through denunciation and compromise and/or through mutual interests, such that their intentions and values become muddled. The following chapter looks at these entangled relationships in greater detail through the case study of rebellion in CAR over the last decade.

Chapter 4

LONG AND SHORT HISTORIES OF REBELLION

> The schism between the two groups is itself the pattern of their integration into one community. (Gluckman 1940: 14)

> To sum up the situation at the bridge, one may say that the groups and individuals present behave as they do because the bridge, which is the centre of their interests, associates them in a common celebration. As a result of their common interest they act by customs of co-operation and communication, even though the two colour-groups are divided according to the pattern of the social structure. (Gluckman 1940: 28)

Introduction

Equatorial Africa has a long history of insurgency and armed actors and groups of different kinds. In a process that began in the 1980s, these rural rebellions have become both internationalized and conventionalized – that is, their features and appearance have become standardized – in concert with the perceptional frames of the international actors who take an interest in conflict in this part of the world. Through a process of mutual adaptation, rebels and international organizations/humanitarians and regional leaders have all helped to conventionalize rebellion as something these international actors notice and can engage with given the international laws and arrangements that guide their work. The core thrust of conventionalization is to make the armed actors' relationship to the state ideal explicit, through such things as mode of organization (e.g. officers and ranks), name, and practices (e.g. wearing uniforms, or some fragment thereof), which make them 'regular' according to international law. To borrow Alex de Waal's phrasing, conventionalization can be seen as a means of perfecting the political marketplace (2015: 213): it spurs mechanisms like peace processes and disarmament designed to organize new distributions to the disgruntled rebels.

Concern over the specific challenge a rebel group poses to the nation-state order is a large part of what brings these various actors to the table together – for peace processes, for disarmament, for national dialogue, etc. – and yet that state framework also lets them perpetuate the idea that they are fundamentally different social groups, with different interests, rather than people involved in a joint endeavour. The state is thus a mode of both integration and schism, to paraphrase Gluckman.

This chapter first explores Central African visions of the proper, state-based order of the world, particularly in relation to two main and somewhat contradictory tendencies. To the extent they can, Central Africans decry, prevent, and otherwise avoid coercive elements of governance. At the same time, they seek 'integration' into the state (that is, a state salary), which is a marker of entitlement and dignity at least as much as it is a payment in exchange for carrying out particular tasks. These tendencies have been the core of the rebellion agenda over the past two decades. Next, I will discuss the state-based order of the world that underlies the good intentions crowd and the work diplomats do. Conventionalizing rebellion, as happened in the 2000s, helped align the Central African and international visions of the state order of the world to such an extent that rebels, government officials, and interveners could sit at the table together. However, everyone involved continued to work to create boundaries between each other. When these thus-divided actors fail to achieve common progress on the issues of the day, a consequences gap arises. People at the table will make a good deal of money simply by being involved; rank-and-file fighters and other Central Africans are less likely to receive the distributions they were promised. This perpetuates and even exacerbates grievances on the part of Central Africans. Though conventional rebellion is *more about being threatening* than it is about perpetrating violence (Lombard 2016b), it entails violence as well. That violence can prove difficult to contain, even setting off new grievances and anger, as has occurred in CAR since 2013. (Chapter 6 explores the potential and limits of making sense of violence.)

Insurgency and entitlement in conceptions of the state

Insurgency is one of the means Central Africans have used to protest the violence that has been perpetrated against them on behalf of their would-be governors. Though those governors have generally had greater firepower at their disposal, their position remains highly precarious, and they know it. In the early years of colonization, five out of every six colonial administrators died on the job (Kalck 1971: 53). This was due to disease, and it was also due to Africans' resistance tactics. Africans would use cover of darkness to raid storehouses and kill colonial and concessionary officials in their beds. In other cases, African rebels attacked convoys and prevented access to the rivers that were the administrators' and concession-aires' only exit from the area (Coquéry-Vidrovitch 1972). The most famous of these efforts became known as the Kongo-Wara Rebel-lion, which was led by a charismatic and enigmatic visionary who received the name Karnu in a dream-communication from God, between 1928 and 1931 (Nzabakomada-Yakoma 1986). But for the most part armed opposition during the concessionary period was not articulated as a set of demands. It was often hard to distinguish these operations from those of the robber gangs that have also long existed in the Chad Basin region (Issa 2010), and indeed it would be analytically incorrect to either separate or utterly conflate the two.

In the case of Karnu, his message drew on 'polyvalent symbolic meanings' in communicating general 'opposition to the French and Fulbe rule and exploitation' (Burnham and Christensen 1983: 3, 17). Karnu's message 'was transmitted to peripheral groups only in the sketchiest outline and was usually substantially rephrased in terms of local symbolic systems and political considerations' (ibid.: 17), belying any exclusive explanation of what was going on.[1] It is especially in this respect that Karnu and the Kongo-Wara are similar to the Anti-Balaka, as described further in Chapter 6.

Administrators and concessionary officials confronted the problem that Central Africans did not want to work for them, because Africans saw little benefit in doing so, not valuing the forms of payment offered them. Payment might be increased but that did not make the labour any less forced (moreover, in the early years, payment went to the person identified as 'chief' rather than the labourers themselves). The twenty-two point legal code governing Africans in French Equatorial Africa included the offence 'Failure to accept payment' (Zoctizoum 1983) in part so that Europeans could perpetuate the fiction that their labour projects were categorically different from the unpaid coercion of the trans-Saharan merchants and raiders.

At first, the forced labour was needed for porterage and for concessionary company exploitation of resources such as rubber. With the arrival of automobiles and the end of concessionary company supremacy around 1930, forced labour became a matter of paying the annual head tax, as well as fulfilling the government's new plan for making Oubangui-Chari profitable: cotton. 'When cotton did not cause open rebellion to emerge, it provoked a bad humour and a spirit of revolt as widespread as it was persistent. Everyone had to recognize that Africans detest cotton cultivation' (Brégeon 1998: 172; my translation). It is not hard to understand why people were reluctant to work in the cotton fields. The pay was dismal. In the late 1940s, people cultivating cotton would be paid about 2,500 francs per year. To put that amount in perspective, a medium-quality *pagne* (a several-yard bolt of cloth used for clothing) was 1,000 francs (Brégeon 1998: 179). It is not difficult to see why people had little interest in such intense labour for such slim reward.[2] Even after the formal ending of the *Indigénat* system in 1946, administrators included stipulations making it possible to force people to labour in the cotton fields.

Some elderly Central Africans remember the vagaries of forced labour. The violence was generally carried out by the regional guards, who came from all over French Equatorial Africa and had no local connections that might give them long-term interests in moderating their behaviour. The guards would use the *chicotte* (hippo-skin whip) extensively, and they would tie up their captives in columns one hundred people long. Both the *chicotte* and tying people together were prohibited by the legal code, but it was generally in administrators' interest to turn a blind eye. Doungous Koro, as of 2010 one of the oldest people in the former lands of Sanusi's Dar al-Kuti (the Ndele area today), described being forced to collect rubber. Looking back, he found it bizarre: 'The weird thing was, they would force people to collect rubber, and then they would pay them.' According to Koro, the rates of payment were not bad, and enterprising people could use their time in the forest in search of rubber to gather other profitable items, like honey or fish, and make good money.

The way problems of the state like the need for labour played out varied based on many factors, including the personalities of the particular people involved. In all cases, force was an important element of the governing repertoire, and Africans developed means of avoidance and insurgency at the same time as some were attracted to the new forms of knowledge associated with the colonial incomers. President-turned-Emperor Jean-Bédel Bokassa incarnates these two trends, and the ambivalence that results from them. Orphaned in 1927 (at the age of six) when his village chief father was beaten to death in the centre of Mbaiki after refusing to assemble forced labourers (his mother committed suicide a week later), he received the name Jean-Bédel from a missionary who saw his devotion to the children's grammar of the same name.[3] *Francophilie* became central to Bokassa's conception of self (Smith 2015a). Thus while people may have reviled the coercive incursions, that did not mean they rejected the state, or foreignness, outright.

Koro showed me different sides to these issues of how people conceive of the proper role of the state. One afternoon in Ndele in late 2009, at the end of a long conversation about the history of the Sanusi sultanate, he removed a thick wad of small, square papers from his robes. He said he had been a tax collector, and these small cards – each about 1.5 inches square – were evidence that he, too, had paid his tax. He had one for each year, starting in 1955. The 1955 card read:

OUBANGUI-CHARI
District: Ndele
Village: Zoukoutiniala
Number: 46
Amount: 200 + 20 Francs

In the cards from subsequent years, the header changed to '*République Centrafricaine*' and, briefly at the end of the 1970s, to the '*Empire Centrafricain*'. The name of the tax also changed, from the head tax to the '*Impôt personnel/taxe district/taxes collectives rurales*' (personal tax/district tax/rural collective taxes). And the amounts due also changed, from highs of 3,500 francs to lows of about 1,000 francs. A couple of years in the series 1955 to 1993 were missing, but Koro assured me that he had them at home. Back when the head tax was collected, one had to carry the receipt on one's person. Failure to produce it when asked could result in the demand that it be paid a second time. When Patassé abolished the personal tax in the early 1990s (Smith 2015a), Koro lost his job. The effects of losing a job, and the end of the tax, go beyond changes in one's money supply. For these things are markers of social status. Of his tax cards, Koro said, 'When you have your tax receipt in hand, everyone respects you. *C'était notre dignité à travers ça*' ['it was the source of our dignity']. With this comment, Koro suggested one of the ways that a special relationship to the state – in this case, as a taxpayer – was indicative of a special personal status, one marked by dignity. For Koro this status was doubled by his being a state employee. Though a legacy of the repressive colonial history, at the time it was ended, the head tax was a form of revenue that stayed in local areas and funded health posts and schools. The lost funding was not replaced, and local government service provision became all but nonexistent. (Other Patassé campaign promises – such as the provision of money-printing machines to every village [Smith 2015a] went unfulfilled.) This helps explain why during the local consultations for the national dialogue (the Bangui Forum) in 2015 rural residents repeatedly suggested the reinstatement of the head tax.

Not long after France's African colonies gained independence, Georges Balandier wrote that in Africa one's 'position in relation to the state apparatus' 'determines social status, the form of the relation to the economy and material power' (1970: 168). In other words, one's relationship to the state determined what kind of a person one was, as well as the kinds of entitlements and privileges one enjoyed. Paying taxes was one element of that. But tax paying was also associated with much historical brutality, and as powers of coercion quickly became less centralized after independence official tax paying was overtaken by another path to entitled personhood, namely a civil servant salary.

Amid the general abnegation of authority over public life in favour of concession-management, Equatorial postcolonial leaders used salaried posts as a way of creating loyal citizens and heading off potential opponents (Bayart 2009; Mbembe 2001: 75). Drawing a salary was thus less a matter of engaging in a particular kind of production (i.e. carrying out government functions) than it was about marking one's status as a particular kind of person, namely a person who could claim entitlements through a sort of personal relationship with the president and the state. Thus, in CAR the salient distinction as regards political inclusion is less that of citizens and non-citizens, or even of citizens and subjects, but that of *those who can claim entitlements* and *those who are ignored*. One can be *integrated* into the state – the Central African jargon to describe those with civil service jobs (the unstated implication being that those who do not draw salaries are un-integrated and left out) and thereby have a claim to entitlements. Or one can fall among the *abandoned* (my interlocutors' term of choice) and ignored. The private sector has always been both linked to the government through concessionary politics (Smith 2015b) and feeble, employing hardly anyone, so there are few alternative means to the status of salary other than through the state. The system of salary-personhood meant that involvement with the state/making money had less to do with what one did (that is, with what one produced) and more to do with the social status that a state job conferred.

When the University of Bangui opened in 1969, it offered the surest route to a state job. Most opportunities for government jobs were centralized in Bangui, but there were a few exceptions, like the country's only teacher training centre, which is in Bambari. At the time, there was such a dearth of qualified Central African employees (many jobs were still filled by French people, or by regional expatriates) that every graduate of the university would be integrated into the civil service. This policy continued into the 1980s. At that point, a combination of precipitous economic decline and the imposition of structural adjustment brought an end to that system, while 'ghost workers' and other civil servants whose salaries were deemed inefficient or otherwise redundant were also purged from the public rolls. Though from an accounting perspective these moves made sense and were probably necessary (the university was churning out growing numbers of graduates each year, as government coffers were steadily dwindling), they had consequences beyond the economic realm.

With integration slowing to a trickle, the avenue to becoming a person with entitlements was closed off. Since the president could then only give a few people government posts and hence make entitled persons, he started taking extra care to choose only those he felt he could trust. Ethnicity – previously not much of a factor in Central African politics – became an important means of differentiating among the many competitors (Smith 2015a). This ethnic favouritism ratcheted up feelings of exclusion on the part of everyone else.

From the perspective of the international donors funding governments like CAR's, elections, preferably multi-party, were superior to the old system of making citizens by giving them salaries: now procedural democracy would be the way to claim rights, and all could participate (Englund 2006). However, in places like CAR elections have been marred not just by manipulative practices on the part of incumbents but also by structural problems, making it so no one has confidence that the will of the people has been expressed in any kind of a meaningful way (Lombard 2011). Whatever value they see in voting (and people *do* value it), few have confidence that voting will make it possible for them to later claim entitlements to state largesse. For it is entitlements, not rights, that mark Central African conceptions of the proper order of the world and of states. Rights are abstract principles theoretically held by all; entitlements are privately won and held and when not made good on there are greater possibilities for forcing the issue.

Unsurprisingly, then, salaries have been flash points for conflict over the past several decades. When Bangui politics took a violent turn in the mid-1990s, it was in the form of army mutinies over the issue of salary arrears.[4] Salaries were the demonstration of a kind of material citizenship, a status one could demonstrate through the personal styles one could employ (manner of dress, make of perfume, schools chosen for one's children) and the relations one could cultivate (who one could provide for).

With few public posts to be had, rural areas were left largely to their own devices. In the decades following independence, the government's interest in undertaking grand governing projects involving labourers – whether in the capital or in the hinterlands – has occasionally waxed. For instance, Bokassa began and mostly aborted a number of development schemes. But mostly it has waned. To the extent that there was a project of concern for popular welfare, it consisted largely of state salaries for a few, which marked them as bearing an entitled status. As of 2014, there were about 20,000 civil servants in CAR. The security sector adds about 10,000 to that tally (Fuior and Law 2014). Thus only about one out of every 150 people in CAR has a state job. Since people keep these jobs for life, very few employees are added in any given year.

However, while many people seek entitled personhood through a state salary, there is also a marked tendency among Central Africans to oppose – often effectively – centralized attempts at regulation and control (see Lombard 2016a for discussion of how these dynamics play out in relation to armed conservation). Efforts to govern and control are often seen as capricious and excessive (Lombard 2013a), both in the capital and in the hinterland, and people have developed effective ways of making their discontent known. Though frequently negotiation can be a way of defusing tense situations and finding ways for people to look the other way from their points of conflict, sometimes opposition turns threatening, or even violent.[5]

To take one recent example: at the same time as the Bangui Forum participants were debating the ideal form of the state and better social service provision and inclusiveness, an acrimonious debate was playing out in far northeastern CAR over the legitimacy of government regulation of salaries. An INGO working in the area employs people in a number of towns in Vakaga prefecture to help manage health posts. They are careful to avoid calling these people salaried workers; rather, they are *volunteers* who receive an 'incentive' as a kind of thank you for their efforts. The INGO had set compensation at a rate they found fair – 8,000 CFA/day (about USD16). In May 2015, the government issued a directive mandating a uniform compensation level for all such voluntary workers across the country. The amount was lower than that paid by the INGO. The INGO informed its volunteers of the change in their payment, explaining that the matter was out of their hands. They must follow the law or else risk getting kicked out of the country or otherwise sanctioned. Their position was equivocal: they felt responsibilities to the people they served as well as to the ideals of the organization, but they also depended on the authorization of a government that perhaps had different interests.

People in the area revolted. The INGO's vehicles were stopped from circulating and people promised violence if they tried to continue their work stocking rural health posts. The INGO's field office head reported asking people, 'Wait, you would refuse your families treatment rather than accept the government's terms? You would go back to the way things were before, with no health posts, no doctors, no medicine?' Yes, they replied; we have our traditional means of curing people. Whether this statement was a bluff or a position sincerely held, the INGO found a way to continue paying people the same amount as they had previously, and they did not have to test whether people were ready to follow through on this threat. I offer the story here as one of countless such interactions through which the question of who is in control in rural areas is an open one, with even the most neglected of peasants capable of defending themselves against unwanted centralized regulation they deem out of tune with their needs. In the case of the payments to the 'volunteers', the affront was all the greater because salaries (whether called such or referred to with almost-synonyms like 'incentive') are such central markers of a privileged personhood status in CAR. Dignity has a material component, perhaps especially for the truly poor. But to reduce that to a venal desire for money in and of itself misses the ways that these processes are quests for social status, in a context in which even people in remotest CAR understand their ranking at the 'bottom' of the world and their unlikelihood of touching the real wealth of the world (Piot 2010).

The region, the good intentions crowd, and the problem of the state

All states are relations (Giddens 1985). This is particularly obvious in the case of former colonies that have become quintessentially 'fragile' states like CAR. States that fail to live up to the ideal-type ideas about states that underpin the contemporary international order, and especially those that show little capacity or interest in securing their territories against mobile populations such as armed groups and migrants, raise a variety of concerns and incentives among 'external' actors, to the extent that they step in to play a range of political roles. For the first few decades after independence, France was the main such participant in Central Africa. This was due to the combination of duty, paternalism, pride, and habit that went into the *françafrique* mode of operating. Though only in 1979 with the ousting of Bokassa did France use force to orchestrate a change in power in Bangui, French actors have exerted definitive influence upon other changes in power as well (e.g. in 1981 when David Dacko was replaced by André Kolingba) (Smith 2015a). Through the 1980s, very few humanitarian organizations were in the country, and the UN presence was minimal. The Peace Corps sent volunteers. French advisers ran ministries in the shadow of their Central African boss-advisees.

This began to change in the 1990s. The salary-citizen policy ended, and donors (including France) pushed for multi-party democracy. Army and civil servant salaries went unpaid. Army mutinies brought violence to Bangui. Around the same time, French policy began to change. Tired of being reviled as the 'gendarme of Africa' and no longer needing to shore up Cold War friends, France pulled out the thousands of troops that until then had been stationed in CAR. The pull-out was completed in 1998 (Berman with Lombard 2008). Regional heads of state began to more actively manage and intervene in their neighbours' politics (Marchal 2015b), to such an extent that for CAR the 'typical' mapmaker 'schematic of solid swaths of shaded area representing the control of one or another power' should have been replaced by 'an irregular pattern of contacts and allies that constituted oftentimes tenuous political, commercial and informational networks', as Hubbell (2001: 35) described nineteenth-century Souroudougou (Burkina Faso today). Trans-regional spheres of influence and tutelage became increasingly important to the prosecution of politics.

During the same period, international organizations began playing a greater role in managing conflict internationally. Peacekeeping is almost as old as the UN itself, but it vastly expanded as a response to post-Cold War conflicts. A variety of new agencies emerged: the European Commission Humanitarian Office (ECHO), the UN Peacebuilding Commission, etc. Thus as politics became increasingly militarized in CAR from the 1990s onward, and as trans-regional spheres of influence became increasingly operative, international tools and mechanisms for dealing with conflict in places like CAR were also expanding. Previously, international interests had been focused on political/diplomatic problems such as the French interest in checking Libyan southward adventurism, rather than the creation/preservation of states as such. Now, at the same time as the state has slipped further than ever from its ideal-type form, that ideal-type form has come to play an increasingly important role in the construction of policy. That is, international attention to the area is now officially organized around the danger that a state that is far from ideal (as a possible petri dish for violent conflict – a rear base in the centre of a region with no shortage of rebellions, civil wars, and coups) represents. An aspirational project of state-building has thus become the arena through which a range of actors interact and perform together, and this to a certain extent precludes more realistic assessments of what is going on.

However, far from constant or otherwise hegemonic, international interest in CAR has generally been reluctant, intermittent, and focused on quick fixes (Olin 2015). Central Africans are quick to accuse foreigners of seeking primarily to exploit the country's resources, leaving Central Africans more immiserated than before, and to see international interventions as a means of preparing the field for those corporate interests to step in. This is not to say Central Africans don't want their resources to be exploited; they just argue – with some justification – that it has not ever been conscientiously done. The record on these matters is mixed, but it is embedded in the country's overall downward economic plummet. Internationally-led resource management/exploitation has in some cases had deleterious effects on Central Africans' standards of living (e.g. thirty years of restrictive conservation and timber exploitation in southwestern CAR has dramatically diminished women's nutritional status [Hardin et al. 2014]), but it has also brought a few jobs. Overall, though, international financial interests in CAR are quite small. A few businesspeople are attracted to the countries that rank lowest in the World Bank's Doing Business rankings – as CAR consistently has – but most are repelled.

In fact, it is immensely difficult to drum up support for funding intervention or other measures for 'improving' CAR. Even at times when violent conflict has ebbed, few donors are excited about being seen to support a government with such a questionable record of service toward their citizenry. Even at moments of 'crisis', the good intentions crowd often has to resort to portraying what is going on in CAR in relation to the sexier problems of the moment. In the mid-2000s, this was Darfur (which borders northeastern CAR). More recently, the threat of Islamic extremism has been invoked (e.g. by the then Special Representative of the Secretary General Margaret Vogt in early 2012). While an understandable tactic, portraying CAR's problems less in terms of their own dynamics and more in terms of at best tenuously related problems elsewhere does not prepare the ground for interventions tailored to specific needs in CAR.

Absent a standing audience eager to intervene, those working for international engagement in CAR have had to fight for attention, which is only ever occasional and reluctant. In theory human suffering drives humanitarian interest and action in places of minimal geopolitical importance (Redfield 2013). But to whatever extent this is true, the reality is that different forms of violence entail different possibilities for response, due to practical issues related to both intervention and the international legal architecture. For the last few decades, international interest has mobilized around the deficiencies of the CAR state as regards its failure to credibly claim a monopoly on violence, which causes worries that CAR might become a security vacuum or rear base for armed elements from throughout the region. (These worries allow other actors to arrogate authorities in the name of strengthening the state, but generally they end up 'substituting' for it in exactly the way they say they do not want to do [Lombard 2015].)

However, in the context of the worry over state weakness, responses to violence are differentiated in terms of how the violence relates to the state. Does it self-consciously challenge the state's authority, or does it simply do so *de facto*? An example of the latter is banditry. Road robber gangs have existed in Central Africa for centuries. They became more prevalent and organized during the colonial era, when the creation of prisons meant that people already sceptical of the political order had new opportunities to meet each other and collaborate (Issa 2010). But while road robbery can have major deleterious effects for people living in areas where robbers operate, from the perspective of international legal frameworks it is criminal and economically oriented, and so falls neatly under the government's purview, not theirs.[6] Donors might invoke the existence of road robber gangs in order to justify support for reforming the army, but road robber gangs in and of themselves are not suitable interlocutors from the perspective of international interveners.

In contrast, violence that makes 'the state' its direct object, such as rebellion, renders its threat inherently political and diplomatic. And in that case, international actors have a range of tools they can use to respond and deal with the problem. These tools include peace negotiations, disarmament programmes, humanitarian aid, and so forth (Autesserre 2014).

The crucial distinction is that rebel groups threaten the integrity of the state. That is, they cast the fictive nature of Bangui's control over the hinterlands into relief in a particularly explicit way, which is troubling to the international organizations that take states as their foundational organizational units. The underlying principle of the UN (and similar donor organizations) is that the world consists of states, and that all of those states can and should be made to evolve toward certain ideals that Weber might have recognized, such as defence of territory and provision of certain services. Even though in a place like CAR the government's control of territory is so obviously fictive, international diplomatic and humanitarian actors must act *as if* the state does in fact play the roles ideal types say it should. They are bound to this 'as if' drama even when people working for these organizations realize, as they often do, that it is hampering their ability to make individual context the starting point for their work, which they recognize as a necessity for success (de Waal 2009). In this sense, the state form is fetishized, the object of a simultaneous desire and disavowal arising from the meeting of incommensurate systems of value (one of which is politics 'as they are' – including the use of violent repression – and another the ideal-type state), the grip of which is very hard to escape (Pietz 1985). This is part of the same complex through which Central Africans simultaneously desire state-organized entitlement and disavow coercive state actions in their lives.

And so, in a process that is difficult to treat as a single trajectory, over the past decade international interveners and armed actors have adapted to each other in order to facilitate collaboration with each other. Armed actors, particularly in rural areas, in part through tutelage from interveners and others, have learned to conventionalize various aspects of their organizations such that they are easier to apprehend as *rebels*, rather than criminals. Conventionalization entails such things as a patriotic name and a corresponding acronym, an officer corps, a list of grievances, a desire for DDR. It is a means of signalling a willingness to follow certain rules of a game played

al actors and the president, namely the game of
n. That is, the rebels would describe themselves and
tion to legal and perceptional categories associated
orm. They would permit humanitarian passage (at
hey would consider participating in regional peace
tually agree to do so. They could be *sensitized* (such
nd yet usefully evocative of the top-down nature of
scribed in this way) to international law by the Inter-
ittee of the Red Cross. Thus, with the mediation of
cies, conventional rebellion has a greater chance
nclusion or other largesse for the groups' political
leadership and of bringing some largesse to marginalized youth in
the hinterlands. In short, conventionalization plays into the communicative and perceptional biases of the president and international
agencies and in so doing has made rebellion into a kind of armed
action that – in the context of fitful and reluctant international
attention to aggrieved Central Africans – has a shot at generating
responses with actual material dimensions.

But where some might see Central Africa as a place of war-
profiteering pure and simple – a political marketplace characterized by violence (de Waal 2015), or a site whose violence is seen as
evidence of an all-subsuming capitalism (Hoffman 2011a) – in fact
the various people involved generally see themselves as working to
bring about a statist, entitlement-centred order. While an econo-
mist could still delineate the ways various people make money from
this state of affairs, doing so misses the ways that it is not profit as
such, but people's aspirations to bring about an order organized by
the state and entitlements in a place that is dramatically far from
those ideals, that drives these processes.

Rebellion anew

Armed opposition to coercive operations has a long history in
Equatorial Africa. The shift in recent years has been to frame that

impulse in terms of an aspirational project related to the state, that is, in the form of conventional rebellion. Doing this is both a way of expressing widespread popular grievances related to the decline of salary-citizenship and a means of facilitating collaboration with the good intentions crowd. The increased post-Cold War international interest in intervening in and managing conflicts has repeatedly not achieved its objective of diminishing the importance of rebellion to political opportunity and distribution. Rather, many Central Africans consider rebellion to be more fruitful than ever, as interveners so clearly have vast wealth and promise programmes like DDR, which from armed group members' perspective is their best avenue to a salary and other entitlements. To understand how this works, as well as how it is both similar to and different from previous practices, let's turn to a few incidents in the mid-1980s.

In the 1980s, the northwestern-most Ouham-Pende prefecture (and to a lesser extent its neighbour, Ouham) was the site of the first large-scale post-independence rural armed movement. The most famous person with origins in the prefecture was Ange-Felix Patassé, who had attempted a coup in 1982, so then-president André Kolingba viewed violence in the area with extra suspicion. During a rare visit to the prefectural capital, Paoua, Kolingba and his entourage were fired upon. In revenge, state troops burned a number of villages (Bigo 1988). But observers at the time had trouble parsing whether the non-state armed actors in the area were rebels or bandits:

> The activities of this portion of the opposition have ranged from infrequent public challenges to the regime…, to the more numerous 'bandit' actions aimed at the taxation and disruption of commercial activity. The persistence of this form of opposition stems as much from the economic distress of the region and the physical distance of these two prefectures from the capital than the efforts of a committed and well organized core of supporters. … The amorphous quality of the 'insurgency'

is indicative of both its activity and lack of any identifiable ideology. Except for the coup attempt of March 1982 and a couple of other actions, rebel 'activity' could be equally described as banditry, precisely as the government continually does. ... The majority of 'visible' rebel activity involves stopping government or aid vehicles in the two prefectures and taking anything of value as well as occasional forays into towns during market days. (Webb 1991: 280–281, footnote 36)

Webb's description captures something of how hard it was for outsiders to grasp what this mobilization was. Were they rebels, or just 'rebels'? And what, really, was the difference? The president could and did dismiss them as criminals and take the harsh measures that are designed for such enemies of the state. While these harsh measures elicited some outcry at the time, the country remained under France's thumb and international organizations had not yet begun playing the kind of expanded role in advocating about and managing African conflicts that they do today. For the most part, no one outside the area paid much attention.

While Webb and other observers at the time remained unsure how to characterize these mobilizations, they were already becoming a means of obtaining political power and/or salaries. Patassé's 1982 coup attempt had been led by François Bozizé, with crucial support from General Mbaikoua, who at the time was Minister of Communication. Afterwards, Bozizé was jailed, but Mbaikoua managed to flee to Paoua, where he recruited men to his side both in the area and across the border in Chad, drawing on cross-border ethnolinguistic affinities (e.g. among the Sara-Kaba, Ngambai, Laka, and Mbai) to facilitate the task. This diffuse group became known as the Codo-Mbakaras.[7] When Mbaikoua was killed by one of his officers, the movement lost its leader, which explains part of why its operations were so disorganized. Nevertheless, these men held effective control in the sub-prefectures of Markounda, Batangafo, Kabo, and Moyenne Sido. When Patassé won the presidential election in 1993, many Codo-Mbakara were integrated into the army, especially the Presidential Guard.[8] Thus armed opposition – having proved its ability to threaten – became a means to achieve salaried personhood at the same time as other means, such as a university education, were closing off and discontent within the population was rising. When Bozizé ousted Patassé ten years later, many of the former Codo-Mbakara fled homeward to the northwest.

In October 2005, in the same Ouham-Pende prefecture where the mid-1980s incidents Webb described took place, a truck loaded with cigarettes and other goods that was under guard by Central African soldiers, who were operating as security-for-hire on the bandit-plagued roads, was robbed. The soldiers attacked the population of the town where the robbery took place, who they saw as the authors of this crime. Residents rallied to protest such indiscriminate mistreatment. Who was responsible for the robbery has never been clarified, but reprisals between area residents and soldiers escalated over the next year (Lombard 2012). At first, Bozizé and his military officials pursued the same strategy as Kolingba: they referred to the insecurity in the northwest as the work of 'bandits', plain and simple (IRIN 2006a, 2006b) and burned villages to terrorize and punish people. At the same time, the history of Codo-Mbakaras and amorphous rebellion as a means to participate in the state was likely in their minds. The people who had helped Bozizé take power in 2003 (his 'liberators'), too, got government jobs and/or princely payments for their service (Debos 2008).

In important ways, then, the events of 2005–2006 mirrored those of 1985. They built on the long history of armed opposition in rural areas, and its status as one of the very few ways to claim an entitled position (a salary) after the decline of the salary-citizen mode of politics. But in 2006, there were new players: post-Cold War conflict managers who had an interest in what was going on, and in rebellion in particular. Through emphasis on initiatives like DDR, they ended up facilitating and providing new resources to these processes of threatening in order to claim entitlement. Peacebuilding interventions did not *create* these dynamics, but they have helped transform them and raised their stakes.

Peacebuilder/armed-group-member collaboration is facilitated by making the threat that rebellion represents – revealing the fictive nature of the CAR state – more explicit, and less easily dismissible as banditry or criminality, via a process of conventionalization that everyone interested in these problems participates in. Ousted politicians and members of the Presidential Guard who lost their jobs when Bozizé removed Patassé from the presidency joined forces to give the diffusely-spread people involved in those back-and-forth reprisals with the government a name and a discourse. They became the *Armée populaire pour la restauration de la république et la démocratie* (APRD, a name they eventually shortened to simply the *Armée populaire pour la restauration de la démocratie*). The simple matter of naming could go a long way towards shifting the possibilities for engagement. For instance, in January 2007, the *Front démocratique du peuple centrafricain* (FDPC) signed a peace agreement with the Bozizé government. This previously unknown group was led by Abdulaye Miskine, Chadian-born and with a long history of politico-military entrepreneurialism between CAR and Chad. While Central Africans and many interveners knew that Miskine was 'really' Chadian (in fact, he has double nationality, CAR and Chad) and that he was 'really' a road robber gang leader – both of which should have disqualified him as a political operator – his group's name and tractability when it came to negotiation gave them all a shot at accessing peacebuilding resources.[9]

As the example of Miskine suggests, rebellion and its conventionalization involves people with complicated national backgrounds. Many leaders of Central African rebellions have been accused (with some justification) of 'really' being Chadian, even though in the context of rebellion they present themselves as Central African patriots. Tutelary relationships with men-in-arms who had gained experience navigating war and inter-war in Chad (Debos 2008, 2013) and Sudan are clearly important to rebellion's spread in CAR.

But its spread and accompanying conventionalization cannot be understood as if separate from the new international mechanisms and actors (intermittently) present and responding to conflict in the region. These would-be peacebuilders' priorities and interests direct attention spans, resources, and programming. Interveners thus also end up working to shape rebellion in such a way that it fits the channels.

The extent to which these processes of shaping and adapting entail a real transformation in the organization of rebellion (i.e. from diffuse to centralized and command-controlled) and the extent to which conventionalization is a kind of costume or facade making it easier for people to put on a play together varies depending on the moment and the group. To continue with the case of the APRD, they eventually named an officer corps and zones of operation for various units. However, the number of such zones varied between six and twelve, depending on who one asked (Spittaels and Hilgert 2009), revealing the shakiness of the stated organization in terms of agreed-upon command structures on the ground. Because of these kinds of fluidities, it seems far less interesting to try to pin down the rebel groups' 'real' character and more productive to look at how conventionalization, as a process, involves everyone with concerns about violence in Central Africa, the importance of the aspirational state form to these sometimes unlikely collaborations, and the ways rebellion – far from becoming obsolete – has increased in importance as an element of politics in Central Africa.

We can look in greater depth at the APRD case to see the cross-cutting ties that develop among everyone interested in Central African conflict. When Bozizé's military burned villages in Ouham-Pende in 2006–2007, the actions drew a slew of international condemnation that would have been unheard of two decades earlier. ('State of Anarchy' was the memorable title of a massive Human Rights Watch report.) In addition, it drew (relatively) a lot of people to CAR – UN officials, journalists, etc. – trying to understand what was going on.

Until 2006, UN and other international organization actors made few visits to the northern parts of the country. Very occasional *missions* occurred, and only under armed escort. One of the main reasons for this was that rural insecurity was at the time seen as mostly authored by *coupeurs de route* ('road cutters', also referred to as *zaraguinas* – 'robber bands'). Road robbers did not present themselves for negotiations, and international interveners worried robbers would not respect interveners' untouchable status. Robbers simply held up vehicles and seized their contents, often taking people hostage against a ransom and then disappearing into the bush with impunity. The threat they represented was thus especially troubling to international actors.

However, this picture is only partly accurate. The *coupeurs*, though not vocal about their political aims, were not unknowable. In 2008, the Catholic priest in the northwestern town of Bozoum made overtures toward the closest robber gang and had frequent conversations with them at their base in the bush. They had varied national backgrounds, and included some Central Africans, and many expressed a desire for passage home. Despite their armed operations, few had accumulated much from their work, and they were tired. The priest brought the French general who served as a special adviser to the president to meet them. But though that general was as eager to rid the country of the *zaraguinas* as anyone, he explained that doing so would be legally complicated. Since these actors stated no political agenda and for the most part were not nationals, they fell into the residual category of people using violence for economic gain and hence criminals – not people international actors could be seen to be helping.

When the APRD emerged in 2006, its members described themselves as anti-road-robber and they worked to make the roads more passable for humanitarians and international organization types. APRD members engaged in road banditry from time to time too, but for the most part their extractive practices consisted of mounting roadblocks. While both road robbery and roadblocks are modes of extraction targeting travellers, roadblocks facilitate certain kinds of entitled passage (e.g. by humanitarians) while road robbery does not generally respect those distinctions. Thus though the differences between bandits and rebels converged somewhat in terms of the extent of their organization or their tactics, there was a chasm in terms of their ability to engage and collaborate with international interveners. And what makes a person clearly a rebel is a set of markers related to the ideal-type state play. These range from legal aesthetics (that patriotic name and acronym), to social organization (that officer corps), to the respect of distinctions through which the various people involved understand themselves (e.g. the idea that expatriates should be the first ones to be free from the kinds of molestations that others are subjected to).

Conventionalized rebellion is not just about fronting a superficial face. It is also a mode of affinity. For instance, members of the other major armed group in the 2006–2012 period, the Union of Democratic Forces for Unity (*Union des forces démocratiques pour le rassemblement*, UFDR), were quick to emphasize that they only took up arms in 'legitimate self-defence', a legal category that was central to their understanding of their place in a proper international legal/moral order. Though legal categories generally went unenforced and were maybe even unenforceable in their northeastern CAR context (Lombard 2015), they were nevertheless an important element of how rebel group members understood themselves and justified their undertakings.

Conventionalized rebellion is also opportunistic. This is not a contradictory or competing observation: something can be both deeply felt/justified and opportunistic at the same time. What I mean to highlight with 'opportunistic' is the way that regional politico-military entrepreneurs have learned to use conventionalization as a way to leverage the interest and involvement of international actors in managing African conflicts, and to thereby gain more of a platform for themselves. Miskine, mentioned above, and his FDPC are a good example of this. Other major rebel groups of the time displayed a similar dynamic whereby politico-military entrepreneurs saw rebellion as a means of leveraging international interest in conflict in CAR in such a way that would further their interests. Abakar Sabone, a Chadian who had recruited men to help Bozizé take power but split with his former partner when he felt he had not received sufficient payment for the work, and Michel Djotodia, a civil servant and diplomat with longstanding aspirations to power, are a case in point. While resident in Cotonou, Benin, in the mid-2000s they made contact with and enlisted local militias in northeastern CAR. These militias had mobilized in response to threats in their midst, fighting battles that left hundreds dead between 2002 and 2005 while drawing no humanitarian interest. With Sabone and Djotodia's encouragement the militias incarnated themselves as the UFDR and enacted violence in the form specific to conventional rebellion: the taking of towns, in a progressive march toward the capital. Whereas international journalists tend to assume a baseline of 'inter-communal violence' in places like Central Africa, the taking of a town catapults the undertaking into a different category: one that is political because it is oriented explicitly toward unseating the president or at least making it impossible to ignore the fictiveness of the president's control of territory. When the UFDR took their first town, the northeasternmost Birao, at the end of October 2006, Sabone and Djotodia spoke to journalists on the group's behalf from Cotonou. They described their rebellion as a protest against Bozizé's poor governance. The UFDR ticked various boxes related to conventionalization: a patriotic name/acronym, leaders and spokespeople, a good-governance rhetoric related to the deficiencies of the state, and an ability to take towns on a march toward the capital. As such it drew attention from journalists and interveners, and could be responded to with a range of initiatives.

Few people were killed in UFDR battles, fortunately. In contrast, fallout from the murder of a local leader in Tiringoulou (who had himself killed people he deemed illegal interlopers) in 2002 led to battles in which hundreds had died by 2005. The CAR and Sudanese governments eventually helped broker a negotiation in that case, but the good intentions crowd took little notice of the fighting. This demonstrates, again, that it is not necessarily the extent of the violence that draws international interest and programming, but its form.

Another example of using conventional rebellion as a means to political participation in ways supported by the good intentions crowd is that of Florian Ndjadder, a scion of a prominent military family. Interveners and Central Africans alike knew that Ndjadder's Union of Republican Forces (*Union des forces républicaines*, UFR) did not exist in the form of a group of men ready to fight, but he was nevertheless included in peace processes because he both used the legitimate form for rebellion and had the family history to seem a possible future threat. Yet another example: Charles Massi, a long-time minister who in 2007 had been shunted into the position of minister of rural development and wanted greater prominence. He first tried to get into the UFDR in a leadership position but was rebuffed (ICG 2008). He then developed an alliance with the group that originally called itself *Camp Noir* ('Black Camp', a splinter group of the UFDR). In part because of its name, diplomats described *Camp Noir* as inscrutable. (What kind of a name was that? What did they really want?) Under Massi's tutelage the group became the Convention of Patriots for Justice and Peace (*Convention des patriotes pour la justice et la paix*, CPJP) and gained entry into peace processes. Power-sharing mechanisms can lead to factionalization (see, in particular, Tull and Mehler 2005), and conventional rebellion makes those processes more efficient by helping people collaborate with each other, while also preserving and even hardening the extant hierarchies and other divisions among them.

If thus far it seems that the conventionalization of rebellion is an example of Central African trickery, that view is at best incomplete. For while it would be overstatement to portray international interveners and the good intentions crowd as an army standing at the ready to engage in CAR (remember the general difficulties of mobilizing support for doing anything in this geopolitically marginal place), international interveners can engage in the kind of helping they see as their stock in trade only when they have the 'right' kind of interlocutors for doing so. They can thus end up helping to create those interlocutors.

For instance, in 2006, the UN and regional mediators were preparing peace negotiations between the APRD and the CAR government. When these international interlocutors approached several APRD commanders on the ground to ask who would represent them, the men were unsure who to nominate. In the end, they put forward Laurent Djim Wei, the leader of the Markounda-area band of the APRD. But the mediators rebuffed this choice. Djim Wei was seen as too much of a warlord (and too Chadian). According to high-level APRD leaders, these commanders then asked the international interlocutors to propose someone they would be willing to deal with. The midwives of negotiation proffered a list. It included the name Jean-Jacques Demafouth, a minister of defence under Patassé and long-time aspirant to political prominence. At the time he was living in Paris. The chief mediator, Gabonese President Omar Bongo, invited Demafouth to dinner in Libreville and convinced him to claim the presidency of the APRD. Demafouth was a bit concerned about diplomatic repercussions for joining an armed group (would he get kicked out of France?), but he was assured that arrangements had been made. He agreed to take on the role. The next morning *Radio France Internationale* called and asked him about his platform as president of the APRD. One can imagine a journalist's relief: finally, a person who could speak for this previously inscrutable group, and someone who was easily accessible in Paris to boot. Demafouth became the key APRD representative to international and national forums, such as the Inclusive Political Dialogue held in December 2008. But many, if not most, APRD members on the ground had not known who he was prior to his becoming their titular leader, and he certainly never conducted any operations with them.

Political scientists have looked at how taking on 'insiders' like Demafouth can be useful to rural militias far from the capital's halls of power. They can help overcome the 'knowledge gap' that rural marginality entails. At the same time, it would be wrong to see the process through which Demafouth became president of the APRD as anything but a joint undertaking involving everyone present – the good intentions crowd, APRD members, regional heads of state. Nor is Demafouth's case isolated. For the African Union-led Darfur negotiations, too, mediators needed to find someone to speak on behalf of Darfuri rebels (de Waal 2015). Those rebels were not voiceless in that process, but neither did they act autonomously in their choice of a leader. Moreover, it is questionable whether they would have sought such a leader if not for the need to participate in the internationally-organized negotiations. So rather than a matter of puppeteers and dupes, or profiteers and selfless humanitarians, contemporary rebellion presents complex social situations like those described by Max Gluckman. That is, everyone is participating and collaborating with each other in a collective social situation (engaging in projects with each other), even though certain elements of that social situation have the goal of reifying the divisions between them (such as the division between 'internal' actors and 'external' helpers). The case of DDR, discussed in the following chapter, suggests that these divisions make it harder to tackle the politics of distribution head-on.

When it comes to the rank-and-file members of armed groups, it is tempting to see them as opportunistic, willing participants in corruption (such as through the markets that develop around participation in projects like DDR). After all, most Central Africans *do not* join armed groups – whether for reasons of morals, other occupations, or something else. However, those who do join do so in a context of near-total exclusion from the entitlements they see others enjoying, and – quite reasonably given the ways international aid is prioritized – they see rebel group membership as their only chance of claiming some for themselves, as the following chapter explores.

Chapter 5

DDR AND THE FRUSTRATION OF DESIRES FOR ENTITLEMENT

Introduction

Peacebuilding interventions are built around a hopeful temporal model. In these models, conflict is an aberration, a brief period of upheaval bounded by prior peace (and a state monopoly on force) and a future in which that monopoly has been restored and peace has returned. But in CAR, both intervention and violent conflict have long histories. In particular, pluralized capacities for violence (and ambivalence when not anger toward agents trying to control and punish, such as state forces), and a view that the state should distribute entitlements have long marked Central African politics, particularly in rural areas. The contemporary modes of conventionalized rebellion, then, do not emerge from a blank slate of peace and weak-but-nascent ideal statehood; they reflect long-standing modes of negotiation and threatening that have transformed to accommodate new actors as they arrive in the area. In light of this, it is less interesting to look at whether intervention *causes* violence or peace, and more interesting to see how armed group members, international organization staffers, regional diplomats, and other interested parties adapt to each other, and become entangled in often unexpected ways. Researchers are part of these processes too; for instance, interviewees learn quickly to provide the perpetrator or victim stories they think the (post-)conflict zone researcher wants to hear (Utas 2005).

One advantage of conventional rebellion (as opposed to more inchoate forms of violence) is that as a recognizable and explicit political demand – one that makes clear the kind of threat the rebels are trying to communicate – it actually ends up entailing relatively little physical violence (Lombard 2016b).[1] The paradigmatic form of violence associated with conventional rebellion – the taking of towns just before dawn – causes destruction, but most people (soldiers and civilians alike) are able to flee before violence is unleashed on their bodies. Their suffering comes more in the form of the theft or loss of their few possessions, having to endure the major privations of living displaced in the bush (malaria, snakes), and the trauma of insecurity. Conventional rebellion in this sense is a case of what de Waal (2015) describes as the ways that political marketplaces become more 'efficient' in terms of incorporating people and knowing their price. However, looking only at market functioning misses the emotions and values that feed into and derail these processes even as they are theoretically becoming more efficient. Ultimately, this can lead to more violence (a kind of spectacular inefficiency) in the medium or long term.

And in fact, grievances and a sense that one has been denied one's rightful entitlements are heightened rather than reduced through conventional rebellion. This happens through a range of interconnecting mechanisms, which fall into three broad categories. One is the peacebuilding conveyor belt, which gives people the sense that their grievances should be addressed but keeps moving regardless of how substantively that happens. Another relates to the ways that promissory politics and the hierarchies created by the idea of 'internal' versus 'external' players cause grievances and mistrust related to missing entitlements to grow rather than diminish. A third relates to how, since 'marketplaces' do not stop at national borders, rebellion draws in people not resident in the areas where the rebel groups are operating. Lacking personal ties and long-term interests, these people tend to behave more rapaciously than rebel group members from the area, and residents become angry over the ways these 'foreigners' (who are not necessarily foreign nationals) target them. Disarmament, demobilization, and reintegration (DDR) programmes draw these three elements together, and they will be my primary case for exploring these processes. First, however, it is necessary to look at the temporality of peacebuilding in a more general way.

One of the assumptions of peacebuilding is that war and its aftermath are opportunities to remake social relations, and that violence is in part a problem of culture (e.g. that violence against women during war is caused by problematically patriarchal culture) (Moran 2010). Another assumption runs somewhat counter to this one and is the main current underlying the major peacebuilding policy initiatives: that war is an aberration – that there has been a moment of 'crisis' when armed groups have mobilized, and the 'normal' status of state control and peace can be reinstated through intervention. Previously, there was peace and state presence in rural areas, this reasoning goes. Rebels temporarily disrupted that, and now the rebels must be transformed back into the civilians they once were.

From the perspective of interveners and the tools at their disposal – peace processes, DDR – this temporal trajectory makes sense. But as we have seen, rebellion grows out of a social milieu in which centralized modes of governance have generally been experienced as capricious if not brutal, and even peasants have long had effective means of fighting back and at least forcing negotiation (Lombard 2016a, 2016b). In addition, beyond seeing 'the state' as a predator, people in rural areas also have to deal with the presence of a lot of robbers, foreign armed actors such as Chadian rebels, and increasingly well-armed herder groups. Loosely organized self-defence actors (mobilized on a situational basis) are likely to be present in CAR for the foreseeable future, so the history of armed groups cannot be so neatly divided into a peaceful past, an armed-group present, and an armed-group-free future. This is obvious to many involved in the social situation of rebellion, both members of armed groups and interveners alike.

But, because the focus must always be on 'the state' and its imagined integrity,[2] only people deemed legitimate by virtue of their relationship to the state are allowed on the conveyor belt. As a result, peacebuilding fails to truly engage with the complicated mess of conflict in Central Africa, which does not always take an explicitly state-focused form. New people jump onto the belt (e.g. armed groups keep popping up), but the belt is always separated from messiness below, such that the messy situation on the ground never becomes the starting point for analysis or intervention. On the conveyor belt, one can feel like one is moving forward. At some point, though, it makes a sharp turn back to the starting point, and everyone gets thrown back into the scrum below. This is what happened with rebellion and its conventionalization in CAR.

In the introduction I described the tension and torpor in Bangui that followed Bozizé's coup in 2003. In the following years, while rebel groups continued to emerge in rural areas, Bangui blossomed, as if the dry season had given way to the rainy. Partly, this was due to beautification efforts, such as long-serving mayor Jean-Barkes Ngombe-Kette's 'Bangui Ville Propre' ('Bangui, Clean City') initiative. He erected new monuments (a 'liberator' reminiscent of a G.I. Joe doll and an overstuffed dove), and had their perimeters landscaped. Every year, just before the 1 December National Day, curbs and walls got fresh coats of white paint. New traffic lights were installed and mostly worked (even pedestrian-crossing lights!). A Hollywood-style hillside sign boasting the city's name (and nickname: 'la coquette') frequently blazed at night, and when letters stopped working ('BANG la coquette' always elicited a chuckle from English-speakers) they would eventually get fixed. Perhaps most importantly, civil servants received their salaries mostly on time and, by 2010, they were paid directly through their bank accounts, rather than in person.[3] This regularity supported the economy more broadly. With the exception, perhaps, of some Lebanese-owned groceries, the few private businesses in the country still struggled mightily under oppressive corruption,[4] and almost all would-be international investors still deemed the cost of doing business too high, but even languishing near the bottom of the World Bank's Doing Business index was an improvement over the devastation and uncertainty that immediately followed the 2003 coup. In addition to these developments, one of the biggest changes was the arrival of new humanitarian organizations and UN agencies, in part enabled by the conventionalization of rebellion. Houses, apartments, and office buildings were fixed up to expatriate standards and rented for sky-high amounts. The number of restaurants that had individual printed menus and served meals in less than an hour mushroomed. The international organizations also hired local people. Though the jobs were often short term and required moving away from one's family or other challenges,[5] they were also an avenue for Central Africans to access new networks and careers. Humanitarianism and peacebuilding were, in large part through their incidental (rather than overt policy/project-based) undertakings, rebuilding the economy.

On one level, everyone knew that the rebuilding of the economy around rural rebellion and humanitarian/peacebuilding responses was a fragile and problematic thing. Armed groups had begun to appear in 2005 (the same year Bozizé legitimated his takeover of power with elections) and conventionalized, in part through the various peacebuilding interventions they underwent. But it was also possible to look away from that reality and focus instead on the conveyor belt, which continued to move forward. Though interveners speak of the need to tailor approaches to local contexts, most initiatives tend to be undertaken in a relatively uniform order, the idea being that once a country has passed through them it will be definitively peaceful and the state will be stable and functional. A peace process, national dialogue, planned DDR and SSR, and presidential and legislative elections: all of these initiatives are focused on 'the state' and its ability to play certain ideal-type roles. The 'primal mandate' of the UN and other international interveners means that the nation-state frame and its legal-aesthetic categories shape what can and cannot be said, as well as what can and cannot be done or funded. Thus understanding the 'local context', while nice, often does not neatly align with the programmes and frameworks that shape intervention. Political problems around distribution and accumulation persist, and can only be dealt with to the extent they align with model-state ideals. Everything else must happen off-stage. The problem is that some of the most contentious aspects of those distribution and accumulation struggles fall into the off-stage category, and as such the issues people feel most strongly about often go unaddressed.

Of course, both the national and international actors participating in peacebuilding have more opportunities than they acknowledge to take up questions of distribution and accumulation. National dialogue *could* theoretically provide a forum for re-working politics in the country. But there is nothing *requiring* that to happen. Whether it happens or not, the process moves forward; it is difficult enough to obtain funding for even one peace process or national dialogue, and no donor would want to bankroll a re-do. Instead, these programmes provide a master narrative that makes it easier to downplay the countervailing tendencies, such as the emergence of yet more rebel groups, including immediately after the Inclusive National Political Dialogue – a forum intended to put an end to new rebellions – in 2008. (The irony, of course, is that they end up paying for a do-over once rebellion becomes too blatant and the peace-building process must begin anew.) And at the same time, people get angrier and angrier that the democratic/political forms – such as elections that are democratic in form rather than content – are stripped of transformative promise and potential, leaving people with ever-fewer avenues for expressing discontent over exclusion and the workings of politics (Lombard 2011). Except for taking up arms, of course – rebellion continues to have a low start-up cost in the region. And it continues to be a form of violence that is unique in its ability to channel the interests and priorities of the various people concerned about contemporary CAR.

DDR rationales

> In the past there were leaders enraptured by the taking of power
> by coup d'état in the capital, Bangui, but today the children
> have been initiated into rebellion which remains an incurable
> habit. (Alade 2015: 1)

The fatalism in this characterization might strike some as over-stated. Surely the 'habit' of rebellion can be cured? That, after all, is the premise of international engagement in 'post-conflict' (or, more accurately, the in-between of 'no peace, no war' situations [Richards 2005]). And administering a 'cure' is the particular purpose of DDR programmes, which are the main institutional means of addressing the demands and desires of the people who joined rebellions. An article by a UN news agency about DDR in CAR sums up the reasoning behind these initiatives: 'Any progress on these problems [of insecurity] depends on consolidating peace, which in turn, depends on DDR' (IRIN 2012). Does it, though? For more than a decade (since 2004), CAR has had a DDR programme being planned or carried out. Each time rebellion has abated, new ones have emerged.

Looking at the specific effects of DDR in CAR shows a few things. One is that it has brought people into collaboration who would not otherwise have had anything to do with each other. But while they are working together, the terms of their interactions are structured by the form of the state and the segregation it imposes ('national' versus 'expatriate', 'rebel' versus 'minister'). These social divisions and identity categories are not natural facts of the world; they must be produced through relationships and interaction, and DDR is a key forum for that. The divisions are in part created from the fact that access to resources and information is not equally shared (and in particular, access to *information about resources* is not equally shared), but no clear hierarchy emerges from this. All players have advantages and leverage in relation to the others, and prefer to see someone else as the problematic 'boss'. The consequences of any DDR 'failure' are not borne equally, however. DDR staffers receive their salaries no matter what; armed group members might not be so lucky.

So while DDR is supposed to be a different way of doing politics – and indeed, it mobilizes new resources and people for the purpose of addressing rebels' grievances over the paucity of entitlements available – it becomes yet another instance of the promissory politics 'the state' generally subjects them to. By promissory politics, I mean the use of promises about future agency-generated welfare to demonstrate authority without assuming direct personal responsibility for people's plights or otherwise giving them any direct means to claim entitlements (such as by fundamentally dismantling hierarchies between the promiser and the person to whom the promise is made). Promissory politics is the main mode in which Central African elites (ministers and the like) engage with their ostensible constituents, especially those separated by long distances made all the longer by poor roads and little transport.

After the Cold War, DDR quickly became a standard aspect of internationally brokered peace agreements. From the birth of DDR as such in 1989 (early test cases included the UN interventions in Namibia and Cambodia [Muggah 2005]) to 2009, there were more than sixty DDR initiatives around the world (Muggah 2009: 6–7). The irony is that after more than twenty years of 'assuming' rather than 'proving' the effectiveness of DDR 'as a conflict prevention tool' (Themnér 2011: 12), DDR planners and staffers have begun to recognize its problems and to argue for a different approach,[6] but without taking responsibility for having stoked armed group members' senses of entitlement and grievance and having helped to create the phenomenon of armed groups in the first place. Plebian Central Africans are left feeling more aggrieved than ever, and ever further from the goal of entitled citizenship.

I do not intend this as a 'gotcha' moment. DDR is not *the cause* of rebellion and violence in CAR. However, the terms of DDR

– a joint undertaking by Central Africans and international interveners – are to a large degree dictated by the fundamental linkage
between DDR and an ideal-type idea about the proper role of the
state: before, the state had control; armed groups temporarily
disrupted that; and DDR will bring back/create state control again.
This model bears little resemblance to the workings of politics in
CAR. But it sounds awfully attractive to many people, and when
it fails to operate as advertised people's feelings of grievance and
entitlement may be augmented.

I also do not intend this as a 'gotcha' argument because through
years of studying DDR in CAR I have met many people working on
the programmes who share my criticisms of it, while also adding
their own. These they have earned through long hours at the office –
often thankless work under the stress of deadlines. Too often social
scientists have positioned themselves as uniquely able to pull back
the curtain of ideology that blinds others: 'They *think* they're doing
x, *but really…*' is a classic formulation, with many variants (Maurer
2005). Much of the time, 'they' in fact share the sense of disconnection between stated goals and actual effects, so a social scientist
who sticks to this veil-lifting role adds little. Yet at the same time,
people enmeshed in the world of DDR as practitioners often forget
the weirdness of these modes of international intervention: they are
such recent inventions, and yet it is so difficult to imagine different
terms for international engagement. Why?

I argue that it goes back to the way that the nation-state form
becomes a 'bar' (along the lines of Gluckman's 'colour-bar'
– connections that are also chains) such that the new social situations and collaborations around conflict and its management help
to instantiate hierarchies and distinctions such as 'national' and
'expatriate', and this has consequences for what one is able to know
and the resources one is able to claim. Particular forms of knowledge are dangerous, just as they were for the Banda as described
in Chapter 3, and contribute to the exclusivity of the group. Thus
while the various diagnoses of the shortcomings of peacebuilding

that draw attention to the need to start from 'local context' have a point, that recommendation is quite limited. This is so both because efforts to bring context in are constrained by the need to respect the fundamental primacy of the nation-state form, which denies people a vocabulary to talk about anything else. Moreover, this state of affairs results in shunting off those lower on the hierarchies, who become re-marginalized in turn, even more aware of their marginalization and angrier about it. As such, DDR reminds us that marginalization is not simply something that happens on its own. It is the result of individuals' actions and practices, and the people involved in planning and implementing DDR play central roles in those processes – even as they lament doing so.

In addition to its arguments, this chapter is a chronicle of successive DDR undertakings gone awry, as seen in part from the perspectives of both armed group members and DDR staffers who shared time with me. I think in particular of one person whose organization helped fund DDR in CAR. Echoing the sentiments of many armed group members with whom I spoke, this person argued that I should write about DDR because the fact that so little DDR money went to intended beneficiaries 'should be a scandal'. Yet the term 'scandal', like 'crisis', suggests that these are out-of-the-ordinary happenings (Roitman 2013). In CAR, DDR failures have been all too ordinary. In its small way, this chapter records this latest in the long history of scandals accompanying Central African integration into the world.

The UN definition of DDR restricts itself to the assumed rather than proven effects of DDR. It states that DDR is 'a process that contributes to security and stability in a post-conflict recovery context by removing weapons from the hands of combatants, taking the combatants out of military structures and helping them to integrate socially and economically into society by finding civilian livelihoods' (cited in Jennings 2008: 329–30). Defining a project in terms of the outcomes one hopes it will achieve highlights the often untested assumptions at its foundation.[7] The key terms in the DDR abbreviation are often left undefined or vague, based on general concepts rather than the particularities of the situation to be addressed, and this lack of clarity can produce unintended negative consequences, such as the fact that armed group members so often feel shorted by programmes that had seemed to offer a promise of greater largesse (Jennings 2007). As Jennings diagnoses,

> deliberately or not, the language and promises of transformation are often used, even where the resources, implementation, and forms of control employed are those of expedience. ... The problem is when vague, platitudinal, or contradictory understandings of reintegration translate into ad hoc and disengaged planning processes and programs, lacking a clear strategy and generating overblown expectations. (2008: 332)

Thus Jennings (2008), like others (e.g. Autesserre 2014), argues that a deep understanding of the context should be the basis for designing projects like DDR. While as an anthropologist it would contradict my disciplinary presuppositions to argue against the need for contextual understanding, this still misses a fundamental point. People working for organizations or groups are not free to design policy based purely on knowledge. Their frameworks for engagement orient them, and in the UN world order one of the chief frameworks is the form of the nation-state and the need to respect it. It is a framework that brings together a range of people to work together on DDR, while also mandating divisions and hierarchies in what they say to each other, how they relate to each other, and what entitlements they can expect.

In CAR, there has not been a lack of clarity around, or competing definitions of, what the various components of DDR would entail in substantive terms. Rather, there has been a disconnect between what people said and planned publicly – which aligned more or less with the assumptions entailed in the nation-state form – and what they admitted privately – known secrets that would marginalize their speaker if said aloud. Thus *everyone knew* that disarmament would not entail removing very many guns. (It rarely does, and even if many guns were collected it would remain easy for people to obtain more [Themnér 2011: 11].) *Everyone knew* that demobilization would not entail dismantling armed group structures. (In that respect, too, case after case has shown that the social networks through which people have mobilized to fight persist, in different forms, even after DDR [Bhatia and Muggah 2009; Hoffman 2011b; Persson 2012]). And *everyone knew* that reintegration or reinsertion, as this final phase is sometimes called, was an inherently fuzzy and slippery undertaking.[8] And yet they spoke of these concepts as if the processes they described were clear and automatic. Nor were these problems reserved for the DDR leadership and staffers – armed group members, too, participated in preventing open secrets from being the basis for policy and practice.

The disconnect between the *realpolitik* assessments people made privately and the rhetoric they used publicly created an accountability gap. Ex-combatants could not be expected to be accountable to their promise to step away from threat-based politics (Lombard 2016b), and planners and implementers could not be expected to be accountable to the hoped-for outcomes of DDR. The accountability gap also undermined the symbolic potential of DDR as a confidence-building measure, since the tension between expediency (stepping through the DDR hoops, even if only cursorily) and transformation (creating a basis for sustainable peace, de-militarizing politics) was never acknowledged, but always present. The slippage between transformation and expediency is not just an error or a matter of laziness – it is a tactic.

PRAC (2004–2007)

To say that DDR preceded rebel groups in CAR would be an exaggeration, but not false. CAR saw its first UN peacekeeping mission in 1997. Violent army mutinies and militia operations prompted intervention. The president at the time, Patassé, had sidelined the army in favour of his Presidential Guard and also armed youth both in the capital and rural areas in order to shore up his hold on power. These youth received some military training, but generally only a couple of weeks at most. Rather than standing forces, they lived as civilians but formed loose agglomerations that could fight back when tensions rose. In 2003, the former armed-forces chief of staff Bozizé ousted Patassé with a force of fighters that was between two-thirds (Debos 2008) and seven-eighths (ICG 2007) Chadian. Some of these fighters left for home immediately after taking the capital. They paid themselves on the way, looting and pillaging along the roads north and, in a particularly damaging move to the region's economy, destroyed the local cotton-processing facility. Those who remained in the capital were restive. When, in 2004, they began manifesting their discontent over lack of payment for services rendered, they were transported to Goré, in southern Chad, each paid about USD2,000 cash (Debos 2008), and told to go their separate ways.

Around the same time, Bozizé was negotiating membership for CAR in the Multi-Country Demobilization and Reintegration Program (MDRP), a repository of DDR funding for the Great Lakes Region. (Though CAR is not itself part of the Great Lakes Region, it is proximate to it; moreover, the MDRP had money that needed to be spent.) A CAR government delegation made a presentation to the MDRP explaining the pressing need for DDR for a range of groups of ex-combatants who, the officials argued, posed a grave security risk. For Bozizé, calling for DDR was a no-brainer. At no cost to himself, he would gain largesse he could distribute both to the eventual members of the National DDR Commission as well as to people who had once mobilized against him or might otherwise be hostile toward him. His efforts were successful and resulted in CAR's first major DDR programme, the Programme for Reinsertion and Support to Communities (*Programme de réinsertion et appui aux communautés*, PRAC).

The document the government submitted in support of their accession to the MDRP included a table with the names and precise sizes of various armed groups. There were Patassé's *Karako* ('peanut'), *Balawa* ('shea nut'), and *Sarawi* ('of the Sara ethnicity', who live along the CAR/Chad border) militias; the supporters of André Kolingba's failed 2001 coup; there was the intriguingly named *police parallèle*. The first three were, as described above, loosely organized groups that were less standing forces than networks that could be mobilized as needed. The others were even harder to describe; Kolingba had not used a well-organized force but rather had drawn on disaffected soldiers and neighbourhood people originally from his home region in the south. As for the 'parallel police', shortly after the document was submitted, in August 2004, I asked the minister for public security, Jules-Bernard Ouandé (a Central African Army officer who helped Bozizé take power), who they were. He was unsure. In the end, no one presented himself to the PRAC as a member of the parallel police, and the spaces set aside for them were allocated to the other groups, so that not a slot would be missed.

In part because the groups on the list were not actually groups, the problem of determining who should properly be granted entry to the programme was tricky from the outset. PRAC staff and the National DDR Commission worked with a broad definition: anyone 'associated with an armed group' was an ex-combatant and could join the programme. Beyond that, administrators were dependent on armed group leaders to furnish them with lists of members. Each 'ex-combatant' was to further prove his or her status by handing in a weapon, with 'weapon' defined broadly to include ammunition as well as guns, grenades, and other arms. And each ex-combatant was to sign a statement attesting to his or her status as a former armed group member. These criteria were difficult to put into practice, however. (It did not help that the contracts ex-combatants had to sign were in French, which many did not read with fluency.) For one thing, the rule that each ex-combatant present a weapon was difficult to implement because a number of *ad hoc* disarmament efforts had already been carried out by the various peacekeeping forces in the country, none of which kept thorough records of what had been collected and from whom, so people without weapons could claim theirs had already been taken from them. In the end, the PRAC 'disarmed' nearly 7,500 people but collected only 417 guns. Of those, only 291 were in working order. The majority of the weapons collected were turned in not by 'ex-combatants' but by area residents hoping they would receive some aid in return (Clément et al. 2007).

A mid-project review in 2006 determined that the entry criteria had been too loose and people who were not 'real' ex-combatants were purchasing their way into the programme. Rather than deal with the crux of that problem, project staffers decided that these substitutions of 'fake' combatants could be lessened by simply excluding women and children from the project. The substitution problem was much more extensive than that, however. A single name on the list could be used by three different people: Person A would undergo 'disarmament' and receive its relative perks; Person B would take the demobilization benefit; and Person C would wait for reinsertion assistance. The officers tasked with verifying who was a 'real' ex-combatant were often accused of selling slots in the project. There were vast disparities between the lists of names of ex-combatants prepared by neighbourhood DDR commissions and those furnished by armed group leaders. It was moreover quite difficult for the project staff and others associated with the PRAC to oversee details such as the tracking of ex-combatants and the benefits they received because the accounting mechanisms and databases were unsynchronized and difficult to use, especially for people with limited computer experience, as was the case for the majority of the PRAC staff.

My point here is not that 'fake' combatants made it into DDR. Rather, my point is that the 'group' part of the 'armed group' was created by the process of DDR itself. The people who acceded to the PRAC were not members of standing forces, akin to sports teams that practise daily and are always ready for a game. Rather than being defined by their 'team membership', many people had been called on at some point in the past and might at some point be called on in the future. But in the meantime, they did other things. Since they were not standing forces, they would have to be re-mobilized in order to be de-mobilized; names (including of people who never mobilized in the first place) would be added until all existing DDR slots had been filled.[9] As concerned citizens and occasional members of armed 'groups', a range of people participate in matters of both security and insecurity in CAR. Everyone knew DDR would not change that, though it was hard to express that publicly, because it would compromise the validity of the programme and neither Central Africans nor donors wanted that to happen. Rather, DDR created a stronger sense of group identity around being an 'ex-combatant' than had previously existed. As part of 'demobilization', many project beneficiaries received a poor-quality t-shirt with lopsided printing identifying its wearer as an ex-combatant – exactly the kind of identification the PRAC was meant to undermine, not foster, and which became one of the many small ways that people were encouraged to think of themselves as a new category of aggrieved actor. This is the most pernicious aspect of the process: everyone has incentives to be mistrustful of each other, and some benefits accrue to particular individuals as a result. But overall the sense of being aggrieved, of expectations going unmet, grows. Some swallow that anger and frustration. Others do not.

The gap between what people said publicly about DDR and what they felt privately helped create a climate of mistrust among all the parties involved in the PRAC. Even the funding agencies (the World Bank, the MDRP, and the United Nations Development Programme [UNDP] all contributed money; the semi-independent PRAC implemented the programme, with guidance from the National DDR Commission) found it immensely difficult to work together and speak frankly with each other. Having information was a source and a consequence of power. In some respects, people actively managed what they knew in relation to what others knew. In other respects, the segregation, hierarchies, and rigidity of roles inherent to the project itself shaped who could know what and who could be where.

For instance, according to ex-combatants, PRAC staff never spoke with them and instead only disseminated information through posters. When questioned about their communication strategies, PRAC staff were nonplussed: 'Our door is always open.' They meant that in both literal and metaphorical senses. It may be true that their office doors within the PRAC building were kept ajar. But getting to the building required breaching a high concrete wall topped with broken glass, or making it through the tall gate staffed by private security guards and/or soldiers tasked with limiting entry. The decision to admit someone turned on such factors as the person's ability to present an ID to serve as collateral, as well as other markers of wealth and status, such as skin colour (whites, the dominant race among the purse-string-manager class, always have IDs and are never turned away), fanciness and cleanness of clothing, and whether the person arrives in a private car (sweat smell and/or weathered flip-flop-wearing feet both count against a person seeking entry).

Thus ex-combatants felt utterly excluded from knowing about what was going on with the project. This lack of knowledge became all the more irksome given the massive delays in implementation. The reasons may have been understandable (that is, beyond the control of the PRAC staffers themselves) – the presidential elections held in 2005, budget pipeline issues, the difficulty of procuring items for ex-combatants' demobilization and reintegration 'kits' all had effects – but remained opaque to the project participants, who had no one to consult. Instead, they began to manifest their force outside the PRAC's walls. Remember that many had actually never fought before. But participation in DDR and its terms helped to inculcate in them the feeling that they were aggrieved and mistreated, and that the only way to get those grievances taken seriously was by fighting or being threatening. Throughout 2006, protests by PRAC participants grew in size and vehemence. Hundreds would cluster outside the PRAC building, threatening violence. This further entrenched the PRAC staff behind an even larger security presence, which only fed participants' anger and frustration.

Presumed segregation (such as between PRAC staffers and PRAC participants) and the information blockages it fostered had tragic consequences. For instance, in Bozoum (a town about a day's drive to the north and west of Bangui) PRAC staffers set fire to a cache of spoiled World Food Programme foodstuffs that had been trucked in for PRAC participants. From the participants' perspective, the food had gone bad due to the staff's laziness and failure to distribute it on time. From the staffers' perspective, the foodstuffs had arrived already rotten. The truth remains obscure. What is clear is that the incident, and others like it, stoked mutual mistrust.

However much 'failure' one can ascribe to the PRAC, one could nevertheless argue that injecting any resources into impoverished communities is a net good.[10] Whether they are 'real' ex-combatants or not, it is likely that all beneficiaries could make use of the goods, materials, and, in many cases, cash they received. However, the lack of clarity around policies that kept changing and the disinterest PRAC staffers showed in talking with beneficiaries meant that no matter what was given, people always felt they were being shorted. In addition to their suspicions that PRAC was shortchanging them, participants also listened to the radio and watched TV broadcasts describing DDR programmes in the Democratic Republic of the Congo and Côte d'Ivoire, both of which entailed, in the PRAC participants' understanding, vastly better benefits than what PRAC staffers said they would get.

One response to the gaps in communication and slights described above would be a better 'proximity strategy' (how staff would communicate and listen) among the various stakeholders, as the independent evaluation of the PRAC suggested, as well as better technical procedures. A proximity strategy would not hurt. It could at least have been a first step. And technical procedures could have been – and were to a degree – improved. But alone or together, neither of these measures can overcome the deeply-entrenched structural and institutional hierarchies, in which the management of information is a useful skill for everyone involved (even, in their own ways, for project participants, who do not want DDR staffers to know about their other projects, or, for some people, that they never fought), that characterize these kinds of projects. No proximity strategy would disclose information about how much the international staffers earn, for instance. That information seems irrelevant, or too difficult to explain (you have to understand the cost of living in Europe/elsewhere…). Access to this kind of knowledge is intimately tied to one's place in the world, in the manner Giles-Vernick described in the case of the Banda (1996). Like the older men who kept knowledge of the secret dangers of the bush hidden from women, who were seen as not being able to understand them, restricting access to project information is justified on the grounds that sharing such knowledge with the wrong people could be dangerous. Perhaps staffers and officials are correct that this kind of information is irrelevant to programme 'beneficiaries'. But these practices also erode whatever proximity is intended to be created.

Moreover, DDR creates a climate for promissory politics, and improved communication techniques would not be enough to overcome them. As Gluckman observed in apartheid South Africa, differences in personality, temperament, and day-to-day practices could have a big effect on relationships between the governed and their governors ('A sympathetic Commissioner who understood the Zulu would draw them to him, especially from an unsatisfactory chief; a harsh commissioner kept the people away from him, and they went more to their chiefs' [1955: 159]), but ultimately the reality of the 'Colour-Bar' continued to divide and determine life chances in the midst of these cross-linkages and friendships. In DDR, the gap between the ideals of DDR – which stem from an ideal-type model of the state – and the realities of the situation on the ground work to create a kind of bar separating the various parties to these programmes, even as cross-cutting ties are created and strengthened at the same time.

Anders Themnér (2011) argues that whether ex-combatants will return to violence depends on three factors: remarginalization, remobilization, and relationships. His case studies in the Republic of the Congo and Sierra Leone showed that people who felt themselves to have been marginalized politically, economically, and socially, and who remained in close relationships with the people who had been their mid-level commanders ('intermediaries', in Themnér's terminology) were more likely to re-engage in organized violence. Themnér focuses on the mid-level commanders as the chief agents of remobilization, since they have, in his account, a near 'monopoly on the interaction between ex-fighters and entrepreneurs [armed group elites]' (2011: 165). His account of remarginalization, in contrast, is focused on political-economic forces and factors, as if it were simply something that happens. But remarginalization too is the product of active relationships, and those relationships include the people staffing DDR programmes. Together with the armed group elites and mid-level commanders, DDR staffers mediate questions of identity and opportunity for the people participating in DDR. The staffers are also central to the sharing and dissemination of information about future possibilities. So though people running DDR programmes are generally not active remobilizers, their practices too often actively remarginalize. And though marginalization is not in and of itself a determinant of engaging in violence (plenty of people are marginalized but do not take up arms), it is a factor cited by many who end up doing so.

Steering Committee (2009–2012)

My first in-depth exposure to DDR was as a member of the independent evaluation team for the PRAC, in 2007. In addition to ethnographic research, focus groups, and interviews, I pored over thousands of pages of PRAC documents, which included seemingly endless evaluations by staff and outside assessors like me. Each report listed specific problems and the steps to be taken to rectify them, broken down into tasks and deadlines. And yet none of the recommendations made it off the page and into practice. How, then, would the final evaluation that we were conducting be any different? It was yet another reminder that knowledge is not in and of itself sufficient to change policy and practice, and that my job was not 'lifting the veil' to reveal what others could not see, but rather looking critically at the mechanisms, relationships, and hierarchies that those more directly enmeshed in the projects had to take for granted, in order to see where scope for action and change existed and where it was constrained.

The question was all the more pressing because even while we were conducting the evaluation, planning had begun for a new DDR programme in CAR. As one government document put it, 'The government thinks that the UNDP-executed program that is ending did not get to the root of the problem' (Government of CAR 2007). Indeed, a number of armed rebel groups had emerged during the years the PRAC was in operation. A comprehensive peace agreement was developed and signed by most of the armed groups in 2008. It included the provision of DDR for rebel group members, a programme that finally got underway in 2009. The new initiative, which never gained a catchy acronym, was what DDR planners call a 'second generation' effort. In the first generation (until the early/mid-2000s), operations were overseen by national DDR commissions, but they were found to be pits of corruption. In 2006, a UN inter-agency process issued Integrated DDR Standards that proposed mechanisms such as steering committees to provide monitoring and oversight of DDR operations. It was just such a *Comité de pilotage* that was launched in Bangui in August 2009.

Steering committee membership was decided at the Libreville peace talks, in 2008. The Special Representative of the Secretary General of the UN Peacebuilding Support Office in the Central African Republic (BONUCA) was to chair.[11] The first vice chair was Jean-Jacques Demafouth, the president of the APRD, and the second was Cyriaque Gounda, the CAR minister of communication. Representatives of the other 'politico-military groups' party to the comprehensive peace agreement (APRD, UFDR, MLCJ, UFR) would have seats, as would government representatives, the European Commission, the African Union, the World Bank, France, BINUCA, and UNDP (UN 2009). The theory behind the steering committee model was that it would provide a forum for dialogue among the key elite stakeholders, who could address all the 'sensitive' political questions surrounding DDR: how funds would be disbursed, and by whom; the criteria for the selection and verification processes; etc. The military aspects of DDR (the first two D's) would involve military observers sent from elsewhere in the region (Democratic Republic of the Congo, Burundi). Meanwhile, expatriate and local staff working for UNDP would carry out the technical aspects of DDR: developing databases, running 'reinsertion', and so on.

A lack of clarity about what DDR is actually going to do – and especially an oscillation between 'transformational' ideals and more realistic assessments – has consistently been a problem with DDR projects (Jennings 2008), as well as with development/peacebuilding initiatives more broadly. This is the problem the steering committee was meant to fix: it brought together everyone involved in DDR with the idea that they could clarify the political issues that needed to be resolved in order for the technicians to do their work. However, even though the steering committee was a collective endeavour, time and again members used their and each other's respective status in relation to the state as a means of frustrating clarification of the key issues. That is, they were in theory united in their goals (overseeing the running of DDR), but the nation-state form that brought them all to the table together also provided ways for them to see themselves as belonging to different, segregated camps, each with different interests. And one interest that everyone seemed to share was to avoid forcing anyone to reveal information that, though necessary to move the process forward, could potentially compromise his (members were almost all men) position.

For instance, to run a DDR programme, it would be helpful to know about how many people would need to be disarmed and what level of armament they likely possessed and could be expected to turn in. UNDP sent an expatriate staffer to Paoua, a base of the APRD, to write a report on the state of the group. The president of the APRD, Demafouth, responded by accusing the woman of being a spy and meddling unacceptably ('That's not her job!' he told me). Members of the steering committee would make very few decisions, but even the few that they did make would be denied at the subsequent meetings, so the head of the UNDP DDR team (and a steering committee member himself) decided to record a meeting to make it harder for people to walk back from decisions. Armed group and government representatives to the committee protested, calling him an unethical spy. In the wake of these incidents, Demafouth argued that the entire UNDP DDR team should be replaced. (Doing so would have delayed the process by months at least.) The staffers remained in place, but these kinds of manoeuvres show that saying 'let's sit down and clarify what we're doing' or 'let's start from local context' is a lot harder than it might sound at first. One reason it is so difficult is that managing information (deciding who can know what) helps people retain their fictively segregated identities, rather than coming to common definitions (e.g. of 'local context') and in the process diluting their power.

Each steering committee meeting lasted the better part of a workday. Hours would be spent debating small changes in word choice (should it be ' … but the youth … ' or ' … so the young people … '?) and grammar, while big issues about how the DDR process would work (e.g. who would be offered a job in the army?) went unaddressed. The BINUCA head, as chair, could have forced decisions. But though that was part of her position, she had little incentive to do so. These kinds of interactions lead to a depressing question: is it in anyone's interest to move the process forward or to demand accountability? Perhaps it was in the armed group members' interests, but they designated someone else to represent them, and that person's interests overlapped with theirs but also diverged. Demafouth, for instance, was head of the APRD and also running for president.

The criticism that the Special Representatives of the Secretary General in CAR do not take strong enough political stances has dogged everyone who has held the post. Though one might expect that in a country of as little strategic importance as CAR it would be easy for diplomats to set aside diplomatic niceties, the opposite seems more common. One means of advancement in UN political positions is to avoid rocking the boat (such as by standing on principle). Rocking the boat in a place of as little account as CAR would be a double folly because it would not even win many friends. When I have spoken with Special Representatives (I interviewed Lamine Cissé, SRSG in Bangui from 2001 to 2007, several times, Sahle-Work Zewde [2009–2012] once, and participated in several conferences with Margaret Vogt [2011–2013]), they emphasized the delicate situation they were in. On the one hand, human rights organizations expected them to take a hard line and force the government to change its ways of operating; on the other hand, the principle of sovereignty meant that they had to treat their government interlocutors with the deference and respect they demanded. Zewde described her job as a continual quest for an elusive 'equilibrium' between these interests. Though from an analytical perspective we can see how central she is to creating the politics of this thing called CAR, the nation-state world order situates her as an 'external' player who is part of a different 'culture'.

The DDR process was also delayed by debates over the *Prime journalière d'alimentation* (daily food allowance, PJA), an auxiliary payment that, though not technically part of DDR, was considered a necessary first entitlement by armed group members. Funding for the PJA was to come from the government, using money given by Central African Economic and Monetary Community, a Central African regional organization. Over the course of six months, steering committee members debated the details of the PJA. How much should each ex-combatant receive? Should seniority – whether measured in terms of officer status or time spent in rebellion – be factored into the amounts distributed? And, perhaps most importantly, who should hand out the money? The government thought its agents should, as that would help build allegiance to them and establish their authority, while the armed group leaders were adamant that they should have this responsibility, for otherwise *their* authority would be unacceptably compromised. The DDR technical staff suggested that they could distribute the payments themselves and so avoid the dilemma, but none of the others accepted the technicians' claims to neutrality.[12] Finally, after more than a half year of discussion, it was decided that the PJA should be 21,000 CFA (about USD42 in 2010) per month for three months. Field commanders would distribute the funds.

I interviewed ex-combatants both during the deliberations over the PJA and after it had been distributed. Some were aware of the discussions underway and followed them closely. Others were not. In the end, armed group members received substantially less than the officially determined sums. APRD members in the Kaga Bandoro area who had been in the group for some years reported they received a single instalment of 10,000 CFA (about USD20) and never heard another word about the PJA. Those who had joined more recently received just 5,000. (The fact that the stacks of cash that left Bangui contained only 10,000 and 5,000 CFA notes virtually guaranteed that the ex-combatants would not get the full 21,000, given how difficult it is to make change outside of the capital.) It remains unclear what happened to the PJA money that was not distributed. The rank and file were convinced the armed group leaders had 'gobbled' (*bouffé*) it and pointed to the stories that Colonel Lakué of the APRD was building not just a house but a full-on villa in Chad as proof. No legal or other mechanism prevented Bozizé from using the CEMAC funds as he saw fit, and a large portion went to his campaign for re-election.

In the case of the PJA, months had been spent determining a clear plan of action, which in the end was not respected anyway. This contributed to the miasma of distrust that characterized the relations of everyone involved in DDR. In many respects, though, the problem was not a lack of clarity or context. Rather, the problems were the disconnect between the surface that people fronted and what they suspected was going on underneath; the way proprietary information can keep people in their respective places; and the way segregation into 'internal' and 'external' players prevented these issues from being dealt with seriously. For instance, 'everyone knew' that two of the five armed groups that were to participate in DDR did not really exist. That is, they were not standing forces that had participated in hostilities against the government. One was the *Union des forces républicaines* (UFR). The self-proclaimed leader, Florian Ndjadder, had some credibility in that he was the son of a Patassé-era military officer, but he had no fighters standing behind him. This did not stop him from signing the Libreville Peace Agreement, though, and he was treated with the respect due any armed group leader. Another was the *Mouvement des libérateurs centrafricains pour la justice* (MLCJ), a name picked by the former UFDR leader Abakar Sabone, who also found himself without any fighters when he split with Damane Zakaria, the UFDR's on-the-ground leader. In 2009, Sabone signed up a militia in the Birao area to join him, but these men had never formally engaged in rebellion (taking towns, etc.). But in whose interest was it to police participation in DDR and limit its applicability? That is, in whose interest was it to argue that DDR and related programming was affecting people's strategies for political inclusion in unintended ways, and what would recognizing that even do? DDR brought a variety of people together, but not as fellows with shared investments. Rather, they came together as members of superficially collaborating but deeply mistrustful camps.

DDR also helped the two most established armed groups, the APRD and the UFDR, to expand. At the time of its hostilities with the government in 2006–2007, the APRD numbered 1,000 to 1,500 members; at the time of DDR, the ranks had swelled to 6,000 to 6,500. The UFDR was also understood to have grown exponentially since signing the peace agreement, but since its members were never verified for DDR it is difficult to give exact numbers; a good estimate would be that 600 fighters gave way to about 1,500 'ex-combatants'. DDR staffers laughed in amazement at the APRD 'fighters' who presented themselves to the military observers yet could not recall their own names (a sign they had purchased their spots, or been sent on behalf of someone else). But they did not see it as their job to police these 'hoaxes'. That would have been political and not appropriate for technical staff and expatriates. The military observers, too, abnegated responsibility for deciding who should be accepted into the programme and who should not. That was a political matter and above their pay grade. Had any of them tried to take a stance, the armed group members and/or their superiors might have mutinied, accusing them of spying and using other means of making their lives difficult. When DDR finally started creaking into action, the APRD was to be the first group disarmed. But only 2 per cent of those who presented themselves to the military observers for verification as ex-combatants brought a weapon with them. Everyone knew that few guns would be collected, but 2 per cent was extraordinarily few. And yet after a brief hiccup the process proceeded.

Through the two years of steering committee operations (more than fifty meetings), committee members and others responsible for DDR benefited from comfortable per diems and/or salaries as a function of their posts.[13] The Economic Community of Central African States (known by its French acronym, CEEAC) sent military observers to verify the ex-combatants and oversee the disarmament phase. They should have stayed a maximum of six months but they, too, found themselves waiting for the steering committee to make the decisions that would let them do their work. They were in the country for nearly two years, at an overall cost of millions of dollars.[14] The commander of the military observers in Kaga Bandoro fell asleep while I was talking with him and some colleagues one warm midday. Waiting is frustrating, and boring. The observers would likely have preferred to have accomplished the tasks they were brought in to do. The UNDP DDR team worked long hours (staying at the office until after 8 p.m. was common) preparing various 'technical' aspects of the programme.[15] Deadlines hung like heavy weights suspended just above their heads. A superior would say that a certain output absolutely had to be finished by the end of the week, which the employee would struggle to do, and then the materials would not be used for weeks, if ever.

So when I point out that these various people all drew their salaries yet without doing the work they were supposed to do, I don't mean this as an exposé. They worked hard, such as they did. Rather, I mean to suggest that the costs associated with accountability gaps are not shared equally. Some people in the DDR orbit will benefit either way, while others will not. Moreover, there is a gross difference between what DDR participants would receive and what DDR staffers and leaders would receive, with the latter claiming the vast majority. This might seem like a cheap point. After all, it simply is the way of the world that expatriate staffers make orders of magnitude more money than 'local' or 'national' staff, who in turn make more than people benefiting from the projects. It is reflective of the income inequality that exists in the world, which is a fact that surpasses any one institution or project. Disrupting it is not feasible. And yet as tedious as it may be to point this out, removing it from the equation distorts the analysis. For instance, ex-combatants are described as programme 'beneficiaries', but they each receive very little in comparison to the staffers. The 'beneficiaries'' position is one of far less income security than that of those running these undertakings, and recognizing this re-calibrates discussion of 'corruption' around DDR (as in the case of people who pass themselves off as armed group members without having fought). The amounts people gain by doing so are pittances compared to what staffers make. That does not in and of itself excuse trickery, but it does remind us that the implied moral difference between 'transparent' staffers and 'corrupt' Africans rests on a foundation of immense inequality.

Waiting: Promises and threats

Though the people who were to be disarmed, demobilized, and rein-
serted were excluded from most aspects of the preparatory phases
of the project, they were included in one particular way: promises.
Armed group leaders and DDR officials would occasionally alight
in their towns, appearing, generally unannounced, out of the sky
or from Land Cruisers, and make pronouncements about the state
of the programme and what was to happen. People received them
cordially, even warmly. But when the officials left, usually later the
same day or the day after, the armed group members would begin
complaining. They saw themselves as hostages to their leaders' false
promises, and as further constrained by the difficulty they had in
obtaining information about what was really going on.

For instance, by March 2010, the UFDR in Tiringoulou had
received Demafouth twice. Stanislas Mbangot, minister of reconciliation, came once as well, as had Prefect [governor] Raymond
Ndogou. Cyriaque Gounda, co-vice president of the steering
committee, had come and promised shea oil and soap-making
projects for women. He gave the UFDR three million CFA (about
USD6,000) in 'coffee money' – a thank you for attending the
meeting with him. But, as Joseph Zindeko, the UFDR *chef d'état
major*, recognized in telling me about it, that is not how a payment is
supposed to be made. To be official, a money transfer must include
paperwork signed in Bangui. With Gounda's method, they had no
way of knowing whether they had received the full amount they
were due: access to knowledge was a means of keeping people in
their respective places (with 'place' in this case both a location and
a status). Gounda had also given them forms to fill out on which
each person could indicate what profession he wanted to be 'rein-
serted' into: soldier, gendarme, carpenter, livestock raiser, and so
forth. They completed the forms and sent them to Bangui. 'Since
then, silence,' as one UFDR member put it to me. When I asked
DDR officials about these forms, they responded, baffled, that

they had no idea what I was talking about – they had never seen any such forms. Perhaps it had been a personal initiative on the part of the government. Perhaps just a bit of research. Whatever the case, the armed group members took it as a promise (as it was in their interest to do).

Further contributing to this sense of drift was something else openly discussed at DDR headquarters in Bangui but not mentioned during these visits to the UFDR. Owing to the compromised security situation and the coming rainy season, which would have made transporting and delivering equipment like demobilization or reinsertion kits to a place as remote as Tiringoulou extremely diffi-cult, DDR was put on indefinite hold for the UFDR.

Though everyone stated an eagerness for DDR to happen, there was little to push the process forward and much to slow it down. Whether or not there was DDR, the armed group members were unlikely to give up their guns. They had taken on governing func-tions in their areas of operation, and this more or less suited the president, who never saw it as his role to administer or 'develop' the countryside anyway (Smith 2015b) and was unsure whether they would be loyal soldiers. Better to dither on DDR and prioritize the presidential elections, which donors were pushing with greater urgency and which would provide a patina of democratic legitimacy for the government and their engagements with it (Lombard 2011).

As 2010 drew to a close, those oft-postponed presidential elec-tions were finally on the horizon, scheduled for January 2011.[16] If the elections happened without DDR, the armed group members felt it would be taken as their implicit acceptance of Bozizé's rule. (People critiqued the way that elections played out and the manipulations of the ruling party, but they knew that both nationally and internation-ally, even flawed elections counted since the important metric was the election procedure, not its democratic substance. No donors would want to pay for yet another election.) After elections, armed group members could exit the peace process and take up arms again, but that carried two big risks. One, people were tired of fighting.

And two, the groups' status in the diffuse realm of international opinion would be diminished if they reneged on the terms of the peace deal. For the armed groups, their status as legitimate armed opposition depended in large measure on the international actors and the leverage they provided (or did not provide). Postponing DDR, as national and international elites did, was less subject to sanction – delays can always find a reasonable justification.

The entitlements that armed group members felt they had been promised – entitlements both from rebellion itself and from DDR – had proven elusive. The armed group members with whom I spoke around the time of the 2011 elections responded to their fate of perpetual 'waithood' (Honwana 2012) with derision for the Bangui elite. 'This DDR smells bad to us,' was how one UFDR member put it to me. 'It's a business for the state.' Many reflected on how 'discouraged' everyone – armed group members or not – in rural CAR felt at being ignored by the sources of largesse and entitlement ('*Azo ake découragé*' – people are discouraged). The entitlements they sought entailed money, but they were not just about profit as such. They were desired for the way they would mark the bearer as an entitled person, rather than part of the ignorable masses.

Previously, attending university had been a way for people to access the civil servant jobs that remain the gold standard of entitled personhood. Today, more people than ever attend university. (Many more would like to but cannot afford it.) But the post, and the status that people think should follow, never materializes. Again and again, I heard from people that they or their children or friends had 'graduated from the university, but are still waiting'. Waiting for what? 'For integration.' Among the list of complaints Damane Zakaria, operational leader for the UFDR during its existence, presented the government was that 52 people from the northeasternmost Vakaga prefecture had graduated from university but were still waiting for their integration. Many Central Africans thus see a politics of distribution (Ferguson 2015) centred on entitled/salaried personhood as the proper organization of their political-economic order, but have little leverage to force the expansion of such a system. Civil servant salaries are paid by donors. The president and ministers could theoretically use their concession slush funds to hire more people, but concession payments are intermittent, not always transparent, and otherwise not particularly well-suited to the steady and long-term payment of a salary.

With the paucity of state jobs, some university graduates reoriented themselves towards NGOs and international organizations and consultancies. Some preferred this sector, finding it better paid and more transparent than the government. UN and other international organization jobs are the best paid; a lucky few even manage to breach the national/expatriate divide and go to work abroad themselves, with the immense increase in salary and other entitlements that entails. Humanitarian jobs have variable salaries (organizations have to compete for grants, and one way to boost chances is to cut costs) and have shorter terms. Others prefer the stability of a government job, which may pay less but doses money over a lifetime, not just a year or two. But many people, especially those who had not graduated from university, remained left out, at the same time as their desire for entitlement and money was greater than ever. What to do?

For many, joining a rebellion had been a way of threatening the president and donors in order to force one's claim to entitled citizenship to be taken seriously. The promise of DDR helped keep those hopes alive. When it became clear it would fall far short of armed group members' expectations, they began discussing what leverage remained.

One morning in Tiringoulou in March 2010 I stopped by the UFDR-staffed gendarme post to talk with people there about their work. The previously animated men became silent as I stepped from the bright morning sun outside into the post's dim interior. A UFDR spokesman I knew, Hamad Hamadine, was there, together with four other men. Hamad said they had been discussing their frustration over the lack of DDR and the 'top secret' plans they would implement if it did not start soon. The language of secrecy, far from hiding their intentions, made them clear: they would take up arms again. None had any particular interest in taking up arms or engaging in violence. It was simply a way – the only way – they could force their demands for inclusion to be taken seriously.

Armed group members had used threats – namely, rebellion – to force a deliberation on their status as entitled persons. In order to have a chance of obtaining that status, they had to show their good will by signing peace agreements. But once they did so, the source of their leverage (that is, the threat they represented) was removed as well, and they had far less ability to force their integration. Stuck in that hard place, many armed group members returned to threatening. Often, they did so in conversations with me. As one APRD member put it, 'I tell you, this white woman who is among us and who has listened to all the people in charge of this movement must go to her embassy and tell them what we have told her [about their plans for imminent attacks] so that the ambassador will *force* the president to do the disarmament before the elections'. He implied that if this did not happen, there would be mayhem. Mats Utas (2005) coined the term 'victimcy' to refer to how people in humanitarian zones represent themselves as victims in order to align with the priorities of the resources and programmes they observe around them. Because of the gendered assumptions of post-conflict and humanitarian programming, victimcy opportunities are primarily available for women. For men, a similar process of social navigation (Vigh 2009) requires demonstrating their (potential) dangerousness – 'threateningcy', for lack of a better term. As another APRD member warned, if there was no DDR he would become a 'road cutter' (robber):

> We will divide [disperse into hard-to-control small groups] because our leaders lied to us, they misled us. ... We will return to the bush because there are lots of *coupeurs de route* [road robbers] and from the trucks and the travellers we will

be able to find something to eat. ... Me as a lieutenant I will
return to my fighters and we will cut the roads and make
money, cut the road and find money to live and that's enough.
Because we can't go back to our households without money.
No, we cannot.

When the armed group member threatened to engage in road
robbery, he did so in order to indicate how far he would go – that
he would do something as morally questionable as banditry – while
also making a statement of what he needed: the money that would
mark his entitled status. Again, in the Central African context, a
desire for money cannot be reduced to a profit motive; having
money is a marker of status and dignity that for many has become
harder than ever to secure. (In a context of scarcity, the entitlement/
socialist/statist worldview that is a legacy of the French presence in
Africa is not a bearer of solidarity among people but a driver of indi-
vidualism [MacLean 2010].)

The ideal is to have a state salary, which is a long-term source
of money and hence provides greater security as an entitled status.
Once one is a state employee, it is far harder to fall to the status
of peasant. In the private sector or at NGOs, this is not the case,
and so though they may pay better in the short term, this advantage
is mitigated by the difficulties of saving in Central Africa, where
keeping money for oneself is often seen as unacceptable hoarding.
Frequently, when I went to the extortionately priced Lebanese
grocery store in Bangui, I would be greeted outside by a young man
I had met in Birao, where he had had a short-term contract with
a French NGO that had since left the country, depriving him of a
job and recommendation letters. Now, he sold bouquets of flowers
gathered on the hillside or from rich people's gardens. That, at
least, was his pretence for standing there. What he seemed mostly
to be doing was locating people who would see him for the entitled
person he knew himself to be (that is, as the person he had once
been), rather than the young man of the street he had become.

DDR had provided the hope of transformation – not necessarily the transformation of the region from conflict-prone to conflict-free, a future everyone realized would be long in the making, but the transformation of armed group members from ignorable to entitled. But all they had gotten were promises. This left them feeling more aggrieved than before.

The problem was not the need to better align DDR with the 'local context' or provide more clarity about what DDR would actually entail. Both of those objectives were chief among the project's stated goals. Rather, it is necessary to look at the structure of collaborative projects like DDR, and particularly the ways they help to create the notion that the parties are less engaged in a collective enterprise than they are representatives of different camps with competing interests. The nation-state form (and the affinities it assigns) is one element of how that process of segregation and hierarchy occurs even in the midst of the collaborative undertakings that otherwise tie people together. And it is one reason why people are preoccupied by managing information (being very careful about who knows what; fronting one face, while leaving most matters in the unspoken shadows), which can be a source of power. Frank and open discussion about such things as clarity, context, or accountability is one of the main casualties. This seems destined to be the case as long as the people participating in these kinds of endeavours perpetuate the fictions of segregation.

Chapter 6

WAR AS THE VIOLENCE OF THE PACK

Introduction

Many people in Bangui say they cheered when Seleka arrived in March 2013. Hundreds went so far as to join the movement in hopes it would bring them a salary and entitlements, as well as security amid the continuing volatility. Residents of the Seleka-controlled areas quickly became disillusioned, however. They complained that their new governors spoke neither Sango nor French, CAR's two national languages, and that they ruled towns for their own profit, to the detriment of people's security and livelihoods. Robbery and violence were both rampant. The previous violent takeover of power, in 2003, had been the product of a gentlemen's agreement among the leaders of the region's other countries (ICG 2007). In 2013, there was widespread frustration with Bozizé, but leaders in the region and donors and diplomats further afield had only a half-engaged plan for dealing with him. Seleka had attracted disaffected youth and men-in-arms from throughout the region, and Djotodia had little command-control authority over these dispersed and diverse actors. In September, he officially disbanded Seleka, which gave the people who saw themselves as part of the movement even less incentive to work together or respect his dictates.

At the same time, people angry over being dispossessed, yet again, by Muslim-'foreigners' began to rally. These new mobilizations built on the long-standing capacities for self-defence that had endured given the predatory-when-not-absent state and militarized regional neighbourhood. In some cases, ousted soldiers/Presidential Guard members helped these fighters organize, not unlike the Codo-Mbakaras of the 1980s or the APRD of the 2000s. They began to strike back against anyone they saw as either plausibly connected to Seleka, or as having benefited from Seleka. Since the widespread perception was that Seleka's nastiest operators were Muslims from the Chad/Darfur borderlands who had protected Muslims and targeted non-Muslims, the new mobilizations – which called themselves 'Anti-Balaka' – made all Muslims their targets. The Anti-Balaka had no over-arching organization. Like the Kongo-Wara rebellion nearly a century before, the diffuse people adopting the name Anti-Balaka draw on polyvalent symbolic meanings and augment according to what resonates with their needs and interests. But the Anti-Balaka did manage several coordinated assaults, including in Bangui. The first occurred on 5 December 2013 and the second on 25 December.

Peacekeepers were deployed in response to the fighting, and a new transitional president was installed in January 2014. These measures did not in and of themselves quell the violence, however. Anti-Balaka patrolled and battled in frequent smaller-scale skirmishes. Thousands died and were dispossessed of their property. The Anti-Balaka said they were operating in self-defence and that they were continually attacked by Muslims/Seleka, but this became less convincing as the southern and western parts of the country were emptied, through death and flight, of their Muslim populations. Former Seleka members retreated to the northern and eastern parts of the country. The antagonists brushed up against each other in Bambari and Bangui, separated only by the French and AU peacekeepers who began arriving in December 2013 and January 2014, respectively. 'Hell is an understatement,' assessed one journalistic account of the country in early 2014 (Wood 2014a).

How did CAR go from being a place where rebellion was conventionalized, with relatively low levels of related violence, to a place where conflict flared along identitarian lines, involving much greater numbers of violent actors than ever before? That is the question I consider in this chapter. I already began to answer it in the previous chapter, in terms of how people's expectations about entitlements rose in inverse proportion to the likelihood they would receive much of anything, fostering grievance and frustration among marginalized youth.[1] Technically-oriented peacebuilding programmes – that is, programmes that focused on the implementation of technical procedures without forcing any substantive discussion of the dynamics of anger and shame, or the mechanisms of distribution – contributed to this state of affairs because they claimed the space for political discussion but left it vacuous.[2] And the Bozizé government certainly bears some blame for repeatedly refusing to include people who, in the end, proved capable of mounting an impressive challenge to its hold on power.

Yet the intensity and wide popular participation in violence in the aftermath of the Seleka coup demands additional answers. How and why did the violence spread so fast? The journalistic and political answers offered at the time could generally be divided into two categories: first, there was the idea that the conflict was about religion, with Christians fighting Muslims, and vice versa. Second, there was the argument that youth were being manipulated into perpetrating violence by venal politicians intent on grabbing power. For instance, in the midst of the crisis, President Catherine Samba-Panza argued that the widespread violence had been set alight by 'agitators who try to manipulate the youth for purely political reasons'. Her prime minister at the time, André Nzapayeke, took a similar line, saying that it was a 'planned plot' organized by 'politicians very close to power' (AFP 2014). The trinity of Central African religious leaders, Archbishop Dieudonné Nzapalainga, Imam Omar Kabine Layama, and Reverend Nicolas Guérékoyame Gbangou, argued similarly that Central Africans had always lived peacefully together and that this was but an unfortunate mis-remembering and politically motivated distortion of that shared past.

These various explanations may well have been useful from an advocacy perspective, especially as the violence was live and there was the feeling that people needed to be called back to reason. However, from an analytical perspective these explanations are lacking.[3] 'Big men' have certainly played a role in supporting violence, both materially and symbolically, but they have never controlled it. And Central Africans of various faiths have indeed lived and worked and inter-married, for the most part without unusual levels of conflict (Kilembe 2015). However, war is not a social eraser, emerging from nothing to overwrite the past and to create a blank space in which to write the future. It is a social project among other social projects, embedded in social practices that both precede and post-date actual fighting (Richards 2005). Moreover, violence is a collective and inherently emotional project, and as such is the product, too, of effervescence – that is, of the excitement and unpredictability that ensue when humans come together and emotions run high.

In recognition of these factors, this chapter focuses on the sources of the insecurity that Central Africans experience in relation to the micro-level ways people use violence (that is, when, why, and how people come to see violence as a necessary, if often also regrettable, response), both prior to and during the 'crisis'. This approach shows that popular violence – in particular to deal with threats that are all the more frightening given the dissolution of boundaries around the real and the unreal as witchcraft becomes unmanageable (Ceriana Mayneri 2014c) – has long been widespread and has recently been exacerbated. The deliquescence of the CAR state over the past several decades has been accompanied by the popularization of punishment and the entrenchment of vengeance as a tool for the management of danger. The mass-participation aspects and wartime dynamics of the recent crisis can thus be seen as the ramping-up of practices that were already underway.

Though far from sufficient to explain the killings and torture that have been perpetrated as part of the war, the prevalence of vengeance and pluralisation of punishment are important parts of the social substrate that facilitated the spread of wartime violence. This is important because it means that violence has not been a brief and therefore aberrant practice, but something that people have seen as necessary in more normal times as well. And so ending violence will require not just disarmament or some other operation focusing on armed groups and reconciliation after the war, but locally initiated efforts to assess the use and effects of violence in social life.

This chapter begins with a discussion of two nodes of tension and insecurity in Central African life. One is the widespread sense that dangers are steadily rising at the same time as state actors' capacity or willingness to respond to them is declining (Marchal 2015a). These perceptions of rising danger are embedded in a broader context of anomie (Durkheim 1951 [1897]; Bouju and de Bruijn 2008; Lombard and Batianga-Kinzi 2015) – social norms are in flux and impossible to fulfil, and people's desires thus run rampant, creating a tormenting thirst that can never be slaked. As such anomie is integrally linked to the sense of dispossession that has also been widespread over the past century (Ceriana Mayneri 2014a, 2014b, 2014c). Since these lands and the people in them were first intensely caught up in long-distance trades about 150 years ago, Central Africans' active participation in these processes has been accompanied by a combination of fear and anger over their dispossession by more powerful, better organized, and rapacious interlopers. Central Africans are cunning victims in these processes, because while they occupy a largely reactive position in relation to these trends, they have robust capacities to strike back and even to use their victim status as a means of participating in and profiting from these processes.

A second node of tension and insecurity in Central African life is that amid the anomie and dispossession, and the 'weakness' of the state, justice, such as it has existed, has occurred amid effervescence and thus appears more properly as punishment. In this sense, punishment has been both a prerogative of statecraft and a popularized capacity exercised in the place of an idealized conception of state justice that is seen as missing. People engaging in popular actions to physically censure a danger (a thief, a witch, etc.) often describe these undertakings not as a mode of justice, which they see as the prerogative of idealized state courts that lie on the impossible-to-reach horizon, but as a means of enacting solidarity through deterrence (punishment).

These processes of dispossession and punishment all map onto the previously discussed concern over who can move and who cannot (and who profits from policing processes of movement), and the ways that those who move appear dangerous to those who do not, spurring reactive violence against them. In this respect, CAR is another case for Geschiere's observation (2009) that contests over autochthony (who belongs, who is born of the soil) have accompanied globalization.[4] It is a particularly acute concern in CAR, because it is effectively a non-territorialized country. That is to say, controlling a territory has never been a major objective of the government (the borders are porous not only because of a lack of capacity but also a lack of interest), and the country's politics are largely prosecuted outside the national borders – in Paris, Brussels, Nairobi, Ndjamena, New York, etc. 'Foreign' actors are thus part of both the warp and the weft of the country, and it is difficult to imagine what would remain without them. For the most part, Central Africans have welcomed newcomers while also making them targets of especial concern and discrimination (Marchal 2009).

In the rest of this chapter I first discuss social tensions, insecurities, and violence in pre-Seleka CAR, and then relate them to the paradigmatic form of CAR's wartime violence, the lynching. My point in emphasizing social tension and insecurity through time in CAR is not to draw a straight line from pre-war to war, as if these factors necessarily caused and therefore explain the violence that occurred. One always reads the past in relation not to itself but to what happened later, as the cliché 'hindsight is 20/20' puts it. However, it is important to remember that violence is performative and communicative in ways that draw on and transform known social repertoires (Richards 1996). Saying that politicians manipulate youth into perpetrating violence might be a piece of the story, but it is far from sufficient. Politicians are not that powerful; violence occurs in social, emotional, and historical contexts with many components. Moreover, while Hollywood films and popular accounts of African violence alike portray it as an undertaking people are quick to engage in, the social-science literature is much more measured: in Africa as elsewhere, violence is always a difficult undertaking, and in general a variety of mechanisms exist to defuse tensions when they arise (Collins 2009). In that sense, even widespread participation in popular punishment tends to be an attempt to decrease future violence. It is a spectacle meant to dissuade others from engaging in it. Because of effervescence, violence can become a kind of celebration of itself, but that is not how anyone would describe it after the fact. As such, the effectiveness of violence when it comes to dissuading people from anti-social behaviours, and the tendency of violence to escalate once underway, must be subjected to scrutiny.

Making sense of violence at the time and after the fact

Much of the recent ethnography of war has been devoted to showing that war is neither purely a reaction to environmental factors, in the manner of the 'new barbarism' thesis, nor an adaptation that furthers evolutionary and reproductive success, in the manner of Napoleon Chagnon's portrayal of the Yanomami as inherently warlike and war-loving savages.[5] Rather, it is deeply imbued with social meaning and manifold in its effects. However, there are risks in trying to make sense of violence. Despite some scholars' attempts to portray violence as similar to anything else anthropologists study (e.g. Nordstrom 2004), physical violence is different in a few important ways. For one thing, anthropologists are only rarely present for the actual perpetration of the violence. More often, we come to the topic after the violence has been enacted, and thus our accounts are a form of hindsight (Donham 2006). In explaining some of the factors that facilitated the rapid spread and intensity of the wartime violence in CAR, I thus run the risk of giving the impression that these factors somehow fully explain the fighting and its aftermath. And equations of that kind are inherently flawed. As I wrote on my blog while the violence was in full swing in early 2014, there is

a time-disconnect between war and ethnography. Ethnography takes time, and it is difficult to do during war. I know of one intrepid Ph.D. student currently doing ethnographic research in CAR. During my own research there I stayed far from conflict, even as I tried to understand it, because I was concerned for my own safety. I managed to miss the two major attacks on Ndele that occurred during my time in CAR, in both cases by just days. There tends therefore to be an element of hindsight, or an element of pre-sight (in the case of ethnographic projects interrupted by war) to ethnographic accounts of war and violence. This has struck me repeatedly as I struggle to come to terms with what has been going on in CAR and to explain it for the journalists and others whose queries have been filling my inbox. I can point to historical and ethnographic dynamics A, B, C, D, and E that have helped bring people in CAR to their current predicament. And I can cite grievances X, Y, and Z that likely motivate the fighters. But the addition of all those factors does not somehow 'add up' to the violence over the last year and a half. There remains an excess, beyond that which is explainable through reasons – even reasons related to symbolism and performance.

In listening to interviews with Anti-Balaka fighters, I have been struck by the disconnects between why they say they are fighting and what they are actually doing, as well as by the ways they contradict themselves. They claim not to be targeting all Muslims, but only 'enemies' from Chad and Sudan who continue to target them. But then they scrawl graffiti declaring

'No more mosques in CAR.' And mob violence acts first and asks questions later when it comes to assessing the provenance of 'Muslims' who have been identified and targeted. The danger of referring to the situation in CAR as motivated by, or playing out through, religious differences is that it hardens and fixes what are actually fluid – or at least ill-defined – categories and grievances that have other referents (such as 'foreignness') as well.

So as violence is ongoing, I wonder if we should be open to the idea that violence might exceed our attempts to make sense of it. That is not exactly a research agenda, nor does it offer a solution for the journalists tasked with reporting on what is going on in real time. It is, rather, a reminder that when it comes to violence, not everything has a reason. I think frequently of a comment Ed van der Elsken made in the text accompanying his photo-book *Bagara*. To preface his description of a hunting expedition that he was part of and during which a heavily pregnant female elephant was slaughtered in a gruesome manner, he wrote, 'The next story is not meant to illustrate the barbarity of hunting, for this was not hunting. Nor was it an incident. Such things happen, I saw them' (1961: 23). In other words, it was not a scandalous event that set in motion a range of accountability initiatives (legal sanction, self-questioning, the end of the safari, or anything else). It was just the kind of thing that can happen sometimes when people have empowered themselves with violence, whether through guns or other means. (Lombard 2014a)

The social study of war has yielded important insights into the nature of conflict and as such offered ideas for discouraging fighting in the future. These investigations have moreover had a humanizing role: rather than seeing participants in war as driven by animal instincts and therefore without culture – the defining trait of humans – they have shown that war too is embedded in and creative of culture. But as my real-time blog post draws out, different kinds of sense can be made of violence at different times. And there are limits to these endeavours. Frequently, violent things happen in the midst of war that exceed the otherwise expected limits around the exercise of violence. Sometimes people find ways to justify those kinds of happenings; sometimes they remain as unexplainable excesses. Emotions are key, and yet it is difficult to recall precisely a past emotional state – regret, satisfaction, or whatever else one might be experiencing in the moment has a tendency to colour the memory. As Randall Collins describes the particularities of violent effervescence (what he calls 'forward panic'), 'Perpetrators of this kind of violence have occupied a hermetically sealed zone of socially shared emotion, a special reality that not only overpowers all other moral sentiments at the moment, but which cannot be penetrated by memory or moral judgment from outside even in retrospect' (Collins 2009: 119).

So rather than explaining or making sense of violence, the following discussion of violence in Central African life is meant to spur reflection. How and why has Central African extraversion come to seem such a fount of danger, and how and why has violence been one means Central Africans use to respond to those dangers? (There are of course non-violent responses as well, such as certain forms of religious belonging or simply staying close to home, and these most likely far outnumber the violent ones; however, violence and non-violence often blend into each other.[6]) Viewed in this context, violence is itself embedded in these economies of extraversion, this time as a means of striking back against one's position of dispossession by conjuring an audience to witness one's enactment of power over other bodies.

Foreign bodies as dangerous and illegitimate

The Central African Republic is nothing if not the product of encounters between people originally from elsewhere, with different time horizons for their engagements with this space and the other people present. As a result it is a particularly difficult place to define who belongs and who is a 'foreigner' – but perhaps for that reason, such distinctions have come to seem all the more important. French officials justified their assassination of Sanusi in 1911 in part by arguing that he was a 'foreigner' with no right to rule over these lands and the people in them (Prioul 1981). The irony of this position was apparently lost on them, at least at the time. It is, however, evident that the fundamental operation of state-making processes is to use the discourse of sovereignty to 'produce the illusion of a clearly defined interior separated from an exterior' (Dunn 2009: 120). Globalization – that is to say, the current global political-economic order, which has strengthened certain borders and weakened others while making everyone both participants in and subjects of cross-border flows – has been accompanied by a return to autochthony as the most important marker of legitimacy and belonging (Dunn 2009; Geschiere and Jackson 2006; Geschiere and Meyer 1998; in a slightly different vein, Appadurai 2006). It is the

> 'very emptiness' of the concept of autochthony that makes it 'fit so well into the constantly changing boundaries created by globalisation processes and that makes it so politically "useful" and malleable a discourse for ideologies. The "Other" – crucial to any form of identity but especially to such fuzzy ones – can be easily redefined, precisely because autochthony as such has hardly any substance'. (Geschiere and Jackson 2006 quoted in Dunn 2009: 121)

That the French could dismiss Sanusi as an illegitimate foreigner at the same time as they claimed a right to legitimate domination by virtue of their non-native status is a memorable example of this malleability.

In the context of anomie and dispossession that Central Africans feel subjected to, and perhaps especially with the passing of the (relatively) halcyon days of the Bokassa era, the ability to produce a 'clearly defined interior separated from a clearly defined exterior' – even an illusion of one – has become all the more important. This ties back into the dynamics around mobility and the policing of mobility. Those who move also have power; one way of claiming some of that power is to police movement, such as through roadblocks. And though the effects of problematic relationships among mobility, violence, and accumulation may feel particularly acute today, they are in fact of long standing. Southerners' (non-Muslims') memories of the late-nineteenth- and early-twentieth-century raiders who participated in networks that stretched northward remain vivid. Sanusi's and the other sultans' power diminished only a century ago, after all. Some of them stayed in power into the 1920s in the service of indirect-rule policies employed by the French. In my interviews with southerners and the few civil servants present in northeastern CAR, they invoked this history (sometimes explicitly, sometimes implicitly) in describing the people they administered as 'foreigners' – even those who had been settled on the lands for a century or more. They were Muslim, they dressed differently from southerners, they were more hot-headed and quicker to resort to violence: those were the stereotypes people not from the northeast applied. Northwesterners were also the object of suspicion, in part because of the examples of people like the robber-rebel Miskine, who work both sides of the border in their politico-military entrepreneurialism. There is fear in these stereotypes at the same time as there is disparagement; these are two sides of the same descriptive coin.[7]

Again, though, foreignness is a slippery and changeable category. Former markers of foreignness have today become the basis for nationalism. The Sango language is the best example. When French administrators arrived, few people spoke Sango. Needing a way to communicate with people but wary of the expense and challenge of teaching French, the administrators decided to promote Sango as the working language of the colony. It was a trading language and relatively easy for people to learn. Christian missionaries saw it as useful as well. To this day, missionaries are known for speaking the most pure and beautiful Sango, like Muslim clerics and their command of classical Arabic. But while people acquiesced to speaking the language, it still had a distinctly colonial reputation. As surely as the French language, it was a marker of foreign domination. This began to change in the 1950s, with the independence movement and with the diffusion of the music of Sango-speaking guitar-players, which became quite popular (Diki-Kidiri 1979). Today, it is the marker par excellence of Central African belonging. Not every Sango speaker is a Central African, but every Central African must speak Sango, according even to those at the highest level of government. Legally, of course, a person can be a Central African citizen without speaking Sango, but someone presenting a Central African identity card and not speaking Sango would immediately be assumed to have purchased it through corrupt means.

Sango is thus an 'invented tradition' (Hobsbawm and Ranger 1983). That does not, of course, mean it is fake. It is simply yet another demonstration of the recent social and historical creation of supposedly primordial ties. In the context of the massive uncertainty – anomie and dispossession set amid state withering – in CAR today, Sango has become something people can cling to. The corruption assumed by all to be at the core of state administration means that few have confidence in the veracity of state-issued documents. Instead, Sango seems more enduring a firmament of nationhood and belonging – of safety amid danger. And that is the additional element that helps explain the turn to nativism and fear of foreigners: as ways of thinking and rationales for acting, nations and borders promise safety, order, and fixity at times when people feel cast about by upheaval (Kiernan 2007; Appadurai 2006).

Even people others vilify as 'foreign' end up espousing the same nation-state system for ordering the world – they just happen to include themselves. For instance, like people in the south, people in northeastern CAR also blame their problems on the depredations of 'foreigners'. That is, even autochthony's victims have trouble envisioning a world ordered differently. Consider the remarks of Soumaine Ndodeba, a Tiringoulou native, anti-poaching guard, and rebel general. He eventually joined Seleka and explained why their rebellion had led to such chaos:

> You see me I have not placed blame on the Christians. The problem is the foreigners. At the moment we arrived foreigners got into uniform. That is why Central Africans have manifested their discontent. The foreigners took everything. That is not rebellion. Rebellion is a project with an objective. We achieved our objective. We made Bozizé fall – that was our objective. Those others they did whatever they wanted.

The problem, he reiterated, was the mercenaries who had not even asked to join Seleka but looted and pillaged in the group's name and would not listen to reason. This analysis was the same as that of the southerners; they just drew the line of foreignness at a different point. The uncontrollable foreigners versus 'pure' Central Africans cast as these rapacious foreigners' victims: cunning victimhood, deployed again. Soumaine described the Seleka leader Nourreddine Adam as 'a Chadian who grew up in Bangui'. This remark indicates how mere presence on the soil does not determine citizenship in popular perspective; it is, rather, a complicated equation involving such factors as family networks (where does your loyalty really lie? Where does your money end up?) and length of stay. In these ways of thinking, the descriptors 'Chadian' or 'Sudanese' approached the status of epithet even during less tense times.

For all involved in understanding and participating in CAR's troubles, the 'abstract figure of the unknown other easily leads to specific categories of strangers' and those delineated as dangers and enemies follow 'Simmel's well-known characterization of the Stranger, those who are at the same time familiar and foreign, spatially near and socially far' (Bonhomme 2012: 216).

At the same time, there are new stresses between people who are, or should be, socially near. For instance, getting married marks the coming together of families and is an important ritual. But these celebrations have become so expensive, with the groom's family expected to provide so many gifts to the bride's family, and Central Africans have become so poor, that many Central Africans cannot afford it. Instead, they cohabit, which more or less works, except when there is a need for sanction – such as a couple who splits, leaving children whose father has but a weak normative obligation to pay child support. Even the current president, Faustin Archange Toudera, only legally married five days before his investiture (though his reasons for not doing so earlier could not have been solely financial). Moreover, wealth and accumulation are simultaneously valorized – many looking for advice will go not to the person in their neighbourhood with a reputation for wisdom or moderation but to the wealthiest (regardless of what he did to gain that money) – and a source of jealousy, contempt, and/or accusations of witchcraft or otherwise anti-social behaviour. These contradictions also contribute to the sense that the world of their desires exists on a horizon that seems not only impossible to reach, but further away by the day.

Another facet to this anomie regards the desire for security and order. Central Africans and interveners alike share the sense that there is a chasm between the strong state ideals they hold and the state actors and institutions they are forced to deal with on a daily basis. In the words of the primary schoolmaster in Tiringoulou, utterly frustrated by his inability to punish the students who had defaced his desk, 'Centrafrique is a country of laws! It is a country of laws!' He spoke as if holding tightly to the concept could make it real. In the end, he got none of the justice he sought. For members of the good intentions crowd, they feel frustrated with the state of law and order in CAR too, but that frustration does not become anomie because they can tell themselves they have no stake in this place, and because their jobs assure them material success and freedom from Central African accountability mechanisms regardless.

Elsewhere in the region, scholars have documented a social preference for 'disorder' (or phrased more positively, autonomy) (Scheele 2015), and there are elements of that finding in CAR too. However, people's preference for autonomy always exists in relation to their ability to further life projects, which many Central Africans feel has been damagingly compromised by the disordered aspects of life in CAR. Central Africans look at their history and draw the lesson that they have been the losers in a rigged contest.

Justice, punishment, and the invisible world

In Chapter 2, I described how spectacular punishments have long been an element of the Central African political repertoire, and are in certain respects a response to the dilemmas of trying to build such an improbable state given such limited resources. The prerogatives of the Central African state have always been popularized and privatized, and they have long included violence, including execution as spectacle, whether extra-judicial or official, as the history of the concessionary period shows. But in other respects, these trends have accelerated as the Central African state has continued to wither, particularly the feelings of economic unmooring, the loosening of ties to France and the growing importance of regional heads of state (Wohlers 2015). The weakness of the Central African state is in some ways new but in other ways old, as is the move to take punishment and threat-management into one's own hands. This long-standing practice has been revived and has taken on new importance in recent years as the state's inability to combat social dangers has become so apparent, and it is in this context that one must understand the wartime mobilizations and violence. Popular punishment is physical violence enacted against suspected disrupters of the precarious social order, chiefly witches, thieves, and adulterers.

Most often people describe popular mobilizations to counter criminals in their midst as vigilantism or 'popular justice'. But those terms do little to describe the ambivalence people feel about these modes of intervention. In the research project I led on the topic of access to justice in CAR, it would not be an exaggeration to say that every single person interviewed described the state judicial sector as wholly corrupt. Therefore people must find ways to counter threats by themselves. This often takes the form of damaging the body of the wrongdoer, sometimes to the point of death. Punishment figures heavily in many Central Africans' conceptions of justice. As one Central African colleague characterized the former Emperor Bokassa's strength: 'All presidents kill people. Bokassa killed the right people.' That is, what made him stand out as a leader was his ability to align justice and punishment. However, this ideal stands somewhat in tension with the idea of a bureaucratic state judicial system, with trials and prisons, which people also recognize as an ideal. To better capture the spectrum of ways of thinking about justice and punishment and the proper relation between them I thus refer to popular punishment, rather than popular justice.

While popular punishment strikes many (Central Africans and other concerned parties alike) as drastic and potentially dangerous, it also creates fleeting projects of cooperation among people who otherwise feel high levels of mistrust and inefficacy in regard to collective action. For instance, in a recent article with Sylvain Batianga-Kinzi (Lombard and Batianga-Kinzi 2015), we describe several incidents both in Bangui and in rural areas in which people were killed or nearly killed in the name of popular punishment. This mode of punishing is justified through reference to an ideal of solidarity, or empathy, with other possible victims. Consider the following explanations given by two men in Bangui's Combatant quarter, not long after the brutal beating of a suspected thief:

> When you let someone who killed the person next to you go, tomorrow he will come and kill you as well. The big people in our society are not ready to make justice. We do as we do [i.e. inflict popular punishment] in order to prevent these practices

[killings] because the state is always negligent in the face of its responsibilities.

The other is the mirror of the self: I cannot be this assaulted other! The laws protecting the other are also those that protect me, and I therefore cannot accept the violation of these laws, knowing in addition that these sufferings are unbearable. (Cited in Lombard and Batianga-Kinzi 2015: 64)

In these comments, violent popular punishment is described as having a deterrent effect on multiple levels, and therefore as promoting desired social norms (such as freedom from theft). It is also couched as a response to the inability of the state to carry out the functions people expect of it. And moreover, popular punishment is a means of demonstrating power and leaving potential opponents cowed. The execution of a 'criminal' is a spectacular, ceremonial act even though it is also generally improvised and happens quite quickly. The horror that accompanies it shows that instigators intend for these proceedings to terrorize people into submission. Burned and mutilated corpses of presumed thieves have been left in the Bangui streets for days in order to ensure that everyone in the vicinity absorbs the lesson this mangled body is meant to teach. The main difference between these practices and those that occurred during the post-Seleka violence was their extent. During the war they became far more prevalent and harder to characterize as defensive. (Though in these kinds of mobilizations, the line between defence and offence depends on one's position; the participants' energy comes in large part from their lamentation of the death/wrong done to them, and the transformation of that wrong into a source of power by vanquishing the one who inflicted it.) They were also reported on much more widely.

Even state-security-sector employees themselves argue that extreme measures of this kind are necessary. As one military officer who participated in the killing of a suspected thief in Bangui explained,

The use of popular and private justice is generally due to the corruption and impunity – to the poor functioning of justice in our country. Each day, people accused, arrested, and incarcerated for theft, breaking and entering, sorcery, and misappropriation of goods are frequently freed as soon as they are brought before the tribunal, the commission, or the gendarmerie. This activates a collective contempt as regards the guarantees of the law and favors the use of personal and popular vengeance in Bangui's neighbourhoods. (Cited in Lombard and Batianga-Kinzi 2015: 65)

The officer spoke shortly after he participated in popular punishment. He had awoken to find a twenty-year-old man in his house at midnight. The officer called out that he had intercepted a thief and began to beat the man. His family joined in and, hearing the noise, neighbours came and beat and whipped the man as well, using sticks and clubs. The presumed thief declaimed his innocence, but a few members of the crowd had taken control of the verdict. His body was red with blood – his limbs broken, his head smashed, his nose crushed. One of his aggressors was preparing to throw an iron block at his head when the officer and some others decided the thief should be taken to the Central Office for the Repression of Banditry rather than killed on the spot. The police brought the man to the hospital, but he died shortly thereafter from his wounds.

Bystanders interviewed after the fact had mixed opinions about how presumed thieves should be treated. One neighbour said, 'The officer's neighbours armed themselves with sticks and iron rods as if this was an affair of state. But this [the thief] was a human being.' Another invoked a Sango adage: zö tî nzï la fâ lo bîanî (if it's a thief, kill him automatically). The officer himself regretted how quickly things had escalated, even as he justified punishment as a necessary undertaking. This ambivalence is crucial to the functioning of popular punishment. It is able to take place not because there is a social consensus that it is the proper means for dealing with grave threats, but because there are enough people who get drawn into participating, and too few people who are so certain it is wrong that they will intervene against the human tide of effervescence. Trying to recall the emotions and split-second rationales that helped drive such undertakings in the moment is, as Collins (2009) argues, as difficult as recreating a dream state once awake. As such it is a mode of effective (if not wholly desirable) collective expression of the fractured solidarities of urban life.

Also, violence can be a declarative statement of agency when social life is as deeply marked by anomie as it is in CAR today. Arjun Appadurai (1998: 244–5) describes such violence as 'preemptive': 'Let me kill you before you kill me. Uncertainty about identification and violence can lead to actions, reactions, complicities, and anticipations that multiply the pre-existing uncertainty about labels. Together, these forms of uncertainty call for the worst kind of certainty: "dead certainty"' – that is, the kind of certainty that requires killing. For many Central Africans, uncertainty is existential: the very border between the real and the imaginary has been compromised, and people experience this breach as disconnection and dispossession (Ceriana Mayneri 2014c). Thus for Central Africans, the insecurity they have had to endure in recent years is not simply a matter of the presence or absence of guns (and who is holding them) or other visible markers of the threat of violence. Rather, the insecurity operates on an existential level, since people feel threatened by forces that cannot be seen but which are clearly operating everywhere and all the time, as the surfeit of funerals even during the comparatively tranquil mid-2000s suggests.[8]

In specific instances, the effects of this situation show themselves in the form of *violence* – intentional harm that can kill. This can be seen in the kinds of statements that are presented as evidence that the person who made them is a witch, such as one I collected while doing research in the northern town of Ndele in 2009: 'You are going to leave this water pump [site of a dispute between two women] and you are going to give birth through your mouth!' The statement's target, six months pregnant, miscarried two days later.

The woman who had stated her violent sorcery intentions and proved them through the ensuing foetal death was tried and found guilty by the Ndele tribunal. She had been charged under Article 162/162 *bis* of the Central African constitution, which criminalizes the practice of charlatanism and sorcery (*pratique du charlatanisme et sorcellerie*, PCS). This statute dates to the colonial era and has been reinvigorated after independence. During calmer periods in CAR when prisons functioned a little bit better than they do during war, many of the people locked up in prisons, and almost all of the women, were being held on charges of PCS. When it comes to sorcery, this is one domain in which people feel that there is supposed to be a compact between themselves and their governors that the latter will demonstrate competence in providing justice for these kinds of threats and crimes. This was evident in the Azande polities of yore. And it is evident today with Article 162, which the National Assembly, under pressure from international human rights interests, debated removing but ultimately decided to retain in 2010.

In this respect it becomes apposite to shift the line of inquiry away from 'what is the state', which is a palimpsest (of UN world order norms, of what it means to be a citizen, etc.) and instead focus on 'what is government' (Mann 2014) in CAR? That is, what kinds of things do people deem it necessary to govern, who does so, and how do they do it? In this respect sorcery stands out. Note that in areas where rebel groups have established a sedentary presence, one of the two key initiatives all undertake is to require that all witch-craft accusations be brought to them for adjudication. (The other is taxation in the form of roadblocks, which both provides revenue and polices movement.) When it comes to these sorcery cases, rebels are known for being particularly harsh. People living nearby express ambivalence about these measures. Some appreciate that the mercilessness reduces people's misuse of witchcraft. Others find it too draconian. Many hold both stances simultaneously.

Roland Marchal explains the problems of sorcery in CAR through reference to Adam Ashforth's concept of 'spiritual insecurity', which is 'a sense of unease arising from the conditions of knowing that invisible forces are acting upon one's life but not knowing what they are and how to relate to them' (Ashforth 2005: 127). This is a useful formulation, but there is a big difference between the South African context Ashforth describes and that of Equatorial Africa, namely the fact that in the latter regulation and punishment of supernatural violence has long been a popularly ascribed *raison d'être* for government. Historically in Equatorial Africa, what differentiated living in a stratified, state-like society from living in a village not subject to that kind of control was precisely the existence of specialists in the divination and punishment of sorcery. Through Article 162 that continues to be the case, but popular sentiment is clear that government has proven outmatched of late. Thus people see the 'spiritual insecurity' of today as a failure of government that recalls the distant social memory of a time when governors – including or especially those of the state – more effectively controlled these forces.

Moreover, it is specifically through the dynamics of extraversion (which, again, Central Africans experience as dispossession) that anti-social sorcery has become so slippery and powerful. That is to say, occult violence has intensified as a result of the 'destructive understandings' (Bernault 2006) produced by the past century and a half of intense encounters between Central Africans and incomers. In the process, the enchantment of the body – a site of power, not just a bag of bones and organs – has been entrenched. As such, bodies have been stages for the enactment of innovative spectacles of violence meant to demonstrate power. The beating deaths of Boganda's and Bokassa's fathers are examples of this, as are the killings of colonial officials perpetrated by members of the Kongo-Wara rebellion, who, the legend holds, turned their victims into gorillas (Nzabakomada-Yakoma 1986). When a person destroys a body in order to remove its power, this is also a means of recuperating and incorporating that power for oneself. The recuperation and incorporation can be largely implicit or more explicit, such as through cannibalism. This is not to say that Central Africans and incomers engage frequently in cannibalism; time and again, accusations of cannibalism have been found to be the result of misunderstandings. Rather, the importance of cannibalism is seen in its prevalence as a discourse/claim about the sources of occult power (Ndjapou 2008) and as a morally fraught yet nevertheless potentially effective way of striking back against them.

Cannibalism

In Equatorial Africa over the past century and a half, one particularly charged topic in the perpetration and (mis-)understanding of violence has been cannibalism. Cannibalism, after all, was one of the things that initially drew European attention to Equatorial Africa, as the region was seen as a hotbed of this abominable practice: beyond the pale, but useful for science to understand. Adventurists thus looked for evidence of the man-eating practices they were certain were occurring around them. They soon encountered people involved in the specialist role of cutting up the bodies of the dead. Evidence of cannibalism confirmed! Why else would they be slicing dead bodies, and removing choice internal organs if not to eat them? Colonial officials moved quickly to ban these practices.

In fact, the autopsies had nothing to do with preparing bodies for eating. They were necessary medical-spiritual procedures performed in the context of Equatorial understandings of the witch-substance present in every body. When a person dies, the witch-substance can continue living and acting in the world. It can enter into someone else's body. So in order to prevent that witch-substance from doing evil, people with particular expertise needed to perform an autopsy and dispose of the witch-substance in the proper way. Though the colonial officials did not have total control over people's practices, the banning of these autopsies irrevocably compromised people's ability to contain these witch-substances' power and violence (Bernault 2006). This was but one instance of the dispossession that has marked Central Africans' participation in long-distance trades, knowledge, and imperialism.

Stories of European misunderstandings of Central Africans have become commonplace in postcolonial critiques. But the misunderstandings went both ways: many Central Africans, too, were convinced the Europeans in their midst were cannibals and found evidence for it everywhere. Consider the reactions to the German adventurist Georg Schweinfurth as he travelled through Africa (from Khartoum to Mangbetu, in present-day Democratic Republic of the Congo) between 1869 and 1871. Schweinfurth's books about his travels are full of admissions of his fear as he travelled through the homelands of (reputed) cannibals. In keeping with the mores of the time, he was an avid collector: he sought proto-ethnographic information, animal and plant specimens, geographic features. Phrenology was the latest Western scientific innovation, and so he also collected skulls.

Schweinfurth was travelling with armed ivory-buyers from Khartoum. They would occasionally enter into violent altercations with the people they travelled among and did business with. Schweinfurth benefited from these battles by collecting the heads they left behind. He only wanted the skulls, though. So at night, in his camp, he would set a cauldron of water to boil, drop in the heads, and stir until the flesh had fallen off. The odour, he admitted, was terrible. 'From the more dense and stupid natives, the idea could not be eradicated that I wanted the bones for my food,' he wrote (Schweinfurth quoted in Harrison 2012: 64); with hindsight, he seems far the denser.

> Schweinfurth's expedition was, in a sense, a self-fulfilling prophecy. He intended to find evidence of cannibalism and headhunting, and his own actions – especially the collecting practices he employed – were virtually guaranteed to elicit the very evidence he sought. First, he offered trade goods in return for evidence of such savagery. These were exchanges in

which he paid, or otherwise enticed, the peoples he encountered to produce signs of their savage nature, or to enact his own European fantasies of primitiveness. Second, his journey through central Africa, accompanied by a large armed escort and acquiring skulls along the way through a combination of violence and trade, was itself a sort of headhunting expedition. ... Certainly, it was almost bound sometimes to prompt reprisals in kind. Though apparently quite unaware that he was doing so, he was himself reproducing the behavior he was looking for in those whom he encountered, and inducing them to reproduce the same behavior in reply. (Harrison 2012: 65)

I relate these gruesome encounters in some detail for several reasons. One is that they point to the blinding effect that preconceived notions can have. For Schweinfurth, the fact that the people among whom he travelled found his head-collecting and cooking practices depraved was confounding, but to explain it he clung tightly to what he held to be an unassailable truth – that Africans were above all primitives ('dense and stupid') – and so he never managed to consider that they saw him for the head hunter and orchestrator of violence that he was. Another is that they suggest the ways violence in Central Africa has long been bound up in the 'destructive understandings' and de-humanizations that have accompanied the integration of this part of the world into long-distance trades and other imperial processes. And third is that they indicate the ways that bodies, power, illicit and/or occult practice, and violence have long been linked.

In fact, in neither the case of the autopsies nor Schweinfurth's skulls were people actually ingesting human flesh. But both contributed to the pervasive sense that bodies, including dead bodies, could be weirdly powerful, precious, and dangerous. Both show how a failure to recognize the partiality (in both senses of that term) introduced by one's assumptions and desire to accentuate the difference between oneself and the foreigners in one's midst can lead people into erroneous analyses and ultimately damaging courses of action. And both show how violence that oversteps social norms can be a way of demonstrating power in a context marked by danger, fear, and misunderstanding.

Cannibalism returned to Bangui during the war, in January 2014. I saw the video of a man apparently eating a cooked human leg on my Facebook feed and did not want to believe it was real. The grainy footage marked by bright Bangui sunlight showed a young man eating the blackened leg of someone he had deemed his vanquished adversary, an apparently-Muslim man who rode in the wrong minibus. Based on the comments (posted by Central Africans in CAR and in the diaspora), the main reason people shared the video was as a public manifestation of their shock. At the same time, it had the effect of enlarging the incident – allowing people not present to experience it, to relate to it, to fear it.

A couple of days later, a BBC journalist set out to find the man in the video. Ouandja Magloire confessed to/took credit for the crime. He explained that Seleka/Muslims had killed his pregnant wife, his sister-in-law, and her child. He explained to the journalist that he had seen a man who appeared to be a Muslim riding in a minibus. He knew that once the minibus reached the Burundian peace-keepers stationed down the road, the man would be able to continue unmolested, so he and the people he had rallied behind him forced the minibus driver to pull over. They dragged out the 'suspect' and began to beat and stab him. They doused him with kerosene and set him on fire. Afterwards, they dismembered him, and it was then that Ouandja grabbed a leg and bit for the phone-cameras that had been engaged to capture the carnage. Ceriana Mayneri (2014a) cautions that while to call this killing simply a 'performance' is not accurate (it was not just a show – it was a flesh-and-blood killing), 'the gestures by which the murder was carried out (in front of the cameras, with the burning and dismembering of the human body, which was then dragged through the dust) were not accidental but 'say something' about the murderers' need to show their strength, to exalt that strength in front of the community, and to impose it by annihilating the victim and destroying his remains with fire' (Ceriana Mayneri 2014a).

The BBC journalist presented Ouandja's nickname – Mad Dog – as if it spoke for itself. He likely did not realize that this sobriquet has been frequently adopted in Equatorial conflicts in recent years; it is the name of the titular character in Simon's Rock College science professor Emmanuel Dongala's novel (*Johnny Mad Dog*) about a boy-soldier who is both a perpetrator and a victim in the midst of his society's breakdown, the film version of which has been popular in Bangui in pirated DVD form in recent years (Ceriana Mayneri 2014a).

When the journalist asked Ouandja why he had done it, he replied that it was because he was 'angry': 'He had no other explanation. During our interview, he betrayed no sign of that anger, or of pride, or regret, or of any emotion at all. His tone was neutral, his eyes and face blank' (BBC 2014). This extensive editorializing masquerades as straightforward description. The author does not consider how cultures other than his own might express emotions differently, or view the expression of certain emotions differently. Ouandja comes across as animal-like, sub-human. These are the kinds of practices through which journalists present Africa as a dark and demonic place, lacking in reason and fellow feeling.[9]

However, Ouandja's actions must be understood in the context of anger and fear, and in that respect they 'make sense'. In Central Africa, a widespread understanding of how people gain power is that they have ingested dangerous, perhaps even enemy, substances – a human heart, a live snake, etc. They do it secretly, however, leaving people to speculate about what someone must have done in order to attain a high position or money or the like. Here, Ouandja had made his ingestion of these materials into a spectacle. He showed his contempt for those who had eviscerated him – an evisceration made evident by his inability to protect the women closest to him – by himself openly becoming the sorcerer. His actions were a dare, a threat – a way of making his power socially real and striking fear in others. And it worked. Ouandja says that while prior to the attack he was nobody, afterwards he became a big person. When he went out, he had an entourage of five or six swaggering youth. He had jumped out of his 'place' (in the sense of 'know your place!') and become someone who was known beyond his physical location, in part thanks to the stories written by the journalists who came to him in an unending stream.

Until they didn't. Now, Ouandja's acquaintances say he regrets what he did. It was a bit stupid, and he is ashamed to have this be the one thing most people know about him. This, too, points to the challenges of making sense of violence: the reasons Ouandja did what he did include emotional ones that even he has difficulty recreating now that the moment has passed.

The new possibilities for images and video of violence to circulate, as in the case of Ouandja, is one of the big differences between war today and that in the past. Alex de Waal (2015) has argued that the Thuraya satellite phone radically altered the nature of warfare in Sudan, making it possible for people to communicate across long distances in ways they had not previously been able to. In the CAR war, mobile phones with cameras and Facebook played an enlarged role in how people came to know about violence. While chatting with Professor Louis Bainilago, a friend and colleague at the University of Bangui, in December 2014 we lamented the violence that was at that point still festering. After a brief silence (what can you really say about these kinds of things?), he said, 'Those were some terrible images.' Though Louis had a much more direct experience of the war than I did, when it came to the most graphic, up-close violence, we had both come to know about it through Facebook and the images and videos people shared compulsively. Muslims would share the images of violence perpetrated against their co-religionists as evidence of the need to be afraid and as a plea for help; Christians would share stories of Seleka exactions; people of both faiths would share stories of hope (neighbourhoods where people still got along) as well as stories of despair (the corruption of the country's leaders) and videos of small children and large women dancing remarkably well.

Violence has an inherently performative aspect to it (Richards 1996; Dunn 2009). That is, it is a physical and material act whose details communicate particular messages to audiences in addition to the discrete harm done to a person or people. That performative dimension is heightened when it occurs with cameras rolling and the possibilities for diffusing it have become popularized through means such as Facebook. (Facebook Messenger and WhatsApp work fairly well even despite the country's spotty network connections.) So in addition to the ways CAR's wartime violence built on longstanding practices of spectacular, popular punishment, and anger over dispossession and evisceration, it also played out as it did because in many cases the people enacting it were aware they were doing so for a camera, and for a larger audience than that gathered physically around them. In this respect, journalists and lay photographers, too, became part of the war. They did not cause it, but they and people enacting violence were acting in relation to each other, and as such entangled. The following example draws out this entanglement as well.

Soldiers who lynch

Alongside Ouandja's much-discussed and lamented moment in the global spotlight, another murder – also a lynching – captured media accounts of the war, social and otherwise. In early 2014, the French Sangaris peacekeeping mission had deployed to the country, as had the African Union's MISCA. Roadblocks managed by armed groups were still widespread in the capital and beyond, however, and the peacekeepers were dealing with a situation of still-ongoing conflict. One morning in February, the new president, Catherine Samba-Panza, presided over a ceremony at the National School for Magistrates meant to launch the re-instatement of the Central African Armed Forces (FACA), which had disbanded and dispersed in the aftermath of the Seleka take-over. Samba-Panza addressed the soldiers. She told them she was 'proud' of them and called on them to return to duty. As the president's motorcade departed, people clapped and cheered with a middling level of enthusiasm. Then someone identified a man in the crowd as a Seleka fighter/ supporter, and soldiers and other bystanders unleashed violence against him. He was killed, and even after he had died the violence meted against his corpse continued. It looked tiny as it was dragged through the streets, as if the killing had not just claimed the man's life but also his status as an adult of normal stature.

The forms of violence used in the FACA-led lynching were similar to the killing that established Ouandja's notoriety, except for the cannibalistic elements. Another difference was that whereas the incident with Ouandja was part of the Anti-Balaka popular mobilizations, in this case members of the armed forces committed the lynching. Not only that, but it occurred while African Union and French peacekeeping troops stood nearby. While the presence of peacekeepers did not stop the violence from occurring, their presence had other effects. For one thing, they made it easier for journalists to cover the atrocity as it happened. Instead of grainy mobile-phone footage, in this case the images and videos were professional-quality – clear and covering every second of the violence. In the videos one can see international journalists – apparent from their skin tone, backpacks, and large cameras – rushing out of the way and/or trying to get shots. This is not a question of the ethics of war photography (probing accounts of that topic have come from photographers themselves, such as Tim Hetherington in his film *Diary*); the effects of images and videos of violence are manifold, especially now that the participants in war are themselves often both producers and consumers of those materials. Drawing attention to atrocities can serve a useful advocacy purpose, eliciting more resources to deal with the situation.

But it is nevertheless noteworthy that the presence of the peacekeepers as bystanders and protectors made it safer for journalists to be closer to the violence as it played out, yet without stopping the violence from happening. Images of the violence then circulated and helped shape the perceptions of people both in CAR and outside as to the nature of the war and its protagonists. The interesting point here is not that peacekeepers and/or photographers caused – whether directly or indirectly – either the spread or reduction of violence. More interesting is to recognize how complex the webs of social ties are even among actors who see themselves as very different from each other, with actions and their effects enabled, frustrated, or otherwise shaped by one other. The images can even travel on to new conflict zones; the image of the body of this unfortunate young man was recently used to illustrate a blog post about escalating violence in Burundi (with the headline, 'This shocking photo explains the crisis in Burundi', no less!) (Hilekaan 2015).

From the perspective of understanding the workings of violence, photos and videos recorded on the spot can help overcome the inherent challenges of understanding violence-as-it-happens. In the videos and photos of the lynching, some people run away, while others run in: they become the attacking group. The victim is beaten, stabbed, and killed several times over. His corpse is dragged through the streets. Some of the photos show FACA kicking and beating him while others are filming and smoking cigarettes. In the photos and videos, the man appears slim and small, almost child-like. The violence unleashed against him seems both unnecessary and excessive. Could they not see how helpless and puny he was?

However, a question like that fails to capture the spirit animating these kinds of attacks, which draw their force from the attackers' sense that they are the ones who are in danger. As Collins explains,

> Mob violence of this kind is a version of piling-on a temporarily weak victim. The emphasis here should be on temporarily. ... Targets of ethnic violence are perceived as strong, aggressive, and imminently threatening. But they are attackable because

they are found in a local situation where they can be safely attacked. (Collins 2009: 119–20)

The perpetrators of this kind of violence thus begin from the position of feeling existentially threatened. The act of killing itself gives them the sense that the terrorizing stranger was in fact small, insignificant, and no match for them. In this way, fear gets translated into an offensive strategy and the elation of feeling in control, rather than immiserated.

These kinds of attacks are often described as the production of a mob or a crowd, but those terms miss the variations in how people present react. Some people run, some watch. The action is carried out by a group more properly termed a pack: ten to twenty people driven and organized by their emotions and desire for action, particularly action in the form of a hunt. The pack 'is the universal expression of communal excitement. … It consists of a group of men in a state of excitement whose fiercest wish is *to be more*' (Canetti 1962: 93; emphasis in original). Seen from the perspective of the people who participate, acting in a pack is itself a way of productively – if temporarily – transforming one's social and emotional state. These microsociological features are part of the expression of the sentiments of dispossession, fear, and anger, and the historical and social importance of physical violence in demonstrating power, that have characterized the war in CAR. Particular instances when people who are otherwise seen as dangerous and powerful suddenly appear in such a way that they can be safely attacked – such as alone, unarmed – become irresistible opportunities for those mobilized by a combination of anger and fear.

The excessive nature of the killings – that the victims were killed and then subjected to additional violence that would kill them again and again, as if they had multiple lives – is also a telling element of the microsociology of violence in the CAR war. Remember that a widespread understanding in Central Africa holds that all bodies harbour a force within them that can act in the world, in ways cultivatable but not wholly controlled by the person him- or herself. This force does not die when the body's ability to live has been extinguished. Known as the *toro ti kúá* ('spirit of the dead'), it can go on acting in the world. While autopsy practices to de-activate it were disrupted by colonial law, there remain a variety of means that people can employ to encourage it to carry out certain actions, such as wreaking vengeance for a wrongful death (Lombard and Batianga-Kinzi 2015). Violence enacted must thus be understood in the context in which danger takes not just visible forms, but also invisible ones that surround and outlive the people who are killed. Desecrating the body does nothing in and of itself to harm the *toro* it has housed throughout the person's life, but it is a means of showing that people's ability to perpetrate violence knows no limits. Doing so stokes fear in the deceased's associates, with the hope being that then they will refrain from inciting the *toro ti kúá* to respond with vengeance and reprisals.

And yet at the same time as spiritual insecurity and the *toro ti kúá* can encourage particularly forceful killings, they can also make people refrain from violence, out of concern that, as an expression in Bangui puts it, 'Death is not free' (*La mort n'est pas gratuite*) – that is, killing will come back to haunt you, as reflected in the assessment made in regard to tragedy that has befallen a bad person, 'He was given his change' (*On lui a rendu la monnaie*). I first heard these expressions in relation to Levi Yakete. Yakete had been an operative in Bozizé's Kwa na Kwa ('work, nothing but work') political party, and had fled to France after the Seleka coup. From there he worked to provide money and supplies to Anti-Balaka fighters. For this he received a spot on the UN sanctions list. In mid-November 2014, he was driving near his home in southern France when his car broke down. With his wife at the wheel and his children in the back seat, he began pushing the car to the side of the road. But before he got there, another car came up from behind and ploughed into the unexpected, nearly stationary obstruction. Yakete died. That this death was entirely an accident of chance seemed less likely to people than that there was a dimension of vengeance or the righting of morals at work, with the *toro ti kúá* of those dead at Yakete's instigation playing an important role.

Conclusion

Ideally, government fulfils some of the same desires as that of a house. A clear set of people belong inside, where they enjoy a range of comforts and shelter and protection from the dangerous elements outside. Many people in CAR share in these desires, even if their own experience of government has too often been less like making a home inside a solid building than like living at a remote train depot. That is, despite being the 'periphery of a periphery' (Cordell 1985) – marginal in every sense of the term – the country has also been a site of encounter. Rather than a stable and sedentary national population, this place called CAR has long attracted people with varying time horizons and interests as regards their involvement with this territory and the other people they find there. For the most part, people manage quite well, take care of themselves and their families, and engage profitably with interlopers. But sometimes the depot comes to seem unacceptably dangerous, at which point people turn to the house-vision in a bid to erect boundaries so as to separate themselves from the people and forces they see as bent on their evisceration. However, their tools for doing so are not those of the house-dweller, like a lock and key. Instead, repeatedly throughout the history of CAR, the tools people have fashioned have entailed the use of violence, and particularly violence intended as punishment.

Punishment has thus been a technique of statecraft and a prerogative of the state, as well as an authority claimed by a wider range of non-state agents. This overturns classic distinctions between 'the state' and its alternatives. For instance, Pierre Clastres argued that the force of law – that which holds people in awe – is written on the social body in one of two ways. In societies with long histories of strong states, the force of law is written in legal texts. In 'primitive societies' (his term), in contrast, the force of law is written on the body through various modes of 'torture' (also his term), such as the painful body-modification practices that occur during coming-of-age initiations. For CAR and many other postcolonial locales, this distinction does not capture their historical experiences. CAR, the 'unfortunate colony' that became a 'failed state' (Lombard 2014b), is a particularly pronounced case. Here, building the state has long involved writing the law on bodies through torture, and these activities have always involved people beyond the ranks of official state employees.

This is why though recent events have been thoroughly chilling and shocking, they nevertheless uncomfortably echo the past. This suggests that these are not merely the actions of people being manipulated by venal leaders but reflect modes of power that have been seen as necessary (sometimes efficacious, sometimes regrettable) over a longer duration. Central Africans often describe themselves as peaceful and non-violent, especially as a way of differentiating themselves from 'Chadians' and 'Sudanese' who they describe as quick to pull a weapon. And yet: popular punishment escalated into a practice of war.[10] As such, eradicating it will require a more thorough excavation of the place of violence in Central African politics than is possible when the recent war is treated as a tragic, aberrant blip in an otherwise harmonious history.

While I have tried to put the practice of violence into a longer history as a means of laying out the particular factors from which it springs, I do so with the caveat that there are limits to the extent it is possible to make social sense of wartime violence. Ethnographic research can help us understand the grievances, emotions, and historical tendencies that underlie people's actions, but there can be an excess that accompanies collective violent action that, after the fact, has no explanation that can be easily captured (Collins 2009). In part, this has to do with the fact that in the midst of war people are making split-second decisions based on far-from-complete information. When people experience social chaos, 'there may be two roots of dissolution to which hindsight and the neatening of history normally blind us. One is uncertainty. The second is the partial logics people construct to cope with knowing but never-really-knowing' (Simons 1995: 64). Anomie and anxiety over dispossession create a maelstrom of 'knowing but never-really-knowing'. Rather than simply treating outbreaks of violence as spontaneous aberrations and trying to stamp them out, Central Africans and the others working to reduce violence in the country will have to do something about the *sources* of the insecurity (Marchal 2015a). That this is a much more difficult task does not make it any less necessary.

Central Africans have long characterized the authors of dispossession using the language of foreignness, even as they have seen foreigners as useful in a variety of ways, such as to operate concessions (Smith 2015b) and engage in regional trade (Kilembe 2015). (This, too, is part of why I describe Central Africans' predicament as one of cunning victimhood: they are certainly victims, and yet as certainly as that is the case they also make deals to profit from that status. Breaking this dynamic for good will require addressing both the ways it has negatively affected Central Africans and the ways it has brought them benefits.) The war in CAR has drawn in new actors – such as an enlarged UN and humanitarian presence – who provide some security but also contribute to Central Africans' longstanding sense that their country's big problem is its tendency to attract people who temporarily use the place for their own profit while their true allegiances lie elsewhere. In the final chapter, I turn to post-Seleka interventions to look at these entanglements in greater detail. That is, I look at 'destructive understandings' in the making.

Chapter 7

WORLD CHAMPION OF PEACEKEEPING

Introduction

'Central African Republic is the world champion of hosting peace-keeping missions,' said one young man during a discussion in his Bangui neighbourhood in March 2016. He listed off the successive international, regional, and sub-regional missions that have been deployed to the country over the past twenty years. Central Africans both rich and poor, educated and not, often lament their country's position as 'last in the world'. Yet in terms of quantity of peacekeeping missions, they rank at or very near the top, with more than a dozen. To many Central Africans, this set of facts requires explanation: they have had more international intervention than anywhere else, and yet they remain among the very last in terms of virtually any kind of development indicator. For many in the intervener crowd, too, this is a troubling combination. How could things have gotten so bad, considering the resources poured into the country through the years, including as a test case for the UN Peacebuilding Commission/Fund?

This chapter approaches these questions not through after-the-fact analysis of the effectiveness of particular interventions or the spoiler actions of various Central African politicians, but by investigating how the various people involved in these endeavours think about and relate to each other as they try to work together. In public statements, Central Africans are eager for international intervention, even to the extent of asking to be re-colonized. People who have worked in both Equatorial Africa and West Africa often contrast the two places by saying that while West Africans push back on donors' plans and have their own priorities to assure, Equatorial Africans – and particularly Central Africans – leave it to the interveners to develop the plan (e.g. through the concessionary politics dynamic [Smith 2015b]). And yet even without overt differences of opinion, Central Africans and interveners seem rarely to accomplish what they set out to. Why?

The above questions are the crux of this book, and the previous chapters have pursued several lines of inquiry that are necessary to answer them. For instance, DDR shows how the interactional dynamics of peacebuilding projects militate against their achieving stated goals. This chapter focuses on another dimension, namely interpretive baggage that different people bring to the job of figuring out what is going on, and how differences in these processes of interpreting the world lead people to remain divided even when working together. Indeed, the differences in these patterns become what simultaneously unifies and divides people.

As people navigate the world, we look for patterns in the information and impressions we take in. We also look for explanations for our ailments and other unfortunate events (Evans-Pritchard 1936). How we locate those patterns and explanations has cultural and class dimensions. What one person (say, an expatriate UN employee) deems important/credible can be quite different from what a Central African in the neighbourhood deems credible. Or put otherwise, the former and the latter may correlate or otherwise seek explanation for entirely different kinds of information, and do so in entirely different ways. In CAR, these differences feed a hermeneutics[1] of mistrust among everyone living and working there. Publicly, people relate to each other through buzzwords and international project priorities, which let them work together in the extraverted ways they long have. Privately, everyone asks – and answers for themselves – some version of the questions 'Why do they not see x and y as a problem/contradiction? What are they *really* doing?'

The prevalent mistrust is exacerbated by the lack of clarity about who is ultimately in control. This is one of the central questions for people, and it is a source of anxiety – for Central Africans, anxiety that some half-secret puppeteer is pulling the strings in order to make off with their riches; for the good intentions crowd, that the president and ministers are milking them to pursue half-secret personal agendas. At the same time, the lack of clarity about the hierarchies among various people enacting governance also makes it easier for everyone to blame someone else for eventual messes.

Uncertainty

It would be easy to make this chapter a critical post-mortem, in the process forgetting that the 20/20 vision of hindsight is never available to people in the moment of crisis. As former UN Undersecretary General for Peacekeeping Operations (2000–2008) Jean-Marie Guéhenno said of that job, 'The most useless way to pretend to help is to offer detailed, specific solutions, or recipes. … What I needed was the fraternal companionships of other actors before me who had had to deal with confusion, grapple with the unknown, and yet had made decisions' (Guéhenno 2015: xvi). While investigating past failures (e.g. human rights abuses) can help counter impunity and inspire new procedures or institutions, the new procedures will always be met with a changing situation on the ground, potentially compromising even the best planning. As Guéhenno explained, he rarely faced situations in which wrong and right were clear-cut, because the effects of any action are many, and usually both good and bad. He relied on his classical education and moral reasoning more than he had expected. 'One needs a reliable compass to navigate through the fog of peace' (Guéhenno 2015: xvii).

Unfortunately, yet fittingly, compasses do not work in CAR. The Bangui Magnetic Anomaly is a geological formation that distorts compasses' ability to point toward north. Instead, they go 'berserk', in the words of one scientist who studies it (Wood 2014b).[2] To be sure, Guéhenno was speaking of a metaphorical compass, not the kind used by an outdoorsperson. But the Magnetic Anomaly is a convenient reminder of the limits of Guéhenno's (and Clausewitz's before him) metaphor nevertheless. Fog temporarily obscures the distinctive features of the terrain, and a compass can help one navigate even if the usual landmarks are hidden from view. But in 'no peace, no war' (Richards 2005) or 'interwar' (Debos 2013) situations, there is not so much an obscuring fog as there is a surfeit of information and impressions. What is just background? What demands a closer look? What is hiding behind that surface? Making one's way through these questions is like picking one's way through a funhouse, or making sense of a Rorschach blot that itself keeps changing.

There is no impartial tool for determining what a Rorshach blot really is. The destabilizing or disorienting aspects of being in a funhouse might never be relieved by an unobstructed view. Instead, one must use one's wits. Interpretive 'wits' are culturally and materially inflected. Wittingly or not, people use their own assumptions and worldview to filter perceptions and to fill in gaps in what can be known (Simons 1995). Assumptions and worldviews derive from personal, institutional, inter-personal, and cultural factors, and as such they have parameters. Some stories or lines of interpretation will strike one person as far-fetched, but another might find them highly credible. Central Africans, for instance, are suspicious of outsiders' ulterior motives, particularly their illicit exploitation of Central African 'riches'. That suspicion translates into credulousness when it comes to any such tales. Interveners are less likely to focus on the illicit exploitation of natural resources, which they tend to believe is anomalous and rare, if they see it at all. Their suspicion is instead organized around Central Africans' corruption (in both the moral and fiscal senses), such that they are credulous about those kinds of stories.

These processes of interpretation and suspicion are compounded by the opacity and uncertainty that surround who is ultimately in charge. Is it the UN mission? The French? Central African politicians? Perhaps there are complicated legal-technical answers to those questions, but on a day-to-day basis their answers are impossible to determine. This contributes to the sense among everyone involved that the others are not honest, disinterested actors, but rather have vested interests that are served by obscuring who is really in control.

Differing modes of suspicion are not problems in and of themselves. Suspicion and mistrust are arguably well-founded all around, in this place of recurrent scandal (Lombard in preparation). Given the differing parameters for being suspicious in a context of uncertainty and mistrust, people strive to carefully manage the faces they front towards others, saying different things to different people. Rather than engage each other directly on contested points, both donors and Central African politicians/functionaries tend to accept each others' terms without much comment, while tacitly mistrusting their counterparts and expecting to continue evading their direct control. This is an improvised way of working together despite the mistrust. It lets people collaborate who wouldn't be able to if everyone aired their suspicions and concerns freely. In this way, humanitarian assistance can get delivered, and peacebuilding projects can be implemented.

And indeed, though CAR has not sprinted through the MINUS-CA-led peacebuilding obstacle course, it has progressed. Critics like myself have complained about the peacebuilding programme priorities, such as the decision to push for national elections as fast as possible while postponing local and municipal ones. But fears of violence during the election process were not borne out. A new president, Faustin Archange Touadéra, was inaugurated in March 2016, and he is saying and doing things that kindle hopes of a more peaceful future among interveners and Central Africans alike. For instance, he refused the outgoing transitional president Catherine Samba-Panza's budget for the inauguration, arguing it was twice as high as it should be, since the money could be put towards many other needs. In short, a façade has been erected by the peace-building efforts. With time we will see if that façade can become a house capable of keeping out the many armed groups that continue to emerge in and around the country, and of sheltering Central Africans in a dignified way.

My point in focusing on mistrust is thus not intended as a denunciation of MINUSCA-era peacebuilding, but rather to show the importance of suspicion to relationships among people who ostensibly share the same goals. Interveners are suspicious of other interveners; Central Africans collaborating with the good inten-tions crowd are suspicious of these interveners; and the interveners are suspicious of their Central African 'partners'. Rebellion and intervention in CAR create all sorts of information and impres-sions that people work to interpret. Central African and intervener interpretations are often mirror images of each other. But whose explanation is the real one, and whose is a mirror-distortion, depends on who one is and where one sits – and on the interpretive baggage one brings to the situation.

It is therefore not possible to simply lift the fog by providing more context for everyone involved, as if context were neutral and perceived by all in the same manner. The dynamics of suspicion and interpretation, and the dislike and grievances they can engender, are not easily set aside. For the time being, suspicions – e.g. Central Africans' argument that interveners are plundering and fomenting conflict – are not the source of violence in and of themselves. But in the recent moments when we have seen violence, such as fighting that broke out in September–October 2015, it was the international organizations most widely seen to be plundering/fomenting conflict (and helping Muslims) who were targeted first. This suggests at the very least that it is useful to track and understand these dynamics. People might be able to work together while remaining in important ways quite suspicious of each other, and this has consequences.

Social cohesion and suspicion

Since 2014, a few pleasant-sounding words and phrases started appearing all over CAR – on banners suspended beside the road, in NGO project funding requests, in the speeches of *chefs de village* and armed group leaders alike. 'Social cohesion' was particularly popular, and 'reconciliation' joined it on the dais as ideas it would feel weird to criticize. Publicly, everyone agreed: we need to increase social cohesion, and we need to reconcile. Of course, different people had different ideas about what these terms meant in substantive terms, but most discussions did not get to that level of detail. Certainly no banners did.

As an anthropologist, I found this choice of focus curious. Understanding the bases of social cohesion used to be my discipline's specialty. Whether that particular term was used or 'social equilibrium' was used in its place, it was the starting point for the analysis. The task of anthropology, then, was to figure out through which mechanisms social cohesion was established and maintained. As long as anthropologists were studying 'primitive' societies, few saw the problems with this model. But once we turned to urban sites and other situations where people from different backgrounds come to live together, often with high levels of inequality, its hollowness quickly became apparent.

The shift away from social cohesion is entombed in Max Gluckman's writings. Describing the historical Zulu empire, he referred to the Zulu sense of unity and shared strength as its social cohesion. Turning to mid-twentieth-century South Africa, where apartheid laws were becoming ever more cruel, he looked for social cohesion, his usual starting point. He found no unity or strength. Instead, he found an unjust and unequal society that somehow managed to 'keep going' (1955: 137), and that – 'keeping going' – became his new definition of social cohesion. That was an assessment beige enough to help call into question the idea that something called 'social cohesion' is the basis for all societies.

So instead of being something that one can assume inheres in all societies, social cohesion has become a project to work on, something to improve, just as the flotilla of NGOs in CAR are now working to do. Who could oppose such a goal? It would seem unreasonable to do so. Indeed, this is the appeal of terms like social cohesion. Because they are things no one could reasonably oppose, and their meaning is rarely discussed concretely, they give the illusion that simply talking about them brings them into being.[3]

Buzzwords like these provide a shared language. Everyone can immediately agree on them. At least on a superficial level, everyone *should* immediately agree on them. By being unobjectionable, and almost even shared values, they make it possible for diverse actors to collaborate across the lines of their respective clans, whether those of an armed group, a UN agency, or a local NGO or political party. Everyone can safely attend a football match where the pitch is adorned with banners advocating social cohesion and reconciliation. Maybe they'll even have fun, which is valuable in and of itself after violence and upheaval.

The problem with buzzword-projects like social cohesion and reconciliation is thus not that they are 'bad' goals. It's that they are but a few points of orientation in a landscape that contains a far greater number of contradictory signals, which different people perceive and rank differently. This is not to say that buzzword-projects are therefore false or hollow, just that they do not exist independently of all the other stimuli people are also engaging with, or ignoring.

For well over a century, Central Africans have greeted, and sometimes welcomed, outsiders who have claimed benign purposes. European explorers in the area in the late nineteenth century described the people they met as plump and prosperous (Prioul 1981). Yet over the course of this hundred years or so Central Africans' relative position seems only to have deteriorated, particularly in terms of their sense of occupying a dignified place in the world (Giles-Vernick 1996; Ceriana Mayneri 2014c). When Central Africans look backwards, they now conclude that those purposes were not as benign as was claimed, and this makes them wary at the same time as they feel they have no alternatives to greeting the outsiders, since they see themselves as weaker than the other party. An alternate perspective, more common among interveners, would emphasize that good intentions often go awry. These two interpretive frames are in part enabled and sustained by the different material positions and cultural/ideological inclinations of the people doing the interpreting. Neither is, strictly speaking, wholly wrong or wholly right. There are both good and bad sides to most of the collaborations that have produced the mess in CAR.

Therefore, the truth of a situation or relationship is not to be found in an immediately apparent essence. Rather, in different ways for different people, it must be worked out:

> Truth is what lies under multiple layers of often conflicting meanings. In this hermeneutic encoding of the real, the shifting order of visibility works less as a transparent surface, through which deep intensions and knowledge become accessible, than as a mirror, which mimetically doubles what is in front without giving away what is beyond the reflection. The impossibility of appealing to the truth behind the surface makes contestation an integral aspect of arriving at the truth, despite apparent declarations to the contrary on the part of social actors. (Ferme 2001: 7)

The key aspect here is what Ferme calls the 'hermeneutic encoding of the real': put plainly, it means that being safe and successful in the world requires that everyone be something of an investigator and interpreter, making connections and listening for possible evidence (e.g. rumours). This is, then, a different way of saying that suspicion and mistrust are foundational to social life.

At the same time, however, these processes are not necessarily dedicated to detecting a person's essential nature. People recognize that others behave differently in different settings, and that context plays a crucial role in what a person does and whether he or she can therefore be trusted, or at least worked with. In studying African cities, Hecht and Simone argue that:

> In thousands of small ways, African societies 'play' with visibility – fronting masks when nothing is hidden; deploying stark realities as covers for something more complex or uncertain... Religious convictions, ethnic identifications, distinct world views are very real – allegiances are not merely cynical convenience. Muslims take Islamic law seriously even when they are sharing alcoholic drinks with heathen Dinka hustlers in a car junkyard that serves as a makeshift bar. One set of convictions do not preclude other, seemingly contradictory affiliations from taking place. Every smuggling operation in these shantytowns contains individuals from different national religious and ethnic backgrounds who bring to the operation different external alliances, resources, contacts, and access to competing interests at other levels. (Hecht and Simone 1994: 52–53)

This is the case in CAR too. Even as the international media, diplomats, Central African religious authorities, and others were decrying the 'hatred' that characterized Muslims' and Christians' views of each other, some Christians and some Muslims were working together, such as to provision the southern cities with meat, particularly beef. Typically, 'more than a dozen diverse actors may facilitate the trade of' a cow.

> In CAR today in order for cattle to arrive at market, pastoralists who find themselves IDPs or refugees must continue to communicate with butchers and government personnel who remain in Bangui and who may generally be considered enemies. This communication informs pastoralists of demand, prices, and timing of transport and facilitates financial transactions. (Bingham 2015)

Arguably as important as the cooperation between people actively making this trade happen, many other people saw what was happening and did not object. This then suggests that identity in and of itself (e.g. in this case, religious identity) is not so much a problem as the interplay between identity and particular situations.[4]

Similarly, the prevalence of suspicion as a social practice does not in and of itself prevent people from working together. One means of doing so has been to cultivate orientation points, like those buzzwords, which give people's relationships with each other features that are predictable, even scripted, for the parties involved. This facilitates day-to-day interactions and operations. But they do not remove the other stimuli that foster people's intense suspicions about others' hidden motives, interests, and alliances, which may appear to run counter to the stated objectives of their collaborations. Ultimately, this ensures the maintenance of a distinctly colonial dynamic among the people involved. These kinds of processes have long marked collaborations and conflicts between Central Africans and incomers from elsewhere, but with the massive influx of international interveners post-Seleka they have greatly intensified.

On dislike: an interlude

Before more thoroughly analysing the workings of suspicion among the various people present in CAR, there is another dimension to these dynamics that is too frequently ignored: many of the people involved in rebellion and international intervention quite simply do not like each other. And lest this seem a quaint, lamentable problem of Central Africans, dislike and mistrust have been particularly present among the various interveners present, who, far from forming some kind of unitary 'land' (e.g. 'peaceland'), are actually a fractious crowd of people. In theory, ideally, all on the intervener side are supposed to be neutral, disinterested actors working towards the same goals. For instance, a blue-helmeted peacekeeper is imagined as a wholly different person from a national soldier. But blue helmets are mobilized on national lines. Everyone brings their own interests, friendships, and hostilities to these messy situations. In CAR, peacekeepers have often mistrusted each other and taken steps to prevent their ostensible counterparts from sabotaging them. In March 2014, during a period of intense attacks in Bangui, Sangaris and MISCA troops patrolled the city together. Each contingent had a specific area of operations. Rwandan and Burundian MISCA troops covered Muslim enclaves; French Sangaris troops were more focused on Anti-Balaka areas. That this set them up for allegations of partiality is perhaps inevitable. When peacekeepers are working amid ongoing conflict/hostilities, they will always be participants – even if only as bystanders – and there will always be someone who will disagree with their choices. But in CAR, it was not just people with proclaimed partisan interests who suspected peacekeepers of malfeasance and collusion but the peacekeepers themselves. MISCA officers would meet off-base and with mobile phones off in order to prevent French officers from learning their plans. The MISCA officers explained this policy by claiming that French soldiers warned militants of the peacekeepers' planned operations, allowing them to escape.

Nor was MISCA itself a united entity. At first, both Cameroon and Chad had contributed troops, and there was a real fear that they would fight each other rather than protect the population. Luckily, that did not happen, and the Chadian troops were withdrawn, leaving the Cameroonians to their various business affairs. ('They are *gros businesseurs*,' as many Central Africans put it to me; this is a stereotype, of course, but one with some empirical basis.) While direct confrontations were rare, rumours and allegations flew around privately. For instance, one French officer told me it was 'fucking obvious' that Pakistani MINUSCA troops deployed in Kaga Bandoro were actively supporting Seleka. (Whether they were doing that or not, they could not explain themselves to the local population, with whom they shared no languages.) The French officer had arrived at this assessment due to a number of factors, among them that the Pakistanis' mode of comportment was suspicious. They engaged in none of the pleasantries (the 'hello, how are yous') that French and Central Africans alike saw as necessary features of normal social relations. This did not strike me as a compelling piece of evidence, but it did for the officer, and therein lies a clue as to a difference in our pattern-finding interpretive processes.

Rwanda and France have tense diplomatic relationships, and that manifested in their repeated passive-aggressive interactions as peacekeepers in CAR. For instance, in March 2016 Rwandan and French peacekeepers were to conduct a patrol together. The Rwandan commanding officer told the French commanding officer he should take the lead. The French officer told the Rwandan officer that he could not do that, since Sangaris's mandate is to support MINUSCA, not the other way around. The Rwandan countered that he was indeed in charge and was ordering the French officer and his troops to go first. In the end, no patrol took place.

Humanitarian workers were also often suspicious of one another. For example, on a recent trip to Bangui I participated in a conversation in which two expatriate employees of international humanitarian organizations discussed a confidence that a *chef de quartier* had shared with one of them: more than a dozen girls and young women in a town near the capital had been impregnated by peacekeepers. The circumstances of these pregnancies (rape? intimate relationships?) were unclear. The employees wondered who they should tell. Who could they trust with this information? They discussed various possibilities (including UN officials with 'protection' in their job titles) but were sceptical about whether they would respond appropriately. The job title was one data point, but it was only useful if one also understood its relationship to that person's underlying sympathies and priorities.

In short, in CAR today mistrust is prevalent even among the people who are supposedly working most closely together towards the same goals, and who claim no vested interests other than unassailable ideals like peace and security. In light of this, it is perhaps not surprising that Central African 'beneficiaries' of intervention and humanitarian aid (I'll explain the scare quotes below) are also highly sceptical and suspicious of what these interveners are doing in the country. Looking at their comments reveals what Central Africans think (their largely negative opinions of the aid world) and helps us understand why these kinds of ideas are so insidious and are not immediately cleared up by better or more communication.

Divining the truth

When I speak with Central Africans about the enlarged presence of international organizations and peacekeepers in their midst, they often offer a few linked observations. 'Yes, they [interveners] say they are here to protect people and bring peace,' people would begin, often offering an analysis of their mixed results toward that end and then concluding, 'What are they *really* doing?' The second question would be inspired by that poor record of success. It was also supported by the observation that while peacebuilders say they are present to help altruistically, they are also clearly profiting handsomely from the endeavour. That appears to Central Africans as a set of facts that requires explanation. And one explanation that seems plausible is that though the interveners say their objective is to build peace, doing so would put them out of a job. Therefore, they are really sowing discord in order to keep their jobs longer, and as they do so they continually look for illicit means to augment their official forms of income. In other words, 'what they're really doing' is rapacious plundering. (This is part of a long history of Central African anxiety over their evisceration – socioculturally as well as economically – by foreigners [Ceriana Mayneri 2014c; Marchal 2015a].)

They hear the interveners when they say they are in the country for benevolent purposes (protecting civilians, re-building the state, etc.) But they also see the fleets of giant white vehicles and the new luxury apartment buildings, and these become clues that the lofty NGO discourse is but a pretext for other, more sinister, half-hidden objectives. The gap between what people say and other clues as to their motives becomes background knowledge and also a puzzle that must be explained. So Central Africans investigate, perking up at the mention of any claim as to the cost of the rent for one of those apartments, or the salaries expatriates and peacekeepers earn. And when a story of a connection between a peacekeeper or intervener and a rebel emerges, or when someone witnesses (perhaps from afar) what appears to be a suspicious delivery, these become the missing links – the proof that the interveners' real motive is to foment conflict so that they can keep their jobs. Jobs are immensely hard to come by in CAR, and this contributes to the belief that someone would do whatever necessary to keep his or hers, especially since these intervener jobs seem like such plum ones.

That the primary 'beneficiaries' of aid are the aid-givers themselves cannot be denied. Their salaries are enormous by Central African standards. They drive around, alone save for a driver, in giant vehicles; they eat in fancy restaurants and pay rents in the thousands of dollars each month. The situation in CAR today is so dire that even the relatively down-to-earth, volunteer-ethic NGOs are strikingly well-endowed compared to the majority of Central Africans. These disparities are glaring to Central Africans, but generally taken for granted by the good intentions crowd, who can chalk them up to bureaucratic rules (e.g. security policies that forbid taking taxis and mandate a certain height of wall around a residence) (Smirl 2015). Yet even with all the perks, international organizations find it immensely difficult to staff posts in this benighted country. This can be difficult to discuss openly with Central Africans because it would expose the organizations' bifurcated hiring process to critique: if it is so hard to find expatriates, why not simply hire Central Africans? The ready-made explanation, that Central Africans do not have the requisite skills, is generally not very convincing to Central Africans.

Many aid workers find their position as inadvertent economic overlords uncomfortable, but also part of a far bigger problem: that the world, in all its glory, is also immensely unfair. And it is not a problem that I claim to have solved here. Rather, what interests me about these matters is that we can see in them the different processes of interpretation and pattern-divining and the weighing of evidence (scepticism) that people bring to bear, and how they are informed by material realities, especially material inequalities. While they do not often discuss it openly, people in the good intentions crowd and Central Africans alike agree that expatriates are making good money as a result of their work on the crisis. But how they explain that and what that observation predisposes them to believe diverges drastically.

For instance, consider the following extracts from interviews with members of the community organization 'Sharing Knowledge' in Bangui's Gobongo neighbourhood in March 2016.

Man A:
They [peacekeepers] are complicit in all kinds of things and they engage in business. They have transformed their military logistics in order to secure public transport. My younger brother drives one of the trucks in the military contingent. When they leave for Bossangoa and Bouca to do provisioning on the way back the truck transports people and their merchandise. A Cameroonian lieutenant was able to buy a vehicle from an ex-Seleka. The lieutenant has already sent the vehicle to his home in Cameroon. These people came to suck the blood of Central Africans rather than protect them. Maybe, in order to stay indefinitely sucking Central Africans' blood, it is necessary that the crisis persist.

Concerning the protection of the population, they [the peacekeepers] are there to protect the big stores and they import foreign beer and substitute in this way for the national merchants. They do everything to perpetuate the crisis in all its dimensions. The other problem is that CAR is overflowing with important natural resources that provoke greed on the part of all the people intervening on behalf of Central Africans. This can be seen by the way that the international forces fight against the redeployment of national forces. We Central Africans don't understand the logic of these attitudes [meaning, this isn't right].

Man B:

For me, I am tempted to say that the UN has a hidden plan. Pretty much all the actors [elites] in CAR profit from the crisis. The hidden plan for the UN is to permit different countries to exploit our natural resources and to permit their people who are involved in the management of the crisis to buy gold, diamonds, animal pelts and even parrots. This exploitation is under the cover of the UN and escapes the state's control. Is the UN providing a service to the Central African population or is it putting in place the conditions for the next crises? We do not understand anything in this [again, a statement that these kinds of activities are morally compromised, not to say flat-out wrong].

Nor were these attitudes limited to association members. I heard them from Central Africans of all backgrounds. For instance, a former high-level government employee first stated some tactical problems in terms of how the international forces were operating and then continued, 'These forces have morality problems. They are *businesseurs*. They are buying diamonds, gold, other stuff. They do it openly.' I asked how and where, and he explained, 'The days they get their salaries you will see a whole market develop around their bases. This is from about the twenty-third to the fifth of the month. They are buying all sorts of things, including diamonds. Sometimes they get duped by fraudsters! ... All this peacekeeping is a game in order to give them time to go fishing. It's a good job, and they want it to continue.'

Someone else might observe those markets and think the peddlers were rooking their captive market of peacekeepers, or that this is capitalism at work (people with money buy things from people who have things, and everyone is better off). But for this man, in contrast, the peacekeeper markets were evidence *in and of themselves* that the interveners were nefariously exploiting the country's riches. Again, it is possible that all of these things were going on. A few peacekeepers might be buying illicit goods while many others support the petty-goods and food markets in CAR. That is, it's not that one person is right and another is wrong, but that they bring different frames of interpretation and suspicion to the process of figuring out what is going on.

For instance, another question on people's minds was how the armed group members were able to continue fighting. Who was providing them with ammunition so they could keep shooting? As one association member put it, 'This is palpable in Bambari, where Darassa's [leader of the armed group the Union for Peace in Central African Republic, or UPC] men are supplying minerals to the UN personnel. Everyone is implicated in the purchase of gold from the armed groups in Bambari. Can you imagine through what means those armed groups manage to continue to maintain themselves? That's where and why I can speak of the complicity of the UN.'

This was just one level of profiteering, however. He continued,

This complicity plays out on the diplomatic level as well. The UN does everything for French interests. Why, in knowing the effects of French politics in Africa in general and in CAR in particular, does the UN allow the French forces to work parallel to the blue helmets? I am tempted to call this peace-keeping mission a crisis-keeping mission. If the UN is really guided by principles of humanity and impartiality, we would see them helping Central Africans to force the French to take responsibility for what they have done. The puppetry is no longer a secret. Everyone knows that France and the French are the ones who are making Central African blood flow. We can no longer think in terms of colonizer and colonized – those days are over. And the UN should not accept that France makes Central African blood flow, just because CAR is a French territory. At the UN Security Council, all the decisions are in favour of France. ... Now, the French [soldiers] arrived, and they accentuated the division and hatred which had implications for human displacement, death, etc. That's how I can speak of the complicity of the UN in the CAR crisis. The UN implicitly legitimated the French position in CAR.

Others went even further in blaming France. These accounts emphasized both that France was reaping a profit, and that the country has a sadistic interest in keeping CAR down – that is, that they are not friends in either an economic or a social sense. Consider this analysis from a CAR army captain: 'It's the French who brought this war between Christians and Muslims. They intervened. And then it's gotten worse. People killed Christians right in front of the French [and they did nothing]. And then the French fired on us. It's not good. They themselves [French soldiers] give weapons. It's a reality.' He went on to describe illicit French operations to infiltrate the UN peacekeepers with 250 Peulh[5] fighters they flew in by helicopter (they were given Rwandan uniforms), MINUSCA giving out containers of arms and ammunition at the central mosque at PK5, Bangui's main Muslim neighbourhood and market area, and other actions aimed at continuing the war. They do this, he said, because it allows them to continue exploiting diamonds, gold, and other resources illegally. There is no agency at the airport that checks their planes before they depart, and so they are able to put crate after crate of diamonds and gold into their planes. He had it on the authority of a Cameroonian officer who told him not to collaborate with the French thieves.

The captain's account was far more detailed than those most people gave. He was part of communication networks that alerted him to happenings such as the alleged PK5 arms delivery; on his lap he held a folder full of secret documents. But many Central Africans in the neighbourhoods had similar views, based on their own experiences and networks of information. The idea that the French in particular and expatriates in general are specialists in nefarious, anti-social means of enrichment was part of the background knowledge that helped them interpret what was going on.

Among the good intentions crowd, there are also a range of assumptions that help them filter and make sense of the places where they are working. For instance, Autesserre (2009) calls attention to how the 'post-conflict' frame shaped what information would-be peacebuilders in the Democratic Republic of the Congo deemed relevant, and the initiatives they prioritized as a result. She argues that shifting that frame to include ongoing local-level conflict as a problem could have made their efforts more effective. That may well be the case. But the interviews reproduced above suggest that the problem is not just one of shifting the frame such that it includes things that were previously left out. Most interveners who encounter explanations like those above dismiss them not just because they see them as irrelevant, but because they seem like conspiracy theories. Perhaps interesting in terms of how Central Africans understand the world, but demonstrably false. Though I have often critiqued enduring French colonial attitudes in CAR, I too found exposés like the captain's hard to believe. There are limits to my own relativism as well. What would it take to make me believe the captain? What would it take to make the captain believe that the interveners are not primarily interested in their own personal gain? And what are the stakes of our differing assessments?

Even within an international organization office one can see these processes of differentially weighting particular people's evidence and dismissing others' as people try to establish patterns and explanations. In these organizations there are three main tiers of employee: local staff (people resident near the office, who do not travel with the organization); national staff (Central Africans, usually from Bangui, who travel to take up posts); and expatriate staff (in this category there is an additional permeable tier between expatriates from the region and those from outside Africa). A story gets presented at a meeting. It is unverified. A rumour, in other words. In figuring out what to make of it, expatriates will tend to agree with other expatriates. They will value the evidence and reasoning of other expatriates more than that of local or national Central Africans. One explanation for this is the hierarchical nature of these kinds of organizations: people on top agree with others on top. Another could be racism or a superiority complex. All of these factors are likely at work from time to time. But there is another, more insidious factor: the parameters for scepticism and for sifting through information that people bring to these encounters are different, and people tend to agree with those whose parameters align with their own. Who is right? The information available will always be at once too abundant and too partial. There will always be stories that are impossible to verify, or that appear in multiple versions. In fact, the majority of what you 'know' about what's going on in an area marked by violent conflict and state decay might be subject to multiple versions. How different people fill in the gaps helps structure their relationships as well as whether and to what degree they take each other and each others' concerns seriously. A platitudinous call for better understanding of the 'local context' is all well and good, but *whose* account of the local context counts?

Consider an incident that had captured the attention of people in Bambari, in central CAR, just before I visited in June 2015. It had become known to residents that French peacekeepers had formed an alliance with Ali Darassa and his UPC, the strongest armed group in the town. The first pieces of evidence were the French weapons and ammunition that the Anti-Balaka had recovered from UPC fighters. This was suspicious, but not damning in and of itself. Then a protocol had been found. This document, signed by a French official and the UPC's *secrétaire particulier* at the French embassy in Bangui, detailed a pact to work together against CAR's Christians. People in Bambari immediately drew up a petition demanding that the French peacekeepers leave. Bambari residents led peaceful marches during which people called for the removal of the French forces. When the officer in charge of the Sangaris contingent there saw that the townspeople had obtained the protocol, he was shocked, they reported. He could not believe they had obtained it. When I mentioned the protocol to an expatriate civilian staffer at the MINUSCA office in Bambari he brushed it aside. The document was obviously fake, he said. He knew so because it was replete with grammatical errors no self-respecting French diplomat would ever allow, and because the formatting was not credible for a formal document. Such elements were part of the parameters of his scepticism. However, they did not enter into the analysis of people in Bambari who had in almost all cases never used a computer.[6]

Perhaps these analytical differences seem like minor issues, which could easily be clarified with a little more 'ground-truthing', as some quantitative researchers describe their fieldwork. They would likely not show up on interveners' lists of the most pressing problems they face. Interveners might instead mention the perennial shortage of the human and material resources necessary to succeed at the tasks assigned to them – the paradigmatic bureaucratic explanation for shortcomings, but not necessarily wrong for that. In fact, that kind of a complaint reveals the nub of the problem: both interveners and Central Africans are interested in the resources available to interveners, but the conclusions they draw are mirror opposites. For interveners, more people and resources would allow them to end conflict; for Central Africans, greater resources and more people would bolster their sense that interveners foment conflict in order to get rich. Both are fixated on the fact that the other sees a mirror image and not the real thing, and in this way the mirror becomes a fixation that both connects them and divides them. And the problems arising from these different processes of interpretation and drawing conclusions in a context marked by suspicion are not overcome by communication or proximity alone. We can shift the frames through which we perceive things – doing so is a big part of learning. But the processes of sifting, interpreting, being sceptical, and deciding what requires explanation are not so easily changed. They are a part of the baggage and assumptions we carry with us as a result of life experiences, the situations we have been in, and our material statuses.

For instance, though an intervener might be drawn to see natural beauty in Central Africa and might appreciate her or his friendships and work relationships with Central Africans, few investigate how governance and social life work in the country. Instead, they assume – or rather, they *know*, since from their perspective it is fact, not conjecture – that government-elite corruption (in a broad sense) is a main reason for CAR's problems. This makes them suspicious of their Central African interlocutors' ulterior motives. They are sure the ways that Central African politicians and functionaries engage with them is superficial compared to what they do and think in other arenas, such as among them--selves, and that they are primarily interested in accumulating money and power. MINUSCA civilian staff, for example, shook their heads at Transitional President Samba-Panza's naming of a shadow cabinet – a series of presidential advisers that were as numerous as and in some cases more influential than those in the official government. This made it difficult to know what was really going on, how decisions were being made, and who really had the power and influence to make things happen.

These mirror-interpretations find perfect expression in the case of Joseph Bindoumi, who was named minister of defence in the Samba-Panza government at the end of October 2015. Bindoumi occupied several roles: president of the follow-up committee for the Bangui Forum, a deputy in the transitional assembly, and head of the Central African Human Rights League, in addition to his ministerial post. One of his first actions was to activate a network of FACA soldiers – some retired, others former Anti-Balaka, others regular soldiers who had not been working since Seleka's takeover. Rather than work through the ministerial hierarchy as protocol theoretically requires (that is, using the *chef d'état major* as his go-between), he went directly to the soldiers. He paid them a supplement (they were already getting their salary) so they would operate checkpoints in the neighbourhoods. Central Africans rich and poor, young and old, men and women, all credited these soldiers with restoring some security in the neighbourhoods, such that they could stay out late (until 22:00 or 23:00), a sign of ease and normality that they had not been able to enjoy for a long time. More educated people characterize the FACA as *'faux sérieux'* (people who could easily turn against the population), but most people simply credited Bindoumi with putting in place a policy that finally allowed them to relax.

The FACA checkpoints gave Central Africans the sense that national institutions could work, and work even better than international ones – a glimmer of pride amid the humiliation they have long felt, and their all-too-acute awareness that CAR brings up the rear in pretty much any world ranking of states. From the expatriate perspective, in contrast, these checkpoints were primarily a sign of Bindoumi's political acumen (to exploit popular sentiment), and secondarily about creating opportunities for soldiers to racketeer as much as or more than actual provision of security. Their sentiments fell more on the spectrum of eye-rolling or annoyance – clearly Bindoumi was just exploiting popular sentiment in the service of his own aggrandizement. And indeed, Bindoumi might show one face to donors and another to people in Bangui neighbourhoods. But this does not mean one is true and the other false, even if to some extent they contradict each other. This is part of what Hecht and Simone are driving at in saying that Africans 'play with visibility'. But this is not a peculiarly African trait; people in the good intentions crowd do the same.

The mirror that divides as it unites and the ways people show different faces to different people make it difficult to 'get to the bottom of things'. But this difficulty does not extinguish people's desire to do so. So people come up with ways to figure out things about the world that are not immediately apparent, but which may in fact explain it all. One of the main sources of anxiety and interest in this respect is the question of who is ultimately in control. From the Central African perspective, this question is asked in the form of 'who is so intent on immiserating and humiliating CAR?' For interveners, it is expressed more as a frustration about how difficult it is to get anything done ('who is responsible for ensuring progress?').

Who is in charge?

Indeed, who *is* pulling the strings in CAR? (And why?) The president cannot implement his/her own programme, because he/she requires financial and other support from donors, whether regional/bilateral or international, to do so. MINUSCA, the World Bank, and the European Union also cannot undertake their own programmes: they must do so through the Central African government. Diplomatic actors with historically important roles (Chad, France) can be the decisive voices in whether a president stays or goes, but in certain respects they are beholden to their Central African counterparts. The truth is that no one, and everyone, is in control: that is, everyone is entangled in relationships with each other, making it impossible to tease out any single sovereign actor. This means that authorities are plurally held, but ultimate responsibility (accountability) is accordingly difficult to assign. This is among the puzzles that implicitly bedevils the superficially unobjectionable goal of 'fighting impunity'.[7]

For expatriate staff of international organizations, concerns about who is in charge are subordinate to the day-to-day demands of their jobs. That is one of the consequences of bureaucracy without sovereignty: it creates its own logics and its own demands, such that bigger political/justice questions recede into the background and become nearly impossible to address (Banbury 2016; Feldman 2008). But for Central Africans, the question of who is ultimately in charge, and its twin, who is really profiting from this state of affairs, are among the foremost questions they feel must be answered. Again from Central Africans' perspective, the litany of suspicious, if not damning, incidents and practices perpetrated by foreigners lengthens by the day. There is a human tendency to seek explanations to the problems that ail us.

As in the case of the FACA captain described above, most people fall back on France as the ultimate author of CAR's immiseration. But international organizations and humanitarians have also been added to the list. One humanitarian INGO brought in a psychologist after the September–October 2015 violence in Bangui for trauma counselling with all the staff. Many among the national staff said the INGOs and MINUSCA were ultimately at fault for the violence, because they were inciting violence in order to retain their jobs and continue illicitly exploiting CAR's 'riches' (diamonds, gold, ivory, etc.).

Hearing this kind of reasoning from their own staff can be a sobering, not to say frustrating, moment for expatriate interveners. After all, the national staff are among the main beneficiaries of these organizations' presence, in the form of relatively well-paid jobs. But these employees' impulse was *still* to wonder about the nefarious, violence-fostering dealings that humanitarian organizations might be involved in and which they had mostly, but not wholly, managed to obscure. If *even they* held these views, what must those Central Africans not employed by any organization think? One major study assessed the barriers humanitarians face in doing their work and found that the main obstacle was that Central Africans simply did not want the humanitarians, whose assistance they saw as derisive, and whose presence seemed to increase conflict rather than diminish it (Norwegian Refugee Council 2015).

But in certain respects Central African and interveners' perspectives are not as wholly opposed as they might at first seem. After all, interveners often analyse Central African politicians' actions as stemming from a desire to retain their plum posts above all else. This appears to them as 'fact', just as for the Central Africans who consider that whatever token endeavours interveners do on behalf of the common good, they are primarily interested in retaining their own well-paid and well-perked jobs.

This leads to a few conclusions, none of which provide a clear policy prescription but all of which are important. The first is simply that, as I've argued throughout this book, everyone working and living in CAR is part of the same social ecosystem. There are many arenas within that social ecosystem, but ultimately looking at any one of them as if it could be separated from the whole is at best an analytical fiction, and at worst a distortion of what is going on. Another is a call to recognize the central role mistrust plays in the CAR social ecosystem. Suspicion can be useful. But failure to investigate its parameters creates gulfs among the various people ostensibly working toward the same ends, whose pattern-finding interests and skills diverge. In this manner they are divided by the manner of their cooperation, and this can foster anger and grievance in ways that in the past have facilitated violence.

'Crisis' in CAR – an inaccurate term to the extent it implies that the past three years have been an aberrant part of CAR's sad history, rather than the intensification of deeply-rooted problems – has occasioned a vastly expanded international presence in the country. The days of DDR described in Chapter 3 seem quaint. As Benoit Lallau, a French agrarian studies scholar, put it upon return to CAR after a few years away,

I have discovered a new tropical disease (that I have already managed to catch, not bad): the indigestion of 'petits blancs' (they can be black too…). All this little world at the bedside of Central Africans, all these fresh off the boat NGOs, all these evaluation missions, all these gleaming white (UN) vehicles, all this dough to spend, all the lessons to give, all these procedures that cut off contact with the population. I have never seen the like in the 25 years I've known this country. People's situation better improve quickly, otherwise it's the whole population that will complain of this indigestion. And in that case, watch out for convulsions…[8]

Some expatriates might complain: other organizations act that way, but not ours/me. And that may well be the case. Central Africans differentiate among NGOs, recognizing the differing approaches of both organizations and the individuals who comprise them. With the government not particularly functional over the past few years, the raft of newly arriving NGOs set up shop with limited knowledge of CAR's laws and few people to help them. Many, perhaps inadvertently, flouted the law. But ultimately, we are all part of the same social ecosystem, and we will be associated with what others like us do. This of course is true of Central Africans as it is of interveners.

A third, and final, point is that these problems are not wholly overcome by either better communication strategies or more context. Context is not like a fruit, ready to be plucked. Communication and context are themselves embedded in the ways people try to observe patterns among pieces of information under conditions of uncertainty, mistrust/suspicion, and jealousy,[9] as well as structural-relational factors that shape what they can and cannot do.

People for the most part do not present the allegations and theories described in this chapter to each other's faces. Doing so would prevent them from doing anything together. And given their shared commitments to *doing something* – that is, to the modes of intervention that can be mustered for a place like CAR (which everyone agrees are far from perfect, but which are what we've got) – they all need each other.

This means that the problems of CAR will not be solved by more information. In fact, people already have a lot of information, even if it falls primarily on the suspicion side of the factual spectrum. If a MINUSCA staffer *knew more* about the shady dealings of a government minister – say, for the sake of example, the minister of justice – that might change certain elements of how she/he interacted with the minister, but it would be less likely to change her/his assessment that the country needs judicial-sector reform and that this necessitates working with the ministry. At the same time as it is difficult to muster money and staffers for CAR, it is also difficult to totally abandon it to its own fate. The vehicle for engaging remains 'the state', an ideal type organized in a particular way: elections, ministries, an army, etc. Twenty years of this mode of engagement have not yielded much for CAR. In the conclusion, I suggest a different vision, a change of emphasis that could fundamentally shift the country's path.

CONCLUSION

One of the more disquieting conclusions to which thinking about the new states [the postcolonial world] and their problems has led me is that such thinking is rather more effective in exposing the problems than it is in uncovering solutions for them. There is a diagnostic and remedial side to our scientific concern with these societies, and the diagnostic seems, in the very nature of the case, to proceed infinitely faster than the remedial. Therefore, one result of very extended, very thorough, periods of careful research is usually a much keener realization that the new states are indeed in something of a fix. The emotion this sort of reward for patient labors produces is rather like that I imagine Charlie Brown to feel when, in one 'Peanuts' strip, Lucy says to him: 'You know what the trouble with you is Charlie Brown? The trouble with you is you're you.' After a panel of wordless appreciation of the cogency of this observation, Charlie asks: 'Well, whatever can I do about that?' and Lucy replies: 'I don't give advice. I just point out the roots of the problem.' (Geertz 1968: 142)

Of all the discussions I have had about the recursiveness of rebellion in Central Africa, one from early 2010 stands out. I was in the northern town of Kaga Bandoro and had been chatting all morning with Anicet, an older Central African man working for an international humanitarian organization there. Since 2005 Kaga Bandoro had been controlled by a rebel group.

Earlier in his life Anicet had worked as a pastor and for the national sugar production company. He had adapted based on the few opportunities available, and he had also tried to start projects on his own. Now, in addition to his INGO post, he had launched an initiative to help youth get steady employment and to encourage people to care for the elderly. Too often, he said, people would cast off the aged as soon as they could no longer contribute material sustenance to the household. So many people were on the precipice between getting by and falling hard, and that compounded what he saw as some Central Africans' cultural disposition to look out for oneself first. Anicet worried, moreover, that a 'rebellion mentality' had set in, both in Kaga Bandoro and many other parts of the country. Given how few opportunities youth have to make cash livelihoods, he said that rebellion has become a 'way of getting money, of finding work, and of expressing oneself. … It's a vicious circle.'

Anicet was also eager to learn from me. We spent a long time discussing Marcel Mauss's classic sociological theory about the gift and reciprocity. Anicet asked whether I had any books or brochures on anthropology, and specifically on the issue of the bases of social cohesion, that he could take and read. He was hoping to find ways to increase solidarity and decrease the self-interestedness that he had diagnosed in those around him. But he also felt that changing things in CAR would require a complete overhaul, not a piecemeal approach. He asked, 'Tell me, based on all of your studies, do you think a real revolution is possible?'

This, for me, was a difficult question. When one is attuned to the ways that history leaves marks on the present, and particularly the fraught remnants of colonialism (Stoler 2013), even those uprisings labelled 'revolutions' fall short of bringing about a truly clean slate. At the time, my response to Anicet meandered. Effectively, I said 'No, but don't give up hope.' I was unsatisfied with the response, and I expect he was as well.

The years since have only borne out Anicet's observations about a rebellion mentality and the damaging effects of violence on Central African lives and psyches. These years have not made it any easier for me to respond to his query with an unequivocal 'yes'. However, I have come to think that I was approaching it too literally.

In this book, I have shown how as the institutions ostensibly governing people and territory in this centre of Central Africa have become more corrupted, people have yearned ever more fervently for a state that fulfils certain ideals. This is the case both for Central Africans and for the incoming interveners. Despite all this fervent attachment to the state as an idea, the state as expressed through its actual institutions and capacities has remained a 'work in regress'. The state has become a node of anomie: desire made limitless because progress towards it is impossible to discern. It would be tempting, therefore, to suggest that all this attention to the state as an ideal is a form of false consciousness, or cruel optimism (Berlant 2011) – an object of immense hope and yearning that is in fact an obstacle to one's flourishing.

However, there are a few problems with trying to argue away the importance of the state. One is that for all the long-standing problems with the CAR state, it has worked in the past to some degree. So when people aspire to an ideal, they do so based both on an imagining of what could, in an ideal world, be in the future, and also on recent memories of less-straitened times. Thus when people speak of the ideal state, they are expressing not just a desire for a revolution – as Anicet phrased it – but also a desire for a state that simply works perceptibly better than what they have become used to. That is, in CAR today, the state is both an eidolon – a haunting, phantom-like ideal – *and* a collective project made all the more urgent because Central Africans feel that the road of history is leading them in the wrong direction.

Another problem is simply the question of where aid and development efforts would be focused if not upon 'the state'. Perhaps a massive corps of people like Anicet, working in a genuinely grass-roots way, could have significant effects in CAR. But whether in CAR or elsewhere, there are few like Anicet. INGO staff and humanitarians have been reading development methods guru

Robert Chambers's (1983) calls for a more grassroots approach to their field for thirty-five years, with arguably little overall effect. 'Local ownership' is far more often celebrated than achieved in a substantive way. Moreover, on a local level, despite how fervently people call for the state to strongly establish itself, actual attempts to regulate and control are often met with great hostility (Lombard 2015, 2016a). At the very least, Central Africans' feelings about regulation and control are complicated and ambivalent.

When I discuss the dilemma of how to work if not through the state with interveners, they respond with a different concern, namely the problem of how many different actors are part of these peace-building or state-building efforts and the need for their efforts to be at least formally aligned. For instance, during a conversation at the French Ministry of Defence in July 2015, one of the officers present listened patiently to my critique of using far-off state ideals as the basis for projects and other policies. He challenged that those ideals are necessary for the coordination of international and Central African efforts. Without them, how could so many different people possibly work together?

These problems are not easily dismissed. And they lead to a conclusion: that the problem is not the inappropriateness of the state as a form of social organization and governance for Central Africa, but the ways that a rigid set of state ideals has come to stand in the place of any more grounded understanding of what the state currently is and what it could be in CAR.

The rigidity of state ideals as a basis for policy and working together also makes it impossible to capitalize on organic state-building initiatives. For instance, Ali Darassa, leader of the UPC in Bambari, developed a system for taxing long-distance trade in the area. The UN mission in Bambari objected, since it thought the state should be the only one collecting taxes. Peacekeepers were thus dispatched to the roadblock where taxes were to be collected to make sure the state officials they had flown to this post would collect the official taxes. But Darassa continued to tax on the road, meaning that truckers had to pay twice, a crippling sum. In the end, Darassa and state officials worked out a deal: state agents would collect the taxes, and a portion would be given to him and his men for providing security in the area. Diplomats (those paying for the UN mission) refused to accept this kind of arrangement, however. Darassa was sidelined. From these diplomats' perspective, *the state* was the only legitimate regulator/taxer. However, this is an exceptionally blinkered view, given that it was only because of the UN mission's presence that those state actors were able to do anything at all. Similarly, the UN mission would regularly fly government officials to their rural posts because it was so important that 'the state' be present in these places. But the differentiation of state and intervener in this sense is at best an analytical fiction. In these durably fragile places, it is impossible to speak of 'the state' and 'international intervention' as if they could be separated from each other. They exist only through the relationships that entangle them. By focusing on a far-off, rigid, ideal state, as if it could be separated from the actions and presence of the interveners themselves, peacebuilders make intervention itself indispensable, and even permanent, rather than something temporary that actively seeks its own redundancy.

So what are the alternatives, particularly if one is not satisfied with simply withdrawing all aid and other international support?

Saving the state

A first suggestion is analytical-methodological. It concerns being alert to how the interpretive frames one brings to bear are never neutral, and therefore probing both how people understand themselves and how their relationships and interactions with one another structure what they do and why. For instance, to call someone an 'external' actor masks how central she is – whether in a good way or a bad way – to constituting the mess in CAR. Therefore, rather than looking at the various corporate groups working on the problem of CAR as if they existed unto themselves, we must look at their intersections – the cross-cutting ties that simultaneously link and divide them.

A critic might counter that such holism is ideal, but rarely achievable. I agree. But there is a solution. Start with particular social situations. Alert to the roles and positions of everyone present, ask: how do the parameters of their actions and interactions arise? And what are the effects? A social interaction or ritual can be a point of orientation allowing one to range outward, following people and dynamics as the changing situations demand, without getting lost. In this respect, Gluckman's bridge essay (1940) remains an admirable example.

A second suggestion moves into the realm of policy. To the extent that interveners want to actually enact a state along lines that resonate with Central Africans' conception of the proper order of the world, and to the extent that all involved want to find a way to make the country's history an asset rather than an obstacle, they will have to fully embrace a politics of distribution. When Central Africans express nostalgia – in its literal sense of a painful homecoming (quite apt in this place where history is conceived of spatially) – for the state, it evokes a past when the state distributed status, in the form of government jobs and their associated salaries. This is arguably the one aspect of the state that is not contentious: the ability it has to make people entitled, rather than ignorable, with entitlement in large part measurable in the material form of a salary (Lombard 2016b).

State-building and peacebuilding initiatives, as planned by interveners and their CAR government counterparts, have quite a different emphasis. They tend to divide the world into states, which provide certain services, and economies, which produce goods, and therefore also jobs and money. However, this conception is blind to the realities of Central Africa, where there has never been much in the way of a private economy, and where, owing to the legacies of the concessionary system, the whole public/private distinction arguably does not hold anyway.

Central Africans tend to conceive of the proper order of the world, and of the future, not as a matter of increasing economic production so much as increasing material distribution, in the form of state jobs/salaries. As described in the chapter on the histories of rebellion, having a job in CAR is less about what one produces, and more about the entitled status it confers. In this way of thinking, the crucial task for the government is thus to distribute status, rather than to foster a market economy imagined as autonomous from the government.

In the African context, distribution-oriented worldviews have often been described as patrimonial, or neopatrimonial. In this context, 'patrimonial' is often a synonym or explanation for personalized, corrupt practices whereby some are granted material favour at the expense of others. It is thus often invoked as a pathology or otherwise a reason for the failure of African states and economies to fulfil rational-bureaucratic and capitalist ideals, respectively. For instance, in a May 2016 post about policy recommendations for the new CAR government, the International Crisis Group's Thibault Lesueur wrote that it is necessary to break with 'the patrimonialization of power, which has contributed, for thirty years, to the decomposition of the Central African state and the economic fabric' (Lesueur 2016; my translation).

There are multiple problems with this way of thinking, including that it distorts Max Weber's foundational discussion of patrimonialism, which emphasized that patrimonialism is first and foremost a reciprocal system of distribution (Pitcher et al. 2009). 'Nepotism', the lavishing of public goods only on one's family and cronies, would have been a more apt term for Lesueur's context. More fundamentally, it gives the impression that prioritizing distribution reflects a desire for an archaic and fundamentally flawed political-economic mode. At least in the CAR context, in contrast, it is precisely this kind of status distribution that Central Africans see as the primary writ of the modern state. They would agree that distribution has become a mode of nepotism, but not that distribution as such is a drain on both the state and the economy. That is, for Central Africans, distribution is not a traditional, outdated, or otherwise unfit mode of governance. It is a major dimension to people's experience of the good side of living in a state, all the more important given that there has never been much in the way of capitalist production (labour, wages, etc. that do not in some way stem from government or parastatal efforts).

So what if, rather than puffing up the CAR state so that it expands to fulfil certain rational-bureaucratic and territorial ideals, such as by continuously blowing air into ministries despite their many holes (INGOS will continue for the foreseeable future to provide the bulk of social services regardless), the focus for peace- and state-building lay instead on letting the state – an amalgam of national and international actors – assign status through distribution? This could occur through salary provision, and it could also occur through basic income grants of some form. Status and entitlement are after all not just about one's material position and possessions. They are also fundamental to being able to live in a dignified manner. The details of such a proposition would need to be defined. But as it stands, the idea that the state might primarily be a jobs/income provider is not even considered appropriate for debate, and that at the very least needs to change, given how important job/status provision is to Central Africans' understandings of the good that states can do.

Peacebuilding and state-building interventions begin to recognize the centrality of distribution when they focus on 'make-work' projects like high-intensity labour initiatives (road maintenance, building rehabilitation, etc.) or 'cash transfers' or distribution of basic household necessities like jerry cans. The problem with these initiatives is that they focus on people's need for money in a narrow economic sense, rather than its fuller social sense, which includes not just the ability to buy things but also *status* and being *at ease as an entitled person*, rather than being an ignorable peon. Moreover, they are always imagined as stopgaps. In a long-term sense, this reasoning goes, they are unsustainable. They are explicitly imagined to be temporary hand-outs, meant to get people on their feet so they can stand alone. Because of this conception, and because it is clear that the interveners are always benefiting more, no matter how much money is given or spent it generally only appears derisory to Central Africans.

This is particularly the case given how apparent it is to Central Africans that such a large portion of interveners' spending is oriented toward their own entitlements – to salaries and other perks, which, to the extent they are considered at all by the organizations distributing them, are not seen as 'unsustainable' over the long term. What I am suggesting, in other words, is that rather than imagining that the future will bring about some dramatically altered reality – a service-providing, border-controlling state; a job-providing economy – a real revolution in Central Africans' experiences of life and their place in the world would be more likely if interveners first made a commitment to supporting people materially, and proceeded organically from there. The commitment aspect would, hopefully, re-introduce some of the reciprocity that has been in such steady decline since the state stopped being able to provide people with status through salaries. Even though the goal of interventions should be to make themselves obsolete, they never quite manage to do so. Making a commitment to distribution and status would recognize that interveners' role in CAR will likely be long term. Acknowledging this could then change the nature of their role to place the emphasis more thoroughly on Central Africans' immediate needs for material dignity.

Of course, a politics of distribution would raise a plethora of new challenges. One that immediately comes to mind is the difficulty of assessing who is properly Central African, and thus deserving of entitled largesse, given how fraught the question of nationality and foreignness has become. This is a real concern, and it would have to be handled with great care. While delicate, however, it could also usefully give substance to much-needed debates around nationality in CAR, which have to date been dominated by platitude-buzzwords and/or vitriolic statements.

A thoroughgoing politics of distribution and an emphasis on status and entitlements would also not directly address the problem of impunity after years of violence. However, seeking to end impunity is ultimately a quest for values backed by reciprocity and accountability that goes beyond simple judicial punishment. And in that sense, a status-dignity commitment could ultimately prove more useful than a raft of trials or a reconciliation commission. It could also offer a way out of the international actors' inconsistent self-conception – that is, the way they alternately see themselves as incidental (we are only flying government officials around) and as crucial (there would be nothing here without us).

An accountant might add an additional critique: that there simply isn't enough money to provide Central Africans with income grants/salaries over the long term. It would, it is true, require a re-organization of international funding mechanisms. But in the end it could prove less expensive than unending interventions that are conceived of as short term but which end up being at best an 'accordion' – alternately expanding and contracting, but always necessary (Picco 2015). This is particularly so since the shift in emphasis would require less expatriate expertise and logistics, which carry immense costs for limited benefit to the intervention's ultimate goals.

In closing

In this book, I've advocated expanding analysis beyond the narrow conceptions of efficacy (e.g. are rebellion and international inter-vention good or bad?) and quests for the origins of state 'failure' that predominate in studies of the peace-kept world (Ghosh 1994). Instead, I've explored the changing roles of violence in helping to constitute an emerging African state over a long term (150 years), a state that has always been a product of collaborations and conflicts between people resident in the area and interventions by incomers from elsewhere. Doing so has demonstrated the limits of 'state collapse' frameworks, which rely on an unspoken assumption that colonial states worked in ideal-type ways, and that only postcolonial stupidity has caused them to stray from Weberian perfection. In other words, while agreeing that African sovereignty has long been outsourced (granted to and secured by people who do not consider themselves members of the polity [Englebert 2009]), and government never solely a prerogative of 'the state' (Mann 2014), I have turned to what that means in terms of entangled relations of governance among the various people involved, particularly as regards structural inequalities and their effects.

However, it is not enough to conclude, as Lucy might have, above, that the problem with CAR is that it is CAR. Relying as it does on goodwill and collaboration between researcher and the researched, ethnography demands balancing analytical detachment with moral engagement, or cultivation of what Geertz termed 'a kind of caring resilient enough to withstand an enormous tension between moral reaction and scientific observation' (1968: 158). And while that tension is a stress, it is also precisely what makes the whole endeavour worthwhile.

In that spirit, this book argues, ultimately, for taking seriously the challenges of dignity and status in one of the poorest places in the world, and recognizing how current modes of intervention – in which Central Africans and incomers alike participate, though on unequal terms – complicate those challenges all the more. By pulling apart the usual categories of analysis ('the state', 'external', 'internal'), I have striven to provoke in such a way as to inspire new ways of approaching how to help Central Africa.

I do not know what the future holds for CAR, even as I have detailed the changing contours of its long-standing tendencies. Together with others concerned about and committed to this place and its people, I hold tight to the hope of a more peaceful and prosperous future, however unlikely it has seemed at certain dark points in recent years. Perhaps there will be no revolution, in the narrow sense of the term I initially used to interpret Anicet's question. But there are many other possible outcomes that could (re-)instate a more dignified position in the world for Central Africans.

NOTES

Introduction

1   The country's most valuable resource is water – something people in the region themselves need and use, and that is becoming more scarce – but it is often left off these lists.

2   The definitive account of the concessionary period is Catherine Coquéry-Vidrovitch's masterful *Le Congo au temps des grandes compagnies concessionnaires* (1972).

3   Some Christians, particularly Igbo from Nigeria, run shops as well but they are a minority.

4   See Geschiere (1997) and Pietz (1985) for a discussion of the problems with terms like 'witchcraft' and 'sorcery', particularly in African contexts.

5   For a longer-term analysis of the ups and downs of humanitarian aid flows to CAR, see Picco (2015).

1 Conflict and the state

1   United Nations Peacebuilding Support Office in CAR. It became BINUCA (an 'integrated' office) in January 2010.

2   The makeup of the good intentions crowd changes. In terms of donor and diplomatic presences, some of the most important actors have been (in no particular order) the United Nations, the European Union, regional organizations and regional heads of state, including the African Union, the World Bank and IMF, and France. In terms of work carried out on the ground, the United Nations has by far the largest footprint. Dozens of humanitarian organizations have joined the crowd as well, coming and going as budgeting priorities permit.

3   Doctors Without Borders (Médecins Sans Frontières) is the most reflective and critical about this state of affairs, and does the most to tackle it. But it, too, must often respect the state order in ways it ultimately deems counter-productive (Magone et al. 2011).

2 The nativeness of 'foreign' violence

1   Since late 2012, scores of journalists and other newcomers to understanding CAR have called me to fill in context for them. I've found their questions and

formulations – especially the naive ones – useful to think with. For instance, one journalist explained the set-up of his article: CAR is so rich in natural resources (diamonds, uranium, timber, water, land); how could a place with so many advantages fall into such a brutal war? Indeed, how could it? Well, there are indeed resources in CAR, but, like 'Central African culture' they do not exist in their own bounded bubble. They are subject to the same unequal position in the world and cost-benefit calculations that everything else in CAR is. Armed violence has frequently accompanied that unequal position, both in the colonial era, when spectacular displays of punishment were a way for colonial officers to govern on the cheap (Lombard and Batanga-Kinzi 2015), and today, when only armed violence draws much sustained international attention to the predicament of people here.

2   Gentil is often called an explorer, and Sanusi a sultan. But these terms have racial connotations that make it harder to see the similarities in the two men's orientations toward the world. For that reason, I use adventurist, for its close connection to adventurism, a willingness to take risks in business dealings, broadly construed, especially abroad, which aptly describes both men.

3   However, this position was always precarious, as I explore in a book manuscript currently in preparation.

4   Mollion (1992) has written the definitive history of the tragic history of porterage in CAR. In a book manuscript in preparation, I further explore the effects of manhunt-as-governance.

5   See Coquéry-Vidrovitch (1972, 2014) for a full account of these investigative efforts and their findings.

6   They already held tightly to the idea that development failures stem from technical rather than political problems: in a 1907 article, French administrator-scholar Pierre Prins (1907) related the story of some Americans who had taken Cuban refugees to Central Africa in order to impart superior peanut-farming techniques. It was a disaster. Most of the Cubans died from the diseases to which they were unaccustomed, and the Africans assumed they were slaves, thus confirming their understanding that whites were slavers first and foremost.

7   See Autesserre (2009) for discussion of how the neo-Hobbesian bias misled would-be peacebuilders in the Congo, with negative consequences for peace.

8   Abel Goumba (1926–2009) was an associate of independence leader Barthélemy Boganda. He had been vice president and prime minister just prior to independence. Later, he burnished his reputation for a commitment to democracy and integrity by speaking out against presidents' abuses, and was at various points *persona non grata* in CAR. During these periods of exile he worked as a medical doctor. He briefly served as prime minister just after Bozizé took power in 2003.

9   In certain respects, this shift is not as great as it might at first seem, since old actors tend to dominate these new forums. For instance, France is often a

driving force behind the EU's CAR policy. This is not always for self-interested reasons. It can also simply be because no one else wants to take on CAR's challenges, and everyone expects France to raise a metaphorical hand first.

10 To give just one example: the expatriate head of mission of a bilateral aid project discovered the adjunct minister working with the project submitted a range of un-allowed expenses to the project, related to a trip to South Africa to attend a conference. The receipts included some for baby clothes and electronics, which the head of mission refused. The adjunct minister threatened to block the project. The head of mission's boss arrived for a week-long visit to see how things were going. He told the head of mission to accept the receipts. What was the use of standing on principle when it would compromise the project in multiple ways (the minister would block them, and the harmonious relations the organization wanted to project would be disrupted) and hence also the organization's shot at renewed funding? Extraversion has real consequences for interpersonal relationships, hierarchies, and integrity, as different priorities and values meet and end in compromise, given that oversight is either absent or faraway.

3 Mobility as power

1 Ethnic group might be something of a misnomer, though, because the Banda are a highly diverse assortment of people, jostled together into one over-arching category by having all fled to the same region during the trans-Saharan raiding processes and having formed new solidarities in its wake, such as in the form of uniting militarily against the raiders.

2 Harri Englund (2006) has argued that the elite/non-elite distinction is too simplistic. He argues that in order to understand how these hierarchies become tenacious, we must also look to the would-be elites, who can be even more hardline in their production and reproduction of these hierarchies. With that point taken, what I have elsewhere (Lombard 2012) referred to as a bifurcation is really a spectrum from powerful/elite to powerless/non-elite. I refer to it as a bifurcation to emphasize how it can feel like a total exclusion to those who are on the powerless side of that spectrum.

3 In Bangui, there is much talk of the need for 'the next generation' to take over, and though this is generally meant in a non-specific sense, it could also be interpreted quite literally: much of the political class consists of the sons of formerly-prominent politicians. Politics is a hereditary profession in Central Africa.

4 Long and short histories of rebellion

1 For instance, though his movement is often described as a Gbaya undertaking, people of other ethnic groups joined as well. While also described as of a particular region, people inspired by him were active in a range of places.

Workers' rights activists saw in Karnu a warrior against unfair labour regimes. Christians saw him as a human vessel channelling God.

2   Interestingly, cotton production eventually became a source of power. When Bierschenk and Olivier de Sardan (1997) conducted research in the cotton-growing hub of northwestern CAR in the late 1990s, they found that the leaders of locally-based cotton growing associations were among the most powerful people present because they had the ability to compel people to pay dues, unlike all the other officials.

3   Jean-Bédel is a contraction of the children's textbook *Jean-Baptiste de la Salle*.

4   As president, Patassé had been starving the army, which he did not trust, in favor of the Presidential Guard and a range of militias.

5   See Lombard (2016a) for more examples of the threats and hiding that are central to these processes.

6   In the international division of labour, international agencies must defer to states when violence is 'criminal'; such violence is generally considered the state's responsibility, even though many states neglect that role. Explicitly state-challenging violence, on the other hand, creates opportunities for international mediation and programming.

7   'Codo' is slang for commando, and Mbakara is the name of a poisonous snake.

8   I am grateful to Sylvain Batianga-Kinzi for his unparalleled research on this history, which he generously shared with me. The Presidential Guard was officially integrated into the armed forces under Patassé, but both during his tenure and that of his successor, Bozizé, it operated substantially autonomously, under the president's direct control.

9   Born Martin Koumta Madji to a Chadian father and a Central African mother and raised in a Chadian town near the Central African border ('*miskine*' means poor, and it was the affectionate epithet by which he became known since his father died when he was young [Debos 2008]), he became the leader of a group of road robbers operating largely in northwestern CAR. When Patassé felt his hold on power slipping, he drew on Miskine and his men, giving them a new name, the *Batallion de sécurité territoriale* (Territorial Security Batallion) and officially making them a part of the army (Berman with Lombard 2008). He fled following Patassé's ouster and risked indictment by the International Criminal Court (ICC) for his group's crimes. He lived for a time in the Middle East, or so rumour had it, while his men remained in a kind of purgatory along the Chad/ CAR border. (They often had trouble raising him on the phone/Thuraya.) Then, in January 2007, Miskine appeared in Sirte, Libya, alongside President Bozizé as they both signed a peace agreement, Miskine on behalf of his *Forces démocratiques pour le peuple centrafricain* (FDPC). The name 'FDPC' was evidence of the usefulness of conventionalizing rebellion in order to participate in the opportunities available at the time. Miskine wanted an entry point back into CAR politics; Bozizé needed to sign a peace agreement with a rebel group

in order to attract more peacekeeping and humanitarian aid. In the end, the ICC worries prevented Miskine from being a credible political player in CAR, but his men still desired DDR. Their nationality (largely Chadian) disqualified them, however, and instead they held up humanitarian and other vehicles to get by – pretty much what they had always done. So conventionalization did not yield the results Miskine and his men were hoping for, but it allowed them a chance to play the game.

5 DDR and the frustration of desires for entitlement

1   Conventionalization clearly draws more people into the orbit of armed groups, but during the pre-peace agreement phase the levels of associated physical violence were actually relatively restrained. The form of rebel attacks was itself conventionalized: rebels would attack a town before dawn. Any state security forces present would flee, as would the civilian population. The rebels (and any other opportunists) would pillage and gather whatever they could of the government force's arsenal. Then a spokesperson (often someone far from the scene of the fighting, such as in Cotonou or Paris) would issue a statement that the group had 'taken' the town and was making an advance on the capital, thereby providing the first indication that the group was a force that should be approached about peace negotiations. Violence against civilians and others did occur (see Human Rights Watch 2007 for a good account of the 2005–2007 period), and people certainly suffered. But, the form of the attack and its conventionalization helped limit the amount of violence. However, when rebel leaders like General Damane Zakaria of the UFDR gained a presidential adviser position and privileged access to diamond mining and diamond-related security concessions, violence usually described with the catch-all of 'inter-communal' (that is, not occurring on the national scale and therefore less readily adapted to the perceptional biases and programmes of humanitarians and other interveners) arguably increased in certain areas. Moreover, conventional rebellion raises expectations on the part of armed group members, and hence also their grievances; it makes violence an established element of national politics; and it can quickly surpass conventionalized limits and become uncontrollable.

2   State- or peacebuilding efforts seem to assume that the CAR state is an infantile form of an ideal-type state, and has only to be helped to grow up into the proper, adult form. This is incorrect. The CAR state has its own well-developed historical dynamics and context, as this book has shown. Any wholesale transformation for the better must begin with these dynamics.

3   The same was true of taxes, which were now to be paid at the Special Window at Ecobank, rather than to individual collectors. Tax receipts were regularly two to three times what they had been previously thanks to this technical fix.

4   Following Daniel Jordan Smith (2007), I retain the term 'corruption', despite its inherently normative connotation, which may or may not capture the multivalent ways people engage in, justify, and criticize practices they label 'corrupt'.

5   For more on internal migration of national aid workers, see Abramowitz (2015), which focuses on Liberia.

6   As with so many other development and humanitarian initiatives, DDR conceives of political problems in technical terms. In this way, the response to 'failure' is generally to re-jig the technical specifics rather than to engage in a wholesale reconsideration of the dynamics of distribution, accumulation, and power (Ferguson 1990; de Waal 1997). In this vein, among DDR planners and staffers recognition of the failures of such programs has carried with it a standard response: DDR must simply be done differently. Thus it has now become possible to speak of 'first-generation DDR' and 'second-generation DDR'. More recently, international organization DDR officials in Bangui have been speaking of DDR that is not DDR – that is, calling the process that they are engaging in DDR but departing from standard practice by not differentiating between armed group members and others when it comes to distributing goods and other support. While this could avoid some of the paradoxes described above, it does nothing about the expectations that several generations of failed DDR programmes in CAR have fostered on the part of armed group members. Failures have effects, and those effects are not suffered equally.

7   See Jennings (2008) for a full discussion of these interlocking, and often questionable when not faulty, assumptions.

8   See Jennings (2008) for more on the lack of clarity around reintegration in particular.

9   Jennings (2008) also draws attention to the tendency for DDR to 'harden group membership' rather than dismantle it, which suggests this has been a frequent occurrence in DDR programmes.

10 When it came to conceptualization, the PRAC employed the best practices of its time, such as working through an implementing agency (called the PRAC, composed of international and national staffers hired by UNDP), with key decisions taken by a national DDR commission. (National DDR commissions have since become associated with gross corruption, and been abandoned.) The PRAC also innovated in ways that have since become standard. For instance, in addition to the disarmament, demobilization, and skills-training of those identified as ex-combatants, the project was also to include assistance to the towns and neighbourhoods ex-fighters hailed from. Planners hoped the community support elements would also lessen people's feeling that the 'bad guys' were getting paid off for their bad behaviour. The exact projects to be undertaken were to be decided by local councils, which would propose things like building public toilets or refurbishing markets or schools. In the end, most of these projects were neglected to the point of farce. Sixty-nine community projects were initially

planned. PRAC reports claimed that forty-one were completed. An independent evaluation visited thirty-five of these and found seventeen completed and eighteen abandoned and unfinished (Clément et al. 2007: 28).

11 Sahle-Work Zewde occupied this post from 2009 to 2011, when she was replaced by Margaret Vogt. In January 2010, BONUCA became BINUCA, the UN Integrated Peacebuilding Support Office in CAR.

12 Another idea put forth by technical staff was that the money could be handled by Ecobank, the largest bank in CAR (with offices in thirty-six African countries). Though there are no bank branches in the parts of CAR home to the rebellions, Ecobank in Bangui could prepare envelopes of cash with the name of each ex-combatant on them. These sealed envelopes could then be transported north and distributed. This option was never seriously considered.

13 For the ten expatriates working on the project, annual salaries and benefits ran to USD2.04 million per year. For the sake of comparison, the non-personnel costs for the entire disarmament component ran to less than USD500,000, and demobilization was USD1.761 million (DDR Steering Committee 2010a). The steering committee was also expensive, especially the trips its members made to visit the ex-combatants. A brief mission to Tiringoulou or Paoua (by plane) cost around USD10,000 (DDR Steering Committee 2010b), and seems even costlier when one considers that rather than making armed group members feel heard, these visits only compounded their sense of subjection to promissory politics and their frustration over their failure to receive the entitlements they sought. Politico-military group representatives to the steering committee each made indemnities of USD1,000/month, and government representatives received USD1,000.

14 The military observers cost approximately USD1.3 million per six months (DDR Steering Committee 2010a).

15 For instance, employees developed a sophisticated database that would allow a user to sort ex-combatants based on a range of demographic and other identifying characteristics. Each person's photo would be uploaded into the system to verify that the correct person was presenting for each distribution. This would also allow for the tracking of data such as whether someone who presented a Kalashnikov at the verification phase actually ended up turning that weapon in. Designing a database of this type requires not just the attention to detail of a computer programmer, but also skill in thinking through all the possible configurations of personal data that could arise so that every situation is accounted for in the database's decision tree. In a place like CAR, it is especially complicated to do so, because the data is frequently incomplete (last names or birth dates or similar details are missing, or else spellings are not standardized). The system they eventually designed was recognized by higher-ups in New York as a model of elegant design, and the employee who started it went on to a job travelling between different countries with DDR programmes

(Liberia, Democratic Republic of the Congo) to develop similar databases. In CAR, however, the system was never put to use. The technical staff saw these systems as a way to take politics out of the program and make the process smoother, but the steering committee members saw them as challenges to their authority. In theory, of course, DDR was supposed to dismantle their authority, and in theory that would have been possible to articulate publicly. But in practice, doing so could draw retaliation of one kind or another.

16 The initial timeline for the steering committee would have meant completion of the program prior to the March 2010 presidential elections. This seemed the best formula for election fairness and stability. But both procedures were repeatedly delayed. And while for the first half of 2010 Bozizé spoke of the need to do DDR prior to elections, by the later months of the year DDR had dropped from his speeches and statements altogether. Finally, the Independent [in name only] Election Commission set a date for the elections: 23 January 2011. DDR would never happen that quickly. In the end, the elections – far from free and fair, but a procedure that was completed – occurred on that date.

6 War as the violence of the pack

1 These frustrated and aggrieved youth were a minority (most people went about their lives with minimal complaint), but they were a noisy one. The re-opening of the cotton-processing plant in northwestern CAR in 2011 helped reboot livelihoods there, but people still felt a pervasive abandonment.

2 In a similar vein, but less violent-conflict-affected context, see Englund (2006) on the effects of human rights discourse in Malawi.

3 As I argued even at the time – see for instance Lombard (2013b); Lombard and Batianga-Kinzi (2015).

4 Use of the term 'globalization' has been much critiqued, and with good reason (e.g. Cooper 2000). In using it here, I am drawing on Appadurai's (2006) definition: 1) the role of finance capital; 2) the revolution in electronic information; 3) the fact that the new forms of wealth appear magical (what is being produced is often obscure).

5 For a critique of Chagnon's work, see Ferguson (1995).

6 Some people have sought answers from the growing Pentecostal churches, which promise to cure the scourge of witchcraft and, often, poverty. Though the prosperity gospel that many of these churches preach can seem quite predatory in the context of people who have so little, it is hard to deny the ecstasy of many of the churches' members. At the same time, these churches have been key vectors of the dissemination of anti-Muslim sentiment, including in Bozizé's own Celestial Christian congregation (the Celestial Christians are a Benin-based organization, and Bozizé was instrumental in opening a Bangui branch) (Marchal 2015b).

7   See Lombard (2015) for further discussion of the danger-foreignness assigned to people from northeastern CAR.

8   Illness and poor health facilities explain some of these many deaths. More importantly, people seek reasons for their misfortunes, such as untimely deaths, and Central Africans have had more to deal with than most. This helps blur the line between biomedical and social (witchcraft) explanations, as journalist Shaun Raviv (2015) shows beautifully in the case of Swaziland.

9   Many journalistic reports connected this incident to the cannibalism ascribed to Jean-Bédel Bokassa. Rumour had it he kept freezers stocked with human flesh. That is not true. These were colourful stories that a French mercenary told to a journalist, which then got repeated as fact, perhaps because they aligned with people's pre-existing stereotypes (their partial knowledge) about Africa. The mercenary counted the circulation of these stories as perhaps his greatest achievement; he was tickled to see how efficacious his story-telling could be in the world.

10 In a similar vein, there is another movement, or slippage, that bears looking at, namely the ways that the high levels of 'ordinary' or everyday violence in CAR (Batianga-Kinzi 2012) themselves contribute to the use of violence in public, associational life. In CAR, everyday violence might include rubbing pepper in a disobedient child's eyes or beating a family member in order to induce a confession. Anthropologists and other scholars of Africa have often refrained from addressing these modes of violence, or at least from describing them as violence, with that term's normative charge, instead leaving the topics to NGOs and advocacy groups with their agendas (Bouju and De Bruijn 2008). In part, this hesitancy stems from an interest in correcting what are seen as inaccurate popular portrayals of Africa as an exceptionally violent place. Though different forms of violence (everyday, political, structural, symbolic) can in some senses be seen as a continuum (Scheper-Hughes and Bourgois 2004), it is simultaneously important not to portray these different processes as mechanically or even necessarily related to each other (as suggested by Bourdieu's 'law of conservation of violence'). That is, different forms of violence often bundle and blend together, but they do so in contingent and unpredictable ways. Many people experiencing structural violence, for instance, strenuously avoid situations involving political, physical, or everyday violence. And yet: for others these do bundle together, and we need a more granular understanding of how and why that happens.

7 World champion of peacekeeping

1   Hermeneutics refers to the art and science of interpretation, and those are the processes to which I refer here.

2   The reason for this anomaly is not known, but at 600 miles wide it is perhaps

the largest such area the world. The leading hypothesis is that a giant meteor landed here some billion years ago, heating the iron deposits in the area such that their magnetic characteristics remain altered to this day (Wood 2014b).

3 The details of what social cohesion or reconciliation might mean and whom they will implicate are far less frequently delved into. Who exactly should be reconciling with whom, and what does reconciliation entail? The three Central African religious authorities stepped forward to speak on behalf of reconciliation, which is to their credit. The downside was that this made it all the easier to describe reconciliation as the preserve of the religious establishment, rather than something that implicated politicians, businesspeople, peasants, etc. Meanwhile, people from across the social spectrum also avowed an objective that to an extent conflicted with reconciliation, namely ending 'impunity' (*'la lutte contre l'impunité'*). About this goal, too, no one could plausibly disagree. The total lack of judicial accountability in CAR is a serious problem, and it strikes everyone this way. That is, it strikes everyone as a major problem when it is being discussed as an abstract principle. And it strikes people as a major problem when they are diagnosing the unfair advantages enjoyed by others. But at the same time as, say, a MINUSCA official proclaims the importance of ending impunity, he will justify not arresting known criminals because it could disrupt the peace process. Hypocrisy might well be the best policy, but you cannot pretend that it is therefore not still hypocrisy.

4 Schlee (2004) makes a similar point. Identity in and of itself is not the problem – we must instead look to the particular situations when identity becomes a cause for violence, as well as those when it does not.

5 Peulh is the local term for the larger ethnic category Fulani, whose members spread from West to East Africa. Many are herders and itinerant if not nomadic; they often have trouble obtaining nationality given these border-crossing lives.

6 The accusation that the French were supporting a Muslim group like the UPC struck him as particularly laughable given that those same French officers had accused him of supporting Muslim 'terrorists' in town, such as one young man he had recruited for a youth politics project. The young man in question was not a 'PK5 terrorist' as the French officer described him, but a denizen of Bambari with a master's degree in geology.

7 To their credit, this is one dimension of what certain people at the UN are targeting with the new UN-government compact initiative, and it is one dimension of what Central African politicians are aiming for with the proposed NGO law. Whether either will achieve these objectives remains to seen.

8 Private Facebook post, 15 March 2016, quoted with permission. My translation.

9 For more on jealousy in particular, see Marchal (2015a) and Ceriana Mayneri (2014c).

REFERENCES

Abramowitz, S. A. (2015) *Searching for Normal in the Wake of the Liberian War.* Philadelphia, PA: University of Pennsylvania Press.

Africa Confidential (2014) 'Central African Republic: allies lose faith', *Africa Confidential* 55(17).

AFP (Agence France Presse) (2014) 'Centrafrique: les violences à Bangui dues à des manipulations « politiques »', selon Samba-Panza', *Jeune Afrique*, 1 June.

Alade, K. (2015) 'La Gerre ethnique et la rébellion'. Unpublished manuscript.

Allen, T. (2015) 'Life beyond the bubbles: cognitive dissonance and humanitarian impunity in Northern Uganda' in S. Abramowitz and C. Panter-Brick (eds) *Medical Humanitarianism: Ethnographies of Practice.* Philadelphia, PA: University of Pennsylvania Press, pp. 96–118.

Appadurai, A. (1998) 'Dead certainty: ethnic violence in the era of globalization', *Public Culture* 10(2): 225–47.

—— (2006) *Fear of Small Numbers: An Essay on the Geography of Anger.* Durham, NC: Duke University Press.

Appel, H. C. (2012) 'Walls and white elephants: oil extraction, responsibility, and infrastructural violence in Equatorial Guinea', *Ethnography* 13(4): 1–27.

Ashforth, A. (2005) *Witchcraft, Violence, and Democracy in South Africa.* Chicago, IL: University of Chicago Press.

Autesserre, S. (2009) 'Hobbes and the Congo: frames, local violence, and international intervention', *International Organization* 63(2): 249–80.

—— (2014) *Peaceland: Conflict Resolution and the Everyday Politics of International Intervention.* New York: Cambridge University Press.

Balandier, G. (1970) *Political Anthropology.* New York: Pantheon.

Banbury, A. (2016) 'I love the U.N., but it is failing', *New York Times*, 16 March.

Bayart, J.-F. (2000) 'Africa in the world: a history of extraversion', *African Affairs* 99(395): 217–67.

—— (2009) *The State in Africa: The Politics of the Belly.* Cambridge, Polity Press.

BBC (2014) 'CAR cannibal: why I ate a man's leg', BBC News, 13 January.

Berlant, L. G. (2011) *Cruel Optimism.* Durham, NC: Duke University Press.

Berman, E. G. and L. Lombard (2008) *The Central African Republic and Small Arms: A Regional Tinderbox.* Geneva: Oxford University Press/Small Arms Survey.

Bernault, F. (2006) 'Body, power and sacrifice in Equatorial Africa', *Journal of African History* 36(1): 207–39.

Bertrand, R. (2002) *Indonésie, la démocratie invisible: Violence, magie et politique à Java*. Paris: Karthala.

Bhatia, M. V. and R. Muggah (2009) 'The politics of demobilization in Afghanistan' in R. Muggah (ed.) *Security and Post-Conflict Reconstruction: Dealing with Fighters in the Aftermath of War*. London: Routledge, pp. 126–64.

Bierschenk, T. and J.-P. Olivier de Sardan (1997) 'Local powers and a distant state in rural Central African Republic', *Journal of Modern African Studies* 35(3): 441–68.

Bigo, D. (1988) *Pouvoir et obéissance en Centrafrique*. Paris: Karthala.

Bingham, R. (2015) 'Cattle trade in CAR: demonstrating the peace-building capacity of micro-economic relationships', Washington, DC: Social, Urban, Rural, and Resilience Unit, World Bank.

Bissakonou, J. V. (2015) *L'autre version de la crise centrafricaine*. Paris: L'Harmattan.

Boltanski, L. (1999) *Distant Suffering: Morality, Media and Politics*. New York: Cambridge University Press.

Bonhomme, J. (2012) 'The dangers of anonymity: witchcraft, rumor, and modernity in Africa', *Hau: Journal of Ethnographic Theory* 2(2): 205–33.

Bouju, J. and M. De Bruijn (2008) 'Violences structurelles et violences systemiques. La violence ordinaire des rapports sociaux en Afrique', *Bulletin de l'APAD* 27–28: 2–9.

Brégeon, J.-J. (1998) *Un rêve d'Afrique, Administrateurs en Oubangui-Chari: la cendrillon de l'empire*. Paris: Denoël.

Brown, M. F. (2014) *Upriver: The Turbulent Life and Times of an Amazonian People*. Cambridge, MA: Harvard University Press.

Burnham, P. and T. Christensen (1983) 'Karnu's message and the "war of the hoe handle": interpreting a Central African resistance movement', *Africa* 53(4): 3–22.

Canetti, E. (1962) *Crowds and Power*, C. Stewart, trans. New York: Viking.

Carayannis, T. and L. Lombard (2015) 'A concluding note on the failure and future of peacebuilding in CAR' in T. Carayannis and L. Lombard (eds) *Making Sense of the Central African Republic*. London: Zed Books, pp. 319–41.

Ceriana Mayneri, A. (2014a) '"Cannibalism" and power: violence, mass media, and the conflict in the Central African Republic', Hot Spots, *Cultural Anthropology* website, 11 June. https://culanth.org/fieldsights/543-cannibalism-and-power-violence-mass-media-and-the-conflict-in-the-central-african-republic. Accessed 3 October 2016.

—— (2014b) 'La Centrafrique, de la rébellion Séléka aux groupes anti-balaka (2012–2014): Usages de la violence, schème persécutif et traitement médiatique du conflit', *Politique Africaine* 2(134): 179–93.

—— (2014c) *Sorcellerie et prophétisme en Centrafrique. L'imaginaire de la dépossession en pays banda*. Paris: Karthala.

Chambers, R. (1983) *Rural Development: Putting the Last First*. New York: Routledge.

Chauveau, J.-P., M. Le Pape and J.-P. Olivier de Sardan (2001) 'La pluralité des normes et leurs dynamiques en Afrique', in G. Winter (ed.). *Inégalités et politiques publiques en Afrique : pluralité des normes et jeux d'acteurs*. Paris: Karthala, pp. 145–62.

Cimpric, A. (2010) *Les enfants accusés de sorcellerie: Etude anthropologique des pratiques contemporaines relatives aux enfants en Afrique*. Dakar: UNICEF.

Cinq-Mars, E. (2015) *Too Little, Too Late: Failing to Prevent Atrocities in the Central African Republic*. New York: Global Center for the Responsibility to Protect.

Clastres, P. (1987) *Society against the State: Essays in Political Anthropology*. New York: Zone Books.

Clément, C., L. Lombard, G. Kozo and D. Koyou-Kombele (2007) RCA: DDR Sans GPS. Rapport de la mission indépendante d'évaluation du Programme de Réinsertion des ex-combatants et d'Appui aux Communautés en République Centrafricaine.

Collins, R. (2004) *Interaction Ritual Chains*. Princeton, NJ: Princeton University Press.

—— (2009) *Violence: A Micro-Sociological Theory*. Princeton, NJ: Princeton University Press.

Colonie du Congo (1903) Rapport Général Annuel. Commandant Supérieur des Troupes. Stamped and signed at Brazzaville, 20 October 1903, by the chef de bataillon commandant supérieur des troupes. Archival material available at the Service Historique de la Défense, Vincennes, carton 6H2.

Cooper, F. (2000) 'What is the concept of globalization good for? An African historian's perspective', *African Affairs* 100(399): 189–213.

—— (2014) *Citizenship between Empire and Nation: Remaking France and French Africa, 1945–1960*. Princeton, NJ: Princeton University Press.

Coquéry-Vidrovitch, C. (1972) *Le Congo au temps des grandes compagnies concessionnaires, 1898–1930*. Paris: Mouton.

—— (ed.) (2014) *Le rapport Brazza, Mission d'enquête du Congo: Rapport et documents (1905–1907)*. Paris: Le Passager Clandestin.

Cordell, D. D. (1983) 'The savanna belt of north-central Africa' in D. Birmingham and P. M. Martin (eds) *History of Central Africa*, vol. 1. New York: Longman, pp. 30–74.

—— (1985) *Dar al-Kuti and the Last Years of the Trans-Saharan Slave Trade*. Madison, WI: University of Wisconsin Press.

—— (2003) 'The myth of inevitability and invincibility: resistance to slavers and the slave trade in Central Africa, 1850–1910' in S. A. Diouf (ed.) *Fighting the Slave Trade: West African Strategies*. Athens, OH: Ohio University Press, pp 31–49.

DDR Steering Committee (2010a) 'Tableau de projection budgetaire cumulee [sic] PBF & BCPR au 31 decembre [sic] 2010'.

—— (2010b) 'Rapport narratif financier du budget DDR'. Bangui: DDR Steering Committee.

Das, V. (2006) *Life and Words: Violence and the Descent into the Ordinary*. Berkeley, CA: University of California Press.

de Waal, A. (1997) *Famine Crimes: Politics and the Disaster Relief Industry in Africa*. Bloomington, IN: Indiana University Press.

—— (2009) 'Fixing the political marketplace: how can we make peace without functioning state institutions?', Christen Michelsen lecture, Christen Michelsen Institute, Bergen, Norway.

—— (2013) 'Playing the genocide card', *New York Times*, 19 December.

—— (2015) *The Real Politics of the Horn of Africa: Money, War and the Business of Power*. Cambridge: Polity Press.

Debos, M. (2008) 'Fluid loyalties in a regional crisis: Chadian "ex-liberators" in the Central African Republic', *African Affairs* 107(427): 225–41.

—— (2013) *Le Métier des armes au Tchad: Le gouvernement de l'entre guerres*. Paris: Karthala.

—— (2014) '"Hate" and "security vacuum": how not to ask the right questions about a confusing crisis', Hot Spots, *Cultural Anthropology* website, 11 June. https://culanth.org/fieldsights/545-hate-and-security-vacuum-how-not-to-ask-the-right-questions-about-a-confusing-crisis. Accessed 3 October 2016.

Diki-Kidiri, M. (1979) 'L'émergence du sango comme langue nationale centrafricaine', *Pédagogie et Culture* 43: 36–9.

Donham, D. L. (2006) 'Staring at suffering: violence as a subject' in E. G. Bay and D. L. Donham (eds) *States of Violence: Politics, Youth, and Memory in Contemporary Africa*. Durham, NC: Duke University Press, pp. 16–33.

Dunn, K. C. (2009) 'Environmental security, spatial preservation, and state sovereignty in Central Africa' in D. Howland and L. White (eds) *The State of Sovereignty: Territories, Laws, Populations*. Bloomington, IN: Indiana University Press, pp. 222–47.

Durkheim, E. (1951 [1897]) *Suicide: A Study in Sociology*, J. A. Spaulding and G. Simpson, trans. New York: The Free Press.

—— (1995 [1912]) *The Elementary Forms of Religious Life*, K. E. Fields, trans. New York: The Free Press.

Englebert, P. (2009) *Africa: Unity, Sovereignty, and Sorrow*. Boulder, CO: Lynne Rienner.

—— (2015) 'The "real" map of Africa', *Foreign Affairs*, November 8.

Englund, H. (2006) *Prisoners of Freedom: Human Rights and the African Poor*. Berkeley, CA: University of California Press.

Eubank, N. (2012) 'Taxation, political accountability and foreign aid: lessons from Somaliland', *Journal of Development Studies* 48(4): 465–80.

Evans-Pritchard, E. E. (1936) *Witchcraft, Oracles, and Magic among the Azande*. London: Clarendon Press.

Feldman, I. (2008) *Governing Gaza: Bureaucracy, Authority, and the Work of Rule, 1917–1967*. Durham, NC: Duke University Press.

Ferguson, J. (1990) *The Anti-Politics Machine: 'Development,' Depoliticization, and Bureaucratic Power in Lesotho.* Minneapolis, MN: University of Minnesota Press.

—— (2006) *Global Shadows: Africa in the Neoliberal World Order.* Durham, NC: Duke University Press.

—— (2015) *Give a Man a Fish: Reflections on the New Politics of Distribution.* Durham, NC: Duke University Press.

Ferguson, R. B. (1995) *Yanomami Warfare: A Political History.* Santa Fe, NM: School of American Research Press.

Ferme, M. C. (2001) *The Underneath of Things: Violence, History, and the Everyday in Sierra Leone.* Berkeley, CA: University of California Press.

Ferme, M. C. and D. Hoffman (2004) 'Hunter militias and the international human rights discourse in Sierra Leone and beyond', *Africa Today* 50(4): 73–95.

Filakota, R. (2009) *Le Renoveau Islamique en Afrique Noire.* Paris: L'Harmattan.

Fuior, T. and D. Law (2014) 'Security sector reform in the Central African Republic: chronicle of a death foretold', *SSR 2.0 Brief* 1: 1–12. Kitchener, ON: Centre for Security Governance.

Geertz, C. (1968) 'Thinking as a moral act: ethical dimensions of anthropological fieldwork in the new states', *Antioch Review* 28(2): 139–58.

Geschiere, P. (1997) *The Modernity of Witchcraft.* Charlottesville, VA: University Press of Virginia.

—— (2009) *The Perils of Belonging: Autochthony, Citizenship, and Exclusion in Africa and Europe.* Chicago, IL: University of Chicago Press.

Geschiere, P. and S. Jackson (2006) 'Autochthony and the crisis of citizenship: democratization, decentralization, and the politics of belonging', *African Studies Review* 49(2): 1–7.

Geschiere, P. and B. Meyer (1998) 'Globalization and identity: dialectics of flow and closure, introduction', *Development and Change* 29(4): 601–15.

Ghosh, A. (1994) 'The global reservation: notes toward an ethnography of international peacekeeping', *Cultural Anthropology* 9(3): 1–27.

Giddens, A. (1985) *The Nation-State and Violence.* Berkeley, CA: University of California Press.

Gide, A. (1927) *Voyage au Congo: carnets de route.* Paris: Gallimard.

Giles-Vernick, T. (1996) 'Na lege ti guiriri (On the road of history): mapping out the past and present in M'Bres region, Central African Republic', *Ethnohistory* 43(2): 245–75.

Gluckman, M. (1940) 'Analysis of a social situation in modern Zululand', *Bantu Studies* 14(1): 1–30.

—— (1955) *Custom and Conflict in Africa.* Oxford: Blackwell Publishers.

Goffman, E. (1961) *Asylums: Essays on the Social Situation of Mental Patients and Other Inmates.* New York, Anchor Books.

Government of CAR (2007) 'Termes de référence: Analyse de la situation post-PRAC, options envisageables par le gouvernement.'

Guéhenno, J.-M. (2015) *The Fog of Peace: A Memoir of International Peacekeeping in the 21st Century.* Washington, DC: The Brookings Institution.

Guyer, J. I. (1993) 'Wealth in people and self-realization in Equatorial Africa', *Man* 28(2): 243–65.

Hardin, R., M. Remis and C. A. Jost Robinson (2014) 'From abundance to acute marginality: farms, arms, and forests in the Central African Republic', Hot Spots, *Cultural Anthropology* website, 11 June. https://culanth.org/fieldsights/542-from-abundance-to-acute-marginality-farms-arms-and-forests-in-the-central-african-republic-1988-2014. Accessed 3 October 2016.

Harrison, S. (2012) *Dark Trophies: Hunting and the Enemy Body in Modern War.* New York: Berghahn Books.

Hecht, D. and A. Simone (1994) *Invisible Governance: The Art of African Micropolitics.* Brooklyn, NY: Autonomedia.

Hilekaan, F. (2015) 'This shocking picture explains the crisis in Burundi', *Nigerian Nation*, 18 December. http://newspapers.nigeriannation.com/this-shocking-picture-explains-the-crisis-in-burundi-3.

Hobsbawm, E. and T. Ranger (eds) (1983) *The Invention of Tradition.* Cambridge: Cambridge University Press.

Hoffman, D. (2011a) 'Violence, just in time: war and work in contemporary West Africa', *Cultural Anthropology* 26: 1–34.

—— (2011b) *The War Machines: Young Men and Violence in Sierra Leone and Liberia.* Durham, NC: Duke University Press.

Honwana, A. (2012) *The Time of Youth: Work, Social Change, and Politics in Africa.* Sterling, VA: Kumarian.

Hubbell, A. (2001) 'A view of the slave trade from the margin: Souroudougou in the late nineteenth century slave trade in the Niger bend', *Journal of African History* 42(1): 25–47.

Human Rights Watch (2007) *State of Anarchy: Rebellion and Abuses against Civilians*, vol. 19, no. 14(A). New York: Human Rights Watch.

—— (2013) *'They Came to Kill': Escalating Atrocities in the Central African Republic.* New York: Human Rights Watch.

Huntington, S. P. (1996) *The Clash of Civilizations and the Remaking of World Order.* New York: Simon & Schuster.

Hyndman, J. (2000) *Managing Displacement: Refugees and the Politics of Humanitarianism.* Minneapolis, MN: University of Minnesota Press.

ICG (International Crisis Group) (2007) 'Central African Republic: anatomy of a phantom state', *Africa Report* 136.

—— (2008) 'Central African Republic: untangling the political dialogue', *Africa Briefing* 55.

IRIN (2006a) 'Thousands of civilians flee as army fights bandits', IRIN News, 7 February. https://www.irinnews.org/fr/node/225385. Accessed 3 October 2016.

—— (2006b) 'Violence in the northwest claimed 27, Red Cross says', IRIN News, 17 February. http://www.irinnews.org/report/58179/central-african-republic-violence-northwest-claimed-27-red-cross-says. Accessed 3 October 2016.

—— (2012) 'DDR in CAR: hopes and hurdles', IRIN News, 19 April. http://www.irinnews.org/report/95321/briefing-ddr-car-hopes-and-hurdles. Accessed 3 October 2016.

Issa, S. (2010) *Les coupeurs de route: histoire du banditisme rural et transfrontalier dans le bassin du lac Tchad*. Paris: Karthala.

Jennings, K. M. (2007) 'The struggle to satisfy: DDR through the eyes of ex-combatants in Liberia', *International Peacekeeping* 14(2): 204–18.

—— (2008) 'Unclear ends, unclear means: reintegration in postwar societies, the case of Liberia', *Global Governance* 14(3): 327–45.

Kalck, P. (1959) *Réalités oubanguiennes*. Paris: Berger-Levrault.

—— (1971) *Central African Republic: a failure in de-colonisation*. London: Pall Mall Press.

Kaldor, M. (1999) *New and Old Wars*. Cambridge: Polity Press.

—— (2013) 'In defense of new wars', *Stability: Journal of Security and Development* 2(1): 1–16.

Kaplan, R. D. (1994) 'The coming anarchy: how scarcity, crime, overpopulation, tribalism, and disease are rapidly destroying the social fabric of our planet', *Atlantic Monthly*, February.

Kiernan, B. (2007) *Blood and Soil: A World History of Genocide and Extermination from Sparta to Darfur*. New Haven, CT: Yale University Press.

Kilembe, F. (2015) 'Local dynamics in the Pk5 district of Bangui' in T. Carayannis and L. Lombard (eds) *Making Sense of the Central African Republic*. London: Zed Books, pp. 76–101.

Lallau, B. (2016) Facebook post, March 15.

Le Roux, H. (1919) *Oubangui-Chari: Mission Hugues Le Roux*. Paris: Jean Cussac.

Lesueur, T. (2016) 'Centrafrique: quatre priorités pour le nouveau président', International Crisis Group blog post, 10 May. http://blog.crisisgroup.org/africa/central-african-republic/2016/05/10/centrafrique-quatre-priorites-pour-le-nouveau-president. Accessed 3 October 2016.

La Lettre du Continent (2015) 'Les présidentiables livrent bataille... à l'étranger', *La Lettre du continent*, no. 710, 15 July.

Lindqvist, S. (1993) *'Exterminate All the Brutes': One Man's Odyssey into the Heart of Darkness and the Origins of European Genocide*. New York: The New Press.

Lipsky, M. (2010 [1980]) *Street-Level Bureaucracy: Dilemmas of the Individual in Public Services*. New York: Russel Sage Foundation.

Lombard, L. (2011) 'Election report: Central African Republic', The Monkey Cage blog post. http://themonkeycage.org/2011/01/election_report_central_africa. Accessed 3 October 2016.

—— (2012) 'Rébellion et limites de la consolidation de la paix en République centrafricaine', *Politique Africaine* 1: 189–208.

—— (2013a) 'Navigational tools for Central African roadblocks', *PoLAR: Political and Legal Anthropology Review* 36(1): 157–75.

—— (2013b) 'Is the Central African Republic on the verge of genocide?', Africa is a Country blog post, 5 December. http://africasacountry.com/2013/12/is-the-central-african-republic-on-the-verge-of-genocide. Accessed 3 October 2016.

—— (2014a) 'Religion and the limits of making sense of violence as it happens', Foole's No Man's Land blog post, 21 April. http://foolesnomansland.blogspot.com/2014/04/religion-and-limits-of-making-sense-of.html. Accessed 3 October 2016.

—— (2014b) 'A brief political history of the Central African Republic', Hot Spots, *Cultural Anthropology* website, 11 June. https://culanth.org/fieldsights/539-a-brief-political-history-of-the-central-african-republic. Accessed 3 October 2016.

—— (2015) 'The autonomous zone conundrum: armed conservation and rebellion in north-eastern CAR' in T. Carayannis and L. Lombard (eds) *Making Sense of the Central African Republic*. London: Zed Books, pp. 142–65.

—— (2016a) 'Threat economies and armed conservation in north-eastern Central African Republic', *Geoforum* 69: 218–26.

—— (2016b) 'The threat of rebellion: claiming entitled personhood in Central Africa', *Journal of the Royal Anthropological Institute* 22(3): 552–69.

—— (in preparation) *Hunting Game.*

Lombard, L. and S. Batianga-Kinzi (2015) 'Violence, popular punishment, and war in the Central African Republic', *African Affairs* 114(454): 52–71.

MacLean, L. M. (2010) *Informal Institutions and Citizenship in Rural Africa: Risk and Reciprocity in Ghana and Côte d'Ivoire.* New York: Cambridge University Press.

Magone, C., M. Neuman and F. Weissman (eds) (2011) *Humanitarian Negotiations Revealed: The MSF Experience.* London: Hurst & Co.

Mann, G. (2014) *From Empires to NGOs in the West African Sahel: The Road to Nongovernmentality.* New York: Cambridge University Press.

Marchal, R. (2009) 'Aux marges du monde, en Afrique centrale', *Les Études du CERI*, no. 153–154, March. Paris: CERI.

—— (2015a) 'Being rich, being poor: wealth and fear in the Central African Republic' in T. Carayannis and L. Lombard (eds) *Making Sense of the Central African Republic*. London: Zed Books, pp. 53–75.

—— (2015b) 'CAR and the regional (dis)order' in T. Carayannis and L. Lombard (eds) *Making Sense of the Central African Republic*. London: Zed Books, pp. 166–93.

Martinelli, B. (2014) 'La mémoire de la violence en Centrafrique', Hot Spots, *Cultural Anthropology* website, 11 June. https://culanth.org/fieldsights/548-la-memoire-de-la-violence-en-centrafrique. Accessed 3 October 2016.

Maurer, B. (2005) *Mutual Life, Limited: Islamic Banking, Alternative Currencies, Lateral Reason.* Princeton, NJ: Princeton University Press.

Mbembe, A. (2000) 'At the edge of the world: boundaries, territoriality, and sovereignty in Africa', *Public Culture* 12(1): 259–84.

—— (2001) *On the Postcolony*. Durham, NC: Duke University Press.

—— (2006) 'On politics as a form of expenditure' in J. Comaroff and J. L. Comaroff (eds) *Law and Disorder in the Postcolony*. Chicago, IL: University of Chicago Press, pp. 299–335.

Modat (1909) Letter 48, dated 30 November 1909. Archival material available at Archives nationales de l'outre mer (ANOM), Carton 6H124.

Mollion, P. (1992) *Sur les pistes de l'Oubangui-Chari au Tchad, 1890-1930: le drame du portage en Afrique Centrale*. Paris: L'Harmattan.

Moran, M. H. (2010) 'Gender, militarism, and peace-building: projects of the postconflict moment', *Annual Review of Anthropology* 39: 261–74.

Mosse, D. (ed.) (2011) *Adventures in Aidland: The Anthropology of Professionals in International Development*. Oxford: Berghahn Books.

Muggah, R. (2005) 'No magic bullet: a critical perspective on disarmament, demobilization and reintegration (DDR) and weapons reduction in post-conflict contexts', *The Commonwealth Journal of International Affairs* 94(379): 239–52.

—— (2009) 'Introduction: the emperor's clothes?' in R. Muggah (ed.) *Security and Post-Conflict Reconstruction: Dealing with Fighters in the Aftermath of War*. London: Routledge, pp. 1–29.

Ndjapou, E. (2008) 'Au nom de la sorcellerie, je te tue!', *Revue Centre-Africaine d'Anthropologie* 2: 1–11.

Nordstrom, C. (2004) *Shadows of War: Violence, Power, and International Profiteering in the Twenty-First Century*. Berkeley, CA: University of California Press.

Norwegian Refugee Council (2015) *Engage to Stay and Deliver: Humanitarian Access in the Central African Republic*, study led by J. S. Renouf. Oslo: Norwegian Refugee Council.

Nzabakomada-Yakoma, R. (1986) *L'Afrique Centrale insurgée: La guerre du Congo-Wara, 1928–1931*. Paris: L'Harmattan.

Olin, N. (2015) 'Pathologies of peacekeeping and peacebuilding' in T. Carayannis and L. Lombard (eds) *Making Sense of the Central African Republic*. London: Zed Books, pp. 194–218.

Oubangui-Chari (n.d.) Présentation sommaire du territoire de l'Oubangui-Chari, marked 'très secret'. Service historique de l'armée de la terre. Carton 6H 127.

Persson, M. (2012) 'Demobilized or remobilized? Lingering rebel structures in post-war Liberia' in M. Utas (ed.) *African Conflicts and Informal Power: Big Men and Networks*. London: Zed Books, pp. 101–18.

Picco, E. (2015) 'From being forgotten to being ignored: international humanitarian interventions in the Central African Republic' in T. Carayannis and L. Lombard (eds) *Making Sense of the Central African Republic*. London: Zed Books, pp. 219–43.

Pietz, W. (1985) 'The problem of the fetish, I', *Anthropology and Aesthetics* 9: 5–17.

Piot, C. (2010) *Nostalgia for the Future: West Africa after the Cold War*. Chicago, IL: University of Chicago Press.

Pitcher, A., M. H. Moran and M. Johnston (2009) 'Rethinking patrimonialism and neopatrimonialism in Africa', *African Studies Review* 52(1): 125–56.

Polgreen, L. (2006) 'On the run as war crosses another line in Africa', *New York Times*, 10 December, p. A1. http://www.nytimes.com/2006/12/10/world/africa/10africa.html?_r=0. Accessed 3 October 2016.

Prendergast, J. (2015) 'How to destroy a war economy', *Foreign Policy*, August 10. http://foreignpolicy.com/2015/08/10/how-to-destroy-a-war-economy-sentry-smugglers-africa-conflict-enough-sentry-clooney. Accessed 3 October 2016.

Prins, P. (1907) 'Esclavage et liberté dans les sultanats du Haut-Oubangui', *Révue Indigène* 12 (April): 126–36.

Prioul, C. (1981) *Entre Oubangui et Chari vers 1890*. Paris: Société d'ethnographie.

Raviv, S. (2015) 'The Killers of Swaziland', *The Big Roundtable*, 4 March. www.thebigroundtable.com/stories/killers-swaziland/. Accessed 22 October 2016.

Redfield, P. (2013) *Life in Crisis: The Ethical Journey of Doctors Without Borders*. Berkeley, CA: University of California Press.

Reno, W. (1998) *Warlord Politics and African States*. Boulder, CO: Lynne Rienner Publishers.

Republic of France (1897) Treaty between France and Cheick [Sheikh] Mohamed e Senoussi, signed by Administrator Emile Gentil and Mohamed e Senoussi on 24 August 1897. Archival material available at the Service Historique de la Défense, carton 6H124.

Reuters (2009) 'CAR president's helicopter makes emergency landing', 24 December. http://af.reuters.com/article/topNews/idAFJOE5BN0IB20091224. Accessed 3 October 2016.

Richards, P. (1996) *Fighting for the Rain Forest: War, Youth, and Resources in Sierra Leone*. Portsmouth, NH: Heinemann.

—— (2005) 'New war: an ethnographic approach' in P. Richards (ed.) *No Peace, No War: An Anthropology of Contemporary Armed Conflicts*. Athens, OH: Ohio University Press, pp. 1–21.

Roitman, J. (2013) *Anti-Crisis*. Durham, NC: Duke University Press.

Roscoe, P. (2011) 'Dead birds: the "theater" of war among the Dugum Dani', *American Anthropologist* 113(1): 56–70.

Rutherford, D. (2003) *Raiding the Land of the Foreigners: The Limits of the Nation on an Indonesian Frontier*. Princeton, NJ: Princeton University Press.

Scheele, J. (2015) 'The values of "anarchy": moral autonomy among Tubu-speakers in northern Chad', *Journal of the Royal Anthropological Institute* 21(1): 32–48.

Scheper-Hughes, N. and P. Bourgois (2004) 'Introduction: making sense of violence' in N. Scheper-Hughes and P. Bourgois (eds) *Violence in War and Peace: An Anthology*, pp. 1–32.

Schlee, G. (2004) 'Taking sides and constructing identities: reflections on conflict theory', *Journal of the Royal Anthropological Institute* 10(1): 135–56.

Scott, J. C. (1998) *Seeing like a State: How Certain Schemes to Improve the Human Condition Have Failed*. New Haven, CT: Yale University Press.

Sengupta, S. (2015) 'U.N. official resigns amid accusations of sex abuse by peace-keepers', *New York Times*, 12 August. www.nytimes.com/2015/08/13/world/africa/united-nations-central-african-republic-sexual-abuse.html. Accessed 3 October 2016.

Simons, A. (1995) *Networks of Dissolution: Somalia Undone*. Boulder, CO: Westview Press.

Smirl, L. (2015) *Spaces of Aid: How Cars, Compounds and Hotels Shape Humanitarianism*. London: Zed Books.

Smith, D. J. (2007) *A Culture of Corruption: Everyday Deception and Popular Discontent in Nigeria*. Princeton, NJ: Princeton University Press.

Smith, M. J. (1974) *Corporations and Society*. London: Duckworth.

Smith, S. W. (2015a) 'CAR's history: the past of a tense present' in T. Carayannis and L. Lombard (eds) *Making Sense of the Central African Republic*. London: Zed Books, pp. 17–52.

—— (2015b) 'The elite's road to riches in a poor country' in T. Carayannis and L. Lombard (eds). *Making Sense of the Central African Republic*. London: Zed Books, pp. 102–22.

Spittaels, S. and F. Hilgert (2009) *Mapping Conflict Motives: Central African Republic*. Antwerp: IPIS.

Stoler, A. L. (2013) *Imperial Debris: On Ruins and Ruination*. Durham, NC: Duke University Press.

Taussig, M. (1992) *The Nervous System*. New York: Routledge.

Themnér, A. (2011) *Violence in Post-Conflict Societies: Remarginalization, Remobilizers and Relationships*. New York: Routledge.

Tilly, C. (1985) 'War making and state making as organized crime' in P. B. Evans, D. Rueschemeyer and T. Skocpol (eds) *Bringing the State Back In*. Cambridge: Cambridge University Press, pp. 169–87.

Trouillot, M.-R. (2001) 'The anthropology of the state in the age of globalization', *Current Anthropology* 42(1): 125–38.

Tull, D. M. and A. Mehler (2005) 'The hidden costs of power-sharing: reproducing insurgent violence in Africa', *African Affairs* 104(416): 375–98.

Tumutegyereize, K. and N. Tillon (2013) 'Central African Republic: peace talks without the talks', African Arguments blog post. http://africanarguments.org/2013/03/15/central-african-republic-peace-talks-without-the-talks---by-kennedy-tumutegyereize-and-nicolas-tillon-conciliation-resources. Accessed 3 October 2016.

UN (United Nations) (2009) 'Update on the DDR process, CAR: 29 April 2009'. New York: UN.

UNDP (United Nations Development Programme) (2010) *Rapport narratif financier du budget DDR*. Bangui: UNDP.

UNEP (United Nations Environmental Programme) (2008) *Vital Water Graphics: An Overview of the State of the World's Fresh and Marine Waters*, second edition. Nairobi: UNEP. www.unep.org/dewa/vitalwater/article116.html. Accessed 3 October 2016.

Utas, M. (2005) 'Victimcy, girlfriending, soldiering: tactic agency in a young woman's social navigation of the Liberian war zone', *Anthropological Quarterly* 78(2): 403–30.

Van Creveld, M. (1991) *The Transformation of War*. New York: Free Press.

van der Elsken, E. (1961) *Bagara: Photographs of Equatorial Africa*. London: Abelard-Schuman.

Vigh, H. (2009) 'Motion squared: a second look at the concept of social navigation', *Anthropological Theory* 9(4): 419–39.

Webb, R. P. (1991) 'State politics in the Central African Republic: an original study', *Political Science*. Madison, WI, University of Wisconsin, Madison. Ph.D.

Weiss, H. F. (1967) *Political Protest in the Congo: The Parti solidaire africain during the Independence Struggle*. Princeton, NJ: Princeton University Press.

Wohlers, L. D. (2015) 'A central African elite perspective on the struggles of the Central African Republic' in T. Carayannis and L. Lombard (eds) *Making Sense of the Central African Republic*. London: Zed Books, pp. 295–318.

Wood, G. (2014a) 'Hell is an understatement', *The New Republic*, 1 May.

—— (2014b) 'The African country where compasses go haywire', *Boston Globe*, 22 June.

World Bank (2011) *World Development Report 2011: Conflict, Security, and Development*. Washington, DC: World Bank.

Young, C. (1994) *The African Colonial State in Comparative Perspective*. New Haven, CT: Yale University Press.

Zoctizoum, Y. (1983) *Histoire de la Centrafrique, Tome 1 (1879–1959)*. Paris: l'Harmattan.

INDEX

'abroad', object of desire, 89
accountability, organic processes, 35
Adam, Noureddine, 190
adventurism, US military, 43
adventurist, 256n2
African Union, 162; MISCA, 205;
    mistrust of, 20; peacekeepers, 19; 2014
    peacekeepers, 178
aid, 'givers' primary beneficiaries, 227
Aidland, 42
AIDS Free World, 82
airport(s): access to, 88, 90; enclave
    politics site, 89
Al Hussain, Zeid Ra'ad, 82
Al-Sanusi, Sheikh Mohammed, 65, 72,
    93, 117, 188; assassination of, 73, 187;
    Bazingir armies, 68; -French relations,
    67; sultanate, 118
Ali, Abdulaye, 92
allegiances, multiple, 49
amputations, 33
anaemic bureaucracy, violence of, 109
Anicet, 243, 245
anomie, 57, 87, 187, 191, 196, 212, 245;
    Central Africans lives, 56; context
    of, 181
Anti-Balaka, 22, 48, 116; contradictions,
    184; diversity of, 18; fighters, 206, 209;
    Muslims targeted, 178
anti-Seleka violence, 93
Appadurai, Arjun, 196
APRD rebel group, 100, 133–4, 139–40,
    161, 163, 166–7, 173, 178; emergence of,
    47, 135; Kaga Bandoro members, 165

arbitrary detention, experiences of, 103
armed actors, -interveners symbiosis,
    128; peacebuilder symbiosis, 133 -state
    idea, 114
armed groups, fictional, 166
army mutinies, 1990s salary, 9, 121
Ashforth, Adam, 197–8
Autesserre, Séverine, 232
authority(ies), pluralized, 84
autochthony, 182
autopsies, Central African practices,
    201, 209; colonial misinterpretation
    of, 199
Azande people, 12

Bainilago, Louis, 204
Balandier, Georges, 119
Bambari, 178, 230, 233, 246; teacher
    training centre, 120
Ban Ki-Moon, 82
Banda people, 12, 149, 159, men 87; view
    of history, 86
banditry, 127, 131, 174
Bangui, 1, 5, 22, 25, 27, 47, 52, 59, 174, 178,
    224; airport camps, 88; checkpoints,
    236; Combatant quarter, 193; DDR
    headquarters, 170; Forum, 22, 122,
    235; Gobongo neighbourhood, 228;
    Magnetic Anomaly, 215–16; -Paris
    flight, 89; PK5, 231; Seleka arrival,
    177; suspected thief killing, 194; 2015
    violence, 21; traffic jams, 28 University
    of, 120, 204; 'Villa Propre' initiative,
    144

'barbarism', 33
Barre, Siad, regime collapse, 3
basic income grants, idea of, 250
Bateson, Gregory, 25
Batianga-Kinzi, Sylvain, 193, 258n8, 263n10
Bayart, Jean-François, 64, 70
Berman, Eric, 23
Bernault, Florence, 13–14
Bertrand, Romain, 95
Bindoumi, Joseph, 235–6
BINUCA (UN Integrated Peacebuilding Support Office), 17, 161–3
Birao, 136–7
Bissakanou, Johnny Vianney, 60
Boganda, Barthélemy, 28, 75, 79; death of, 8; father's colonial murder, 198
Bokassa, Jean-Bédel, 8, 80, 118, 122, 193; era of, 188; father's colonial murder, 75, 117, 198; ousting of, 124
Bongo, Omar, 139
BONUCA, 28–9
border security, outsourced, 105
bounded cultures' approach, 42
Bozizé, François, 9, 11, 15–16, 20, 27, 47, 69, 88, 92, 131, 136–7, 144, 154, 165, 177, 179; anti-democratic practices, 107; burning villages, 134; Chadian fighters for, 153 clientilistic mode, 15; Kwa na Kwa party, 209; occult protection narrative, 96; Patasse ousting, 132–3; Presidential Guard, 68; rule of, 170; support compromises rationalisations, 106
Bozoum, 135
Brazzaville, 94; mission report, 76
Britain, 6
Brussels, 71, 182
buzzwords: projects, 220; use of, 223

Cambodia, 148; UN Mission, 34, 40

Cameroon, 5–6, 19, 88, 95; peacekeeping troops, 224
Camp Noir, 138
cannibalism, 199; Bangui 2014, 202; Europeans as belief, 200; self-fulfilling prophecy, 200
capitalist modes of accumulation, suspicions of, 56
CEEAC (Economic Community of Central African States), 167
CEMAC (Central African Economic and Monetary Community), 164–5
centralized power, destruction capacity, 77
Central African Human Rights League, 235
Central Africanness, French project, 103
Central Africans: insecurity, 196; position deterioration, 220
Central African Republic, 3; aid dependency, 9; armed conflict entrenchment, 31; Army reinstatement, 205; Article 162, 197–8; as limiting case, 2; as non-territory, 85; belonging, 186–7; cattle market, 222; Central Office for the Repression of Banditry, 195; colonized, 77, 115; corruption, intervener viewpoint, 235; 'cunning victimhood', 42, 190, 212; ecological diversity, 5; elite foreign homes, 88; entitlements centrality, 121; external important meetings, 71; extraverted state, see below; fictive state, see state, the; first UN mission, 152; French cultural attitudes, 232; funerals, 55; history, 6; humanitarian aid workers, 64; Inclusive National Political Dialogue, 139, 146; interveners, see below; intervention time horizons, 126, 210; irregular war regularized, 47; land and water, 10; location, 1;

long-distance trades integration,
46; militarized politics, 125; Muslim
migration to, 11; name taken, 8;
National DDR Commission, 153–4;
National School for Magistrates,
205; non-territorialized state, 128, 182
non-Muslim people, 12; northeastern,
189; Oubangi-Chari name, see below;
outsourced politics and economy,
32; peackeeping missions number,
213; plural authorities, 65; political
control clarity lack, 215; potential
richness narrative, 59–60, 216, 238;
private economy lack, 248; privileged
personhood status, 123; small arms in,
27; sovereignty external guarantors,
106; Special Representatives in, 164;
state, see state, the; state executions,
192; UN mission, 217; UN Panel of
Experts on, 22
Ceriana Mayneri, Andrea, 95, 202
Chad, 5, 6, 9, 11, 15, 17, 19, 133, 237;
'Chadian', description, 190; /Darfur
borderlands, 47; eastern, 105;
peacekeeping troops, 224; troops
from, 68
Chad Basin region, robber gangs, 115
Chagnon, Napoleon, Yanomani, 183
Chambers, Robert, 245–6
chicotte, 117
christianity, 11; -Muslim relations, 222;
-Muslim sectarianism, 179
civil service: jobs status, 119–20, 171;
numbers purging, 9, 120
Cimpric, Aleksandra, 13
Clastres, Pierre, 210
Codo-Mbarakas, 131–2, 178
coercive operations, armed opposition
to, 129
'coffee money', 169
Collins, Randall, 186, 196, 207
communication strategies, 240

concessionary system: legacies of, 249;
-management, 119; politics, 24
Congo Free State, King Leopold era,
6, 79
Congo, Republic of, 160
conservation, restrictive, 126
context(s), 240; different perspectives
of, 218
Convention of Patriots for Justice and
Peace, 138
Cooperazione internazionale, 27
'corporate category', 48
Côte d'Ivoire, 88, 158
Cotonou, Benin, 88, 136–7
cotton, 8, 116; cultivation of, 8; forced
labour French Equatorial Africa, re,
117; labour reluctance, 116; -processing
facility destroyed, 153
creativity, collective, 57
Crampel, Paul, 66
'crisis', misleading terms, 150, 239
'cunning victimhood', 42, 190, 212

Dacko, David, 8, 106; coup against, 80;
safe 'choice' option, 79
daily practices, sacrality of, 57
Dakar, 88
danger, invisible forms of, 209
Danish Refugee Council, 21
Dar al-Kuti captives from sold, 66
Darassa, Ali, 230, 233, 246–7
Darfur, 11; African Union lead
negotiations, 140; 'sexier' problem,
126; 'spill over', 105
DDR (disarmament demobilization,
and reintegration), 21–2, 130, 140,
143, 145, 147, 214, 239; accountability
gaps, 152, 168; armed groups creation,
166; context design need, 151; daily
food allowance debates, 164–5; elite
stakeholders, 162; ex-combatants
information lack, 157; 'fake'

combatants, 155; funding, 150; group
identity creating, 156, 166; phase of,
100; postponing, 171; promise of, 172;
'proximate strategy', 158–9; purpose
vagueness, 162; re-marginalizing,
150, 160; staffers, 147, 159, 167; state
role link, 149; steering committee
operations, 167; transformation
promises, 175
De Saint Félix, Masson, 77
de Waal, Alex, 45, 114, 142, 204
Déby, Itno, Idriss, 15, 20, 24
de-humanizations, imperial processes,
201
'death is not free', 209
Deleuze, Gilles, 48
Demafouth, Jean-Jacques, 139–40, 161,
163, 169
demobilization, pretend, 152
democracy: democratic participation, 35;
post-Cold War discourse, 70
dependence, rents associated with, 70
desire(s): and disavowal dynamic, 108;
impossible limitless, 55–6, 97, 181, 245
despair, 15
'destructive understandings', 212
development, 'local ownership', 246
diamonds, 61
dignity and status, challenges of, 253
dispossession, Central African sense of,
181, 187, 212
distribution: bureaucratic entitlement,
62; fundamental issues, 45; politics of,
248, 252; status, 249; unified political
economy, 4
Djim Wei, Laurent, 139
Djotodia, Michel, 9, 11, 16–17, 24, 28,
136–7; command control lack, 177;
control loss, 18; step down of, 19
Doctors Without Borders-Spain, 28
Dongala, Emmanuel, Johnny Mad Dog,
203

Donham, Donald L., 54, 57
donor aid, 14; politicians dynamics, 64
Douala, 27, 88
DRC (Democratic Republic of the
Congo), 5, 9, 19, 60, 158, 162;
peacebuilders, 232
'durably fragile', CAR, 1
Durkheim, Emile, 51, 53, 55–7

eating together, importance of, 100–1
elections, 121, 146, 170; electioneering
done abroad, 94, 97; rigged, 106
elites: Bangui, 87; CAR's, 39, 148; CAR,
double passports, 88; CAR travel
patterns, 96; DDR postponement,
171; rare rural visits, 97; shared culture
of, 91
entitled persons, status, 91, 171, 173
entitlement(s): denied, 142; state
salary, 4
equality aphorism, 39
Equatorial Africa: French, 6, 116;
Guinea, 43; insurgency history, 113;
militarized region, 30; -West Africa
difference, 214
'equivocalities', 38
ethnic favouritism, 121
ethno-linguistic affinities, cross-border,
131
European Union, 68, 237; EUFOR, 21
European Commission, 162
European Coordinated Humanitarian
Organisation, 125
evangelical church, 15
ex-combatants: -DDR staffers benefit
difference, 168; fictitious, 167; mid-
level commanders, 160; promises to,
169
'expatriates', 149
expectations, unmet, 156
explanations, cultural and class
explanations, 214

'extraversion', 70–1, 109; danger source, 186; dynamics, 198
FACA, 207 (armed group); checkpoints, 236; network, 235
Facebook, violence impact, 204
farming, 5
FDPC (armed group), 133, 136
Ferme, Mariane C., 221
fictive sovereign states, disarmament programmes, 50
forced labour, 75–6, 116; manhunts for, 81; porterage, 74
foreignness: accusation, 185; slippery notion, 189
'forms', durability of, 68
'fragile states', 24, 30; solutions, 4
'fragility', 30
Francafrique: dynamics, 80; mode of operating, 124
France, 6, 36, 59, 67, 72; African colonies independence, 78; aid, 2; Ali Darassa alliance accusation, 233; Bokassa outing role, 124; CAR blame on, 238; CAR loosening ties, 192; CAR presidents role, 36–7; colonial pullback, 80; DDR steering committee, 162; Equatorial Africa, see above; forced cotton colonialism, 8; indirect rule policies, 188; language of, 177, 189; Ministry of Defence, 246; 1980s dominance, 131; peacekeepers, 19; peacekeepers' sexual abuse, 82; private concessions colonialism, 7; regional interest, 125; role of, 79; -Rwanda diplomatic relations, 225; Sangaris mission, 19, 21, 60, 205, 224, 234; Sanusi assassination, 187; troops pull-out, 124; 2014 peacekeepers, 178; violence blame, 231

gatekeepers, PRAC, 157
Gaye, Babacar, 82; resignation, 83

Gbangou, Reverend Nicolas Guérekoyame, 179
Gbaya people, 12; language 18
Geertz, Clifford, 253
'genocide card', leverage source, 19
Gentil, Emile, 65–6
Geschiere, Peter, 95, 182
Ghosh, Amitav, 34, 40–1, 44–5, 48, 56
Gide, André, 76; Voyage au Congo, 7, 110
Giles-Vernick, Tamara, 159
global commodity prices fall, impact of, 8
globalization, autochthony consequence, 187
Gluckman, Max, 37–8, 49, 56, 62, 114, 140, 149, 159, 219, 248
Goffman, Erving, 50
'good intentions crowd', 30, 91, 109, 114, 126, 138, 140, 191, 227–8, 236; institutionalized, 32
Goré, Chad, 153
Goumba, Abel, 79
Gounda, Cyriaque, 161, 169
governing authority, plural, 63
'government', 197; ideal version of, 4; salaries Regulation, 122
Great Lakes Region, DDR, 153
'ground-truthing', 234
Guattari, Félix, 48
Guéhenno, Jean-Marie, 215–16
guns, as currency, 74

Haiti: post-earthquake cholera, 43; US Stabilization Mission, 43
Hamadine, Hamad, 172
Handicap International, 27
hatred, role of, 54
head tax, 77, 118; forced labour form, 116; reinstatement suggestion, 119
Hecht, David, 222, 236
hierarchies, 50, 149, 151
hoarding, suspicions of, 56

Human Rights Watch, 68
human rights, monitors, 110
humanitarianism, 145; jobs, 172;
   unwanted agents of, 238
hunting and gathering, 5
hunting safari operatrors, 102–3
Huntington, Samuel, 32

inclusiveness, nominal, 15
indigénat, system formal ending, 117
inequality(ies), material, 57
informal taxation, crippling, 10
information: limited power of, 240;
   management, 163, 175; management
   hierarchies, 158; -power link, 156;
   proprietary, 166
infrastructure, costs, 7
insecurity: sources of, 180; trauma of,
   142
Integrated DDR Standards, 161
international aid, prioritized, 140
International Committee of the Red
   Cross, 129
International Crisis Group, 249
international NGOs, 52, 99; Central
   Africans differentiating among, 240;
   numbers of, 21, 29; sexual violence
   within, 83; state projects, 81; volunteer
   payments, 123
international organizations: luxurious
   conditions, 14; offices composition,
   232; 2015 looting rumour, 218
international order, nationalist, 31
interveners: CAR relations, 221, 238,
   247; expertise costs, 252; mutual
   suspicion, 216; -rebellions relation,
   223; peacekeeper relative salaries,
   226; quick fix mentality, 125; spending
   entitlements, 251; suspicion of, 229
'interwar', 216
Islam, 11; extremism priority rating, 126
ivory, 7, 61

Ivory Coast, see Côte d'Ivoire

Jennings, Kathleen M., 151
jobs, as status, 249
justice: access to, 193; as punishment,
   181, 182

Kabine Lyama, Imam Omar, 179
Kaga Bandoro, 224, 243, 244
Kalck, Pierre, 8
Kaldor, Mary, 33–4
Kamoun, Mahamat, 36
Kaplan, Robert D., 32, 34
Karnu, 115–16
killing(s), excessive nature of, 208;
   performance as, 202
knowledge: forms of, 149; privileged, 159
'knowledge gap': forms of, 149;
   gatekeeping of, 169; insufficiency of,
   161; public-private, 151–2, 156; rural
   marginality, 140
Kolingba, André, 130, 132; failed coup,
   154
Kompass, Anders, 82
Kongo-Wara rebellion, 7, 115–16, 178,
   198
Koro, Doungous, 117–18

Lake Chad, 10
Lallau, Benoît, 239
Land Cruisers, social status marker, 91
law of weapons distribution, 86
legal aesthetic, 138; rebel group
   adoption, 137
Lesueur, Thibault, 249
Libreville, Gabon, 16, 139; Peace
   Agreement, 161, 166
Libya, southward adventurism, 125
local chiefs, colonially enlisted, 7
'local' the, fetishized, 109; varying
   perceptions of, 233
Lord's Resistance Army, 105

lynching, 182, 205: FACA, 206; videos of, 207
maize, 6
'make-work' projects, 250
Mandja people, 12, 74
manioc, 5–6
Marchal, Roland, 197
marriage, unaffordable ritual, 191
Massi, Charles, 138
Mauss, Marcel, 244
Mbaiki, CAR, 117
Mbaikoua, General, 131
Mbangot, Stanislas, 169
MDRP (Multi-Country Demobilization and Reintegration Program), 153, 156
Meckassoua Karim, 35–6, 94
MICOPAX (regional peacekeeping mission), 15
micro-rituals, 53, 57
militias, 154
MINUSCA (UN Mission in CAR), 21–2, 82, 225, 231, 234–5, 237–8, 240; Pakistani troops, 224; peacebuilding process, 217; 2014 authorized, 20
MISCA, 19–20, 224; change to MINUSCA, 21
Miskine, Abdulaye, 133, 136, 188
mistrust, 218; central role of, 239; 'hermeneutics' of, 214; intra-peackeeper, 224; prevalence of, 215, 225
MLCJ (armed group), 166
mobility access to, 86, 101; -dignity/status aligned, 94, 99; -exclusion-inclusion dynamics, 89–90; imaginary of, 95; importance of, 87; policing of, 92, 188; power marker, 24, 80, 96, 98
modes of power, centralized, 77
money, status marker, 174
money-printing machine, 119

munju voko, 8
Muslims, 188, 231; Anti-Balaka targeting of, 18, 184–5; businesspeople, 10; family networks, 11 'foreigners' narrative, 28, 93, 177; financial innovation, 94; killings of, 19; traders and raiders, 6

Nairobi, 24, 71, 182
Namibia, 148
nation state, 'primal mandate', 109, ideological aspirational, 40, primacy obstacle, 150
nationalist mobilization, 11
nationality: debates need, 252; fraught question of, 251; 'native' categories, 31; nativism turn to, 189
Ndele, 66–7, 73, 99, 102, 196; attacks on, 184
Ndjadder, Florian, 138, 166
Ndjamena, 24, 71, 182
Ndodeba, Soumaine, 44, 190
Ndogou, Raymond, 169
'nepotism', 249–50
'new barbarism', thesis of, 183
'new wars', 33, 45; non-state actors, 34
New York, 24, 71, 182
Ngombe-Kette, Jean-Barkes, 144
Niamey, 15
Nigeria, 6, 93; CAR takeover rumour, 15; northern, 60
Nordstrom, Carolyn, 29
Nzakara people, 12
Nzanga, Desiré, 94
Nzapayeke, Archbishhop André, 179

occult: foreign countries link, 95; mobility link, 99
'organic solidarity', 51
Ouandé, Jules-Bernard, 154
Ouandja, 202, 204, 205; editorializing, 203

Oubangui-Chari, 6, 76, 116; -CAR
renamed, 8; head taxes, 74; non-
centralized, 73
Ouham-Pende prefecture, rural armed
movement, 130; villages burned,
134

Pakistan, peacekeeping troops, 224
Paoua, 163
'paradox of scarcity', 78, 85
Paris, 24, 71, 88, 94, 182
Patassé, Ange-Félix, 27, 118, 139,
152–3, 166; air flight prevention,
107; Bozizé removal, 133; 1982 coup
attempt, 130–1; ousted, 132; plane
boarding prevention, 88; Sylvian
Ngakoutou, 94
'patrimonial', misleading term, 249
Peace Corps, 124
peacebuilding, 248; assumptions of,
143; conveyor belt, 142, 144–5; façade
erection, 218; interventions, 141;
master narrative, 146
peacekeepers: intra-mistrust, 224–5;
Nepalese, 43; petition against, 233;
post-Cold War, 125
peacekeeping, -Bantustans, 44
'Peaceland', 42–3
Pentecostal churches, anti-Muslim
preaching, 93
Peulh fighters, 231
Pietz, William, 108, 128, 255n4
PK5, arms delivery accusation, 231
police parallèle, militia, 154
politics: Azande, 197; CAR control
clarity lack, 217, 237; concessionary,
109; DDR promissory, 159;
externally determined, 182; France-
CAR relations, 37; militarized, 9;
-military entrepreneurship, 47, 136;
promissory, 97, 142, 148; threat-
based, 152

popular punishment, 195; deterrent
effect, 194
postal service, functioning gone,
98
power: mobility as source of, 86;
powerlessness, 14; substance
ingestion, 203
PRAC, 156; communication strategies,
157; disarmament farce, 155;
independent evaluation team, 160;
participants 2006 protests, 157–8;
rebel groups emergence period, 161;
staff-participant segregation, 158;
steering committee, 163
Prendergast, John, 60
Presidential Guard, 132
Presidential TV debate 2016, 22
prisons, 197; colonial era creation, 127
profiteering, Sudanese/Muslim, 18
Program for Reinsertion and Support to
Communities, 153
punishment, popular, 183, 193, 211;
popularization, 180; spectacular, 192;
statecraft tool, 210; terror function,
194
Puntland, 3

Rabah, 72; French defeat of, 66
'real', 'hermeneutic encoding' of, 221
rebel groups: conventionalization of,
113–15, 128–9, 134, 137, 141–2,
144–5; Chadian leaders, 143;
interveners symbiosis, 130, 137; legal
aesthetics, 136; legitimacy leverage,
171; northern regions, 68; patriotic
names adopting, 46; threats use, 173
rebellion, 81; 'habit' of, 147;
internationalized rural, 113; means
to political party creation, 138;
'mentality', 244; recursiveness of,
243
'reconciliation', 219

reciprocity: decline of, 251; ideal state erosion of, 72
Redfield, Peter, 23
refugee(s), 'right to leave', 41
regional stability lens, 107–8
regional guards, West African and Gabonese, 77
reinsertion, vague, 152
reintegration, vagueness of, 151
resources exploitation greed, 60, 126; focus problem argument, 61
Richards, Paul, 32–4; 'no peace, no war', 147, 216
rights, abstract principles, 121; 'right to return', 41
rituals: collective situations, 53; 'propriety', 51
road robbers, 135
roadblocks, 91–2, 94, 103–4, 135–6, 188, 205
rubber, 7, 117
Ruffel, Inspector, 77
Rutherford, Danilyn, 108
Rwanda, -France relations, 225

Sabone, Abakar, 136–7, 166
salary-citizen policy, 120; decline of, 121, 124, 132
Samba-Panza, Catherine, 19–20, 36, 51, 88, 179, 205–6, 217, 235
sandal-wearers, low status, 90
Sango language, 11, 117; 'invented tradition', 189
Sassou Nguessou, Denis, 94
saving, difficulties of, 174
'scandal', misleading term, 150; repetitive, 81
scepticism, differing parameters, 233–4
schooling, interruptions to, 9
Schweinfurth, Georg, head hunter, 200–1
'second generation' effort, DDR, 161

Second World War, 8
sectarian war 2012, 28
'security vaccuum', fear phrase, 106
segregation, 56; fictions perpetuation, 175; realities of, 37–8
Seleka, 9, 15, 28, 48, 178, 190, 224; ad hoc violence, 17; coup, 179, 209; emergence of, 47, 107; ex-members, 22; leaders, 16; officially disbanded, 18 self-defence actors, loosely organized, 143
Sentinel Project/Enough Project, 60
sexual abuse scandal, 82
sexual violence, unsanctioned, 83
'Sharing Knowledge' organization, Bangui, 228
short funding cycles, 10
Sibut, CAR, 59–60
Sierra Leone, 160; political grievances, 33
Simmel, Georg, 190
Simone, AbdouMaliq, 222, 236
Smith, Stephen W., 101, 108, 214
'social cohesion', 219–20
social complicity, 53
social structure: continual recreation of, 50; networks mobilizations, 152
Sokoto, 6
Somalia, 3, 60
Somaliland, 3
sorcery, 12, 197
South Africa, 20; apartheid era, 49, 159, 219; troops deaths, 16
South Sudan, 5, 60
sovereignty: African outsourced, 9, 253; aspirational, 45; CAR fiction, 36, 50; dependent, 78; discourse of, 187; principle of, 164
spatial conception of the world, 86
spheres of influence, trans-regional, 125
spirits, realm of, 12; 'spiritual insecurity', 197, 209

SSR, century of, 70; disarmament objectives, 69
state, the: as unique problem-solver, 104; aspirational ideological form, 40, 134; attachment to idea, 245; 'collapse' framework limits, 253; conceptions of, 23, 101; constraints, 48; depoliticizing force, 49; desire for, 3; dignified social status provider, 110, 251; 'economy' unhelpful distinction, 3; entitlement-centred, 129; equality among fiction, 35; extraverted, see above; fetishized, 108, 128–9; fictive, 133; 'fragility', 61, 72; functioning, 10; hierarchies, 50, 149, 151; 'hurtful presence', 101; idea of, 63; ideal model, 41, 69; ideal type territoriality, 65; idealized courts, 182; imaginary integrity, 144; insecurity source, 103; insistence on, 35; jobs, 61, 122, 172; monopoly of violence failure, 127; 'phantom' revenue and investment source, 61; porousness, 24; privatized, 61; rational-bureaucratic ideal, 250; rigid ideal as obstacle, 2, 246–7; salary entitlement ideal, 4, 114, 174; UN 'primal mandate' obstacle, 102, 109, 150; 'uselesness', 63; world order, 164; violence role in, 25, 181; Weberian ideal type, 23
state-building: aspirational project, 125; difficulty, 30; initiatives, 15; international 'kit', 2; violence inherent, 77
status, social, 250; accoutrements, 90; personal, 87; smell, 90; state distributing, 248
structural adjustment, 9, 120
Sudan, 5–6, 11, 15, 17, 60, 133; governments, 138; Thuraya satellite phone, 204
'sultans': title, 73; Sultanates, 6

suspicion: interpretation frames, 230; peacekeepers, 227; prevalence of, 223; processes of, 217; resources, 234

Taussig, Michael, 108
taxation: 72; paying, 119; pragmatic, 246
terror tactics, targeted, 74
Themnér, Anders, 160
Thuraya satellite phone, sudan impact, 204
timber, 61
Tiringolou, 103, 136–7, 169–70, 172, 191
tobacco, 6
toro ti kua, 209
torture, state building tool, 211
Touadéra, Faustin Archange, 22, 191, 217
truckers, Sudanese, 92

Ubangui River, 17; 'Ubanguian' peoples, 12
UFDR (rebel group), 136–8, 166, 169, 171; DDR visits to, 170
university graduates, 171
UN (United Nations), 9, 135; advancement style, 164; agencies, 145; BONUCA, see above; Conflict Prevention and Peace Forum, 25; DDR definition, 150; Development Programme, 156, 161–2, 167; employee entitlements, 40; French influence suspicion, 231; gold purchasing allegations, 230; High Commissioner for Human Rights, 82–3; High Commissioner for Refugees, 41; MINUCA, see above; mission pragmatism lack, 247; nation-state 'primal mandate', 71, 102, 151; peace negotiators, 139; Peacebuilding Commission, 125, 213; Peacebuilding Fund, 2; peacekeeping missions increase, 34; states underlying principle, 128; Undersecretary

General for Peacekeeping Operations, 215; UNICEF, 103
Union of Republican Forces, 138
university graduates, jobless, 172
UPC (armed group), 230, 233, 246
urban poor, constarined mobility, 88
USA (United States of America): military aid, 105; military Human Terrain System, 43; State Department, 32
Utas, Mats, 173

van Creveld, Martin, 33
van der Elsken, Ed, 185
vengeance, as tool, 180
'victimicy', 173
villages: burning strategy, 68, 130, 132; forced resettlement, 87
violence, 63; against corpse, 206; agency statement, 196; anthropologists view of, 183; Chadian MISCA troops, 20; changing roles of, 252; credible monopoly on, 65; dynamics of, 115; effervescence of, 186; Equatorial African supernatural, 198; Facebook impact, 205; fear produced, 208; forced labour, 76; images misuse, 207; mobile phone impact, 204; necessary, 181; opportunistic, 48; organization of, 70; performative, 182; pluralized capacities for, 141; political use of, 71; popular participation, 179–80; post-Seleka, 194; 'preemptive', 196; punishment function, 210; response forms, 127, 238; 'spilling over' cliché, 105; structural factors, 81; trans-Saharan adventurists, 75; uncertainty creating, 54–5; useful tool, 78; videos of circulating, 204–6; wartime, 211
visibility, African 'playing' with, 236
Vogt, Margaret, 126, 164

voluntary workers, compensation 'issue, 122

Wadai, 6; sultan of, 66
Wahhabi doctrines, 93
war(s): ethnography of, 183; 'machine', 48; photography ethics, 206; post-Cold War, 33; profitability of, 29; social study of, 185
Wars, post-Cold War, 33
wealthy people, contradictory views of, 191
Webb, Raymond P., 131–2
Weber, Max, 128, 249; ideal state form, 2
witchcraft, 180; accusations, 197; airplane travel link, 95; capacity for, 12–13; substance, 199
women: 'victimicy' opportunities, 173; nutritional status, 126
work, Central African conceptions of, 60; forced, 74
World Bank, 156, 162, 237; Doing Business rankings, 126, 145
worldviews, parameters, 216 CAR, riches narrative, 216

Yakete, Levi, 209–10
Young, Crawford, 85

Zakaria, Damane, 166, 171
Zewde, Sahle-Work, 164
Ziguélé, Martin, 94
Zindeko, Joseph, 169
zo kwe zo, 39
Zulus: allegiance switch, 39; historical empire, 219; micro-level processes, 38